ADVENTURES OF CHARTER SCHOOL CREATORS

Leading from the Ground Up

Terrence E. Deal
Guilbert C. Hentschke
with Kendra Kecker, Christopher Lund,
Scot Oschman, and Rebecca Shore

ScarecrowEducation
Lanham, Maryland • Toronto • Oxford
2004

Published in the United States of America
by ScarecrowEducation
An imprint of The Rowman & Littlefield Publishing Group, Inc.
4501 Forbes Boulevard, Suite 200, Lanham, Maryland 20706
www.scarecroweducation.com

PO Box 317
Oxford
OX2 9RU, UK

British Library Cataloguing in Publication Information Available

Library of Congress Cataloging-in-Publication Data

Deal, Terrence E.
  Adventures of charter school creators : leading from the ground up /
Terrence E. Deal, Guilbert C. Hentschke with Kendra Kecker . . . [et al.].
    p. cm.
  Includes bibliographical references and index.
  ISBN 1-57886-166-7 (pbk. : alk. paper)
  1. Charter schools—United States—Case studies.   I. Hentschke,
Guilbert C.   II. Kecker, Kendra.   III. Title.
  LB2806.36.D43 2004
  371.01—dc22

                                                          2004008590

♾™ The paper used in this publication meets the minimum requirements of
American National Standard for Information Sciences—Permanence of Paper
for Printed Library Materials, ANSI/NISO Z39.48-1992.
Manufactured in the United States of America.

To the courageous developers from the admiring analysts.

To the memory of teacher Robert Deal,
and to Abagail, Sarah . . . and the idea of Elizabeth.

CONTENTS

ACKNOWLEDGMENTS

Some of those who had the greatest influence on this book did (and do) not even know it. Chief among them are a wide range of entrepreneurs who created viable educational organizations. Just a few from a long and diverse list include Mike Sandler (Eduventures), Don Leisey (A+ The Report Card), Chris Yelich (Association of Educators in Private Practice), Elliot Sainer (Aspen Education Group), Norm Avrech (Galaxy Classroom), Barbara and Roger Rossier (Rossier Schools), Marc Tucker and Judy Codding (National Center on Education and the Economy), Gene and Dawn Eidelman (Mosaica Education), Christopher Whittle (Edison Schools), Michael Milken (Knowledge Universe), Nancy Lavelle (Total Education Solutions), Jim Boyle and Lori Sweeney (Ombudsman), Doug Becker (Sylvan), Ellyn Lerner and David Winikur (KIDS1), and Bill Siart (Excellent Education Development). The creative energies of these and many other entrepreneurs are finding an outlet in charter school development. As a group they greatly inspired our work.

Others influenced us more directly, through their passion and commitment to underserved children, using charters as a vehicle to serve them in better ways. A sampling includes but is not limited to Carl Cohn, Penny Wohlstetter, Dave Patterson, Sue Bragato, Eric Premac,

Pam Riley, Scot Hamilton, Sonia Hernandez, Lance Izumi, Roger Lowenstein, Bruno Manno, Billie Orr, Lisa Snell, Anita Landecker, Steve Fish, and Jim Davis.

On the conceptual front, Lee Bolman's long-standing partnership with Terry Deal provided a helpful angle on emerging charters. We appreciate his contribution.

Needless to say, we are most grateful to the many colleagues at ScarecrowEducation who consistently supported us throughout the book writing process. Among those at Scarecrow, we are particularly indebted to Cindy Tursman, and subsequently to Kellie Hagan for patiently but persistently offering assistance.

Production and logistics help from members of the USC Rossier School of Education was crucial. Special thanks to Paul Galvin, Mary Orduno, and Cassandra Davis. The already supportive climate of the USC Rossier School for this work was made even greater through the support, provided respectively through the Irvine R. Melbo Scholar and the Richard T. Cooper and Mary Catherine Cooper Chair in Public School Administration. To all these people, to our spouses, and to others unnamed, we owe a debt of gratitude.

—Terry Deal and Guilbert Hentschke

INTRODUCTION

Since the first one opened in Minnesota in 1992, the number of charter schools has soared to nearly 3,000, serving about 700,000 students.[1] Charter legislation has been passed in 41 states, the District of Columbia, and Puerto Rico.[2] There are over 400 charter schools operating in Arizona and California and roughly 200 each in Florida, Michigan, and Texas.[3] State-by-state variations in laws, from start-up to closing criteria, combined with their localized character, make each charter school one of a kind.

To muddy the waters further, charter school legislation is continually altered at the federal level, state by state, and year to year. In the midst of this organized chaos, there are some enduring principles. For example, laws do not endorse any particular curriculum or learning methodology.[4] The uniform focus on improvement provides each school a different venue for delivering public education.

We have now reached a point where unanswered questions about these new initiatives are being replaced by emerging answers. Initial arguments against and for charter schools—for example, their potential to siphon off talented kids and assertive parents or to provide another choice in public school options—are being proved and disproved in local communities. These initial theoretical concerns have morphed into growing bodies of harder evidence.

Another widespread sense is that charter schools are not public schools but private or independent schools. This misconception is fueled by a surge of recent books such as *The Great School Debate: Choice, Vouchers, and Charters*,[5] *Rhetoric versus Reality: What We Know and What We Need to Know about Vouchers and Charter Schools*,[6] and *The Privatization of Public Education: Charter Schools and Vouchers: A Bibliography*.[7] There is now a sizeable and growing body of research replacing such generalizations about charters with recorded experience, for example, works by Finn et al.[8] and Bulkley and Wohlstetter.[9]

Charter schools emerge from the passion and commitment of a diverse group of founders, based on their sense of educational needs of local constituencies. But even the most talented initiators have found they need help in moving from passion to practice. Organizations have sprung up to provide "how to" technical assistance, information on individual schools, and lobbying strategies in support of (or in opposition to) charter schools. Since the details of charter laws make each state unique, these resource centers are typically state specific, such as the Charter School Development Center at California State University in Sacramento.[10] Similar organizations have been created in Colorado, Michigan, Minnesota, Massachusetts, New Jersey, and Texas—in fact, in most states with charter laws. All these centers offer help and advice, from hands-on technical assistance to leadership training. There are also for-profit vendors who charge for technical assistance and professional services—for example, Arizona's ABS and California's EXED, which contract financial and related services to a number of charter schools in those states.[11]

As state-by-state assistance networks grew, some joined forces and developed into national charter school assistance or informational networks. These associations grow, merge, and sometimes come to an untimely end.[12] The Charter Friends National Network, created in 1997 to facilitate collaboration among state-level organizations through online communications, conferences, grant programs, multi-state projects, and publications,[13] is a project of Hamline University in St. Paul, Minnesota. Another national resource is the National Charter School Clearinghouse (NCSC), one of 26 field-initiated research projects funded by a grant from the U.S. Department of Education, Elementary and Secondary Education Act, Title X, Public Charter Schools Program (Project # S282F010056).[14] NCSC works with charters to provide an interactive website, a monthly newsletter, a quarterly journal, conferences and summits, and a compilation of charter school funding resources and research. Another organization is U.S. Charter Schools, which provides similar services, plus resources for parents, job seekers, and researchers.[15]

Despite the growing mix of theoretical and experience-based generalizations, the challenge of creating each individual charter is unique. There are some common elements (reasons for creation, early advocates, special focus, etc.), but at the individual school level the "story" and distinctive particulars combine in a special way. This is partly why there remains a disconnect between what is written about charter schools by analysts and the day-to-day experiences of leaders who create and operate them.

Do those who create charter schools really have any special perspective to communicate to other educators? Stated more narrowly, does anything set charter school heads apart from traditional public school principals? After all, both run schools. Most charter school heads or founders can describe the mission of their schools, but so can their traditional school counterparts. The difference, as we see it, seems to be that most charter school founders take the school mission much further. Their schools reflect the profound impact of their personal beliefs and life history on the school's mission, passion, and instructional practices. This is not evident *a priori*; it only becomes so after we listen and walk some distance in their shoes.

Most published studies have overlooked this and other differences, trying to capture in aggregate the thinking and behavior of charter school heads and their school communities. In so doing, they have left untold the unique stories of individual schools as seen through the eyes of their founders.

If we were to focus the microscope in this way, what useful generalizations about charter school leadership might we uncover? We wanted to find a way to ferret out the untold stories behind the creation of individual charter schools and, at the same time, place them in a broader context.

It is an old saw in education and many other fields that those who have time to reflect and write about a topic, the analysts, are often not the ones who are busy doing it. Conversely, those doing it don't have the time or inclination to write about it. This led us in the direction of trying to understand more about charter school development *from the perspective of people who were in the mix.* After months of conversations with charter school heads, we marveled at the unique story of each charter school developer and the spacious differences between analysts and developers. Analysts tend to think in terms of general tendencies, broad concepts, and comparative perspectives. They address issues and draw inferences based on abstract data sources. Developers, on the other hand, live almost totally inside their story: their construction of what got them into the game, how their world operates, and what that implies for what they do. For them, the basic questions are "What is so?" "So what?" and "Now what?" Their stories are an interwoven fabric with three different threads: the person (story-teller), the organization (charter school), and the environment.

The work of analysts and developers is framed by different models of causation. Often the analyst describes a general model, whereas developers often resort to analogies: "This situation is like X." The objectivity of the analyst differs from the passion of the developer. The pride in the analyst's written product often deviates from the publicly and forcefully stated pride in the accomplishments of the developer's organization. One is sketched by an aspiration of scientific objectivity and descriptive precision; the other is colored by the conviction of personal belief and communicated by analogies and metaphors. While many analysts study and critique actors and trends, the developer lives out a narrative. Developers create and rely on an array of analogies of causation that guide future behavior. Analysts, on the other hand, begin with the generalizations and then see whether and how they are confirmed with the available evidence.

Our approach places relatively more attention on developers—their understanding and explanation of their behavior, their perspective on their work, their motivation and values as reflected in their words and deeds, and the influence of their background and circumstances on their roles as "accidental leaders." Our use of "accidental" is intentional but not meant to characterize or malign the efforts of those whose stories are reported here—far from it. Rather, these are people who did not plan years ago to become charter school founders. Their past experience and inner compass backed them serendipitously into taking the helm.

Our selection of people and their schools grew out of contacts and relationships, and to some extent notoriety, tempered by a desire for variety. We looked for a collection of charter schools by region of the country, mission, and differences in organizational and political environments. We sought a number small enough to enable individuals to describe their story in sufficient detail and large enough to provide us with the possibility of ascertaining new and different hunches about leadership in charter schools.

We wanted first and foremost to capture the stories of individuals playing critically important roles in the creation and early operation of individual schools. We wanted to hear their versions of the circumstances they faced, their articulation of their roles, and their interpretation of successes and failures.

We identified one individual per charter school as the key story-teller. In several instances, others were subsequently involved in producing the narrative.

The thirteen schools included in this exploration survived the initial years of start-up and lived to tell about it. They all addressed students who were "underserved," many of whom were downright poor. They represent different regions of the country, although a disproportionate number are in California.

The book is organized into three unequal parts. In Part 1, A Bird's-Eye View, we create two contexts for the narratives. Chapter 1, New Issues in an Old Industry, frames today's forces in compulsory-age schooling that give rise to the creation of charter schools and similar initiatives. Faced with wider choices and greater stakes on quality schooling, both households and governments now struggle to discover what works. Proponents and opponents of charter schools are driven by five contradictory sets of beliefs about what works and what is important. Chapter 2, Muddling through Enduring Issues, argues that, despite those new forces in education, the issues of leadership in charter schools are in evidence in most organizations and have been for some time. From this perspective, charter schools are comparable to many other start-up enterprises.

Part 2, A Worm's-Eye View, the thirteen stories of charter school founders, is the heart of the book and feeds other chapters. Chapter 3,

Guarding the Mission, is Odyssey's story. Odyssey Charter's driving concept from its inception was to prepare kids who don't fit into a school environment where compliance is rewarded over all else. The focus of Odyssey and its founder Kathleen O'Sullivan is on character development, academic excellence, and the future through project-based learning. Challenges for Odyssey came when founders realized the difficulties in teaching parents unfamiliar with choices how to make decisions and accept compromise.. Odyssey also learned the value of multiple authorizing agencies when they were denied a charter by the local district and had to seek approval from the county. A split between the founding partners over differences of philosophy, the mutiny of seven families, and initial difficulties with the delivery of special education services added to the school's woes and legal bills. A serious physical injury that required handing over the reins of control taught Odyssey's founder the value of letting go and allowing others to lead. Through all its difficulties, the school began to find its stride, and O' Sullivan is confident they are on the path to success.

Chapter 4, Growing the Grass Roots, is the chronicle of Camino Nuevo Charter Academy, founded by Rev. Philip Lance. It is part of a larger strategy to renew the MacArthur Park neighborhood, one of Los Angeles's poorest and most densely populated communities. The comprehensive scope of this strategy includes creating and growing a church, thrift store, community development corporation, and a worker-owned janitorial company in addition to the school. Rev. Lance enlisted the support of Paul Cummins, the highly respected founder of the Crossroads and New Roads schools, which helped open doors to credibility and financing. The school was located in a renovated mini-mall, which has since won several architectural awards for its unique design. Camino Nuevo now provides support for the community development corporation through the payment of rent, which enhances the ability to embark on new neighborhood development projects. In turn, the community development corporation provides support for the school through its after-school program and wellness center.

Chapter 5, New Kid on the Block, is Vaughn Street's narrative, the first conversion to fully independent status in the Los Angeles Unified School District. Yvonne Chan has turned Vaughn Street School around in many ways during her tenure. She took financial accountability from the district and brought it in-house. She used financial resources far more creatively and effectively than their deployment under traditional school governance arrangements. She reached out and allowed the community to reach in by providing a cultural, educational, and economic center for students and parents. Chan also overhauled teacher recruitment, development, and compensation at the school. Because of her efforts, Vaughn Street School has evolved from an example of an abysmal public school to a model of success and hope for other charter schools.

Chapter 6, A Company School, is the account of Ryder. Michael Lynott's expertise is in real estate law, not education, so he was a bit surprised when his boss asked him to become involved in opening the nation's first workplace charter school for Ryder System, Inc. At first, his responsibilities fell within his comfort zone: site planning, permitting, zoning, roadway access. Educational issues were outsourced to an educational management organization. This EMO had excellent contacts with investment banking, real estate development, and architectural firms, effectively creating a "one-stop shopping" method of getting the school opened on time (within just 14 months). However, inadequate communication among Ryder, the EMO, and the local school board required Lynott's more direct involvement in educational issues. Assembling the right team and ensuring open communication between other involved parties proved critical to opening the school on time—or opening it at all.

Chapter 7, Clawing Your Way, presents Fenton's experience. Joe Lucente took on the role of principal at Fenton Avenue Elementary when it was one of the worst schools in the Los Angeles Unified School District. Single-digit test scores, racial divisions, high administrative turnover—five principals in six years—all predicted an uphill battle. After five years of modest gains under district guidelines and budget, Lucente and the staff decided to pursue a charter even in the face of district resistance. They have never looked back. With control of their destiny and no one else to blame, Fenton has soared to success. It was named a California Distinguished School and received accolades from the state superintendent of public instruction. The school now boasts improved test scores, a family center, and excellent collaboration with the community, and it has been held up as a worldwide model for elementary schools. Its guiding principle is simple: "Do what is in the best interests of our students."

Chapter 8, A Fast Track in Harlem, details the epic of Sisulu. The first challenges faced by Judith Price and the Canaan Baptist Church were physical, rather than intellectual. Time was the largest constraint once it was decided to go ahead in April 1999, leaving just five months to opening day. In that time, the newly formed board of trustees worked out a partnership agreement with an EMO to run the school. The board also identified issues related to curriculum, personnel, ethnicity, and finances, and they found a way to share space in their new building with other Canaan organizations. On top of all this, they were faced with ensuring the complete separation of a state-funded charter school and the church. Everyone pulled together to make real a school's vision of their motto: "Children First!"

Chapter 9, A District School, describes the transformation of Feaster-Edison. It was once considered the worst school in the Chula Vista School District; the local community had accepted school failure as the norm, and morale among staff was very low. Its superintendent, Dr. Libia S. Gil, learned of the Edison Project, a for-profit EMO run by entrepreneur Chris Whittle.[16] Gil and other district administrators took the lead in working with Edison to convert the school into a charter and to allay the fears and questions of the local teachers union, the State Teacher's Retirement System, and the San Diego County Office of Education. When Feaster's charter was approved, the school was reinvented with an infusion of capital for modernization and new classrooms for its rapidly growing student population. In its first five years as a charter, Feaster has seen steady and significant growth in student performance, community involvement, and increased enrollment.

Chapter 10, Building on the Dream, is the account of the Watts Learning Center, a bright spot in an otherwise bleak landscape. Forty-five of its surrounding 49 elementary schools score in the lowest decile on statewide school performance rankings. The remaining four barely make it into the lowest quintile. Despite this, the Watts Learning Center is on its way to becoming a world-class academic institution. The school's success can be attributed to a shared and strong vision of purpose, great teachers with good support, empowered parents, and careful stewardship of resources. These four core themes have helped the school and its current head, Dr. Gene Fisher, carry on founder Nina Hardon Long's original vision—to provide poor, inner-city children with

a world-class education. Civil rights lawyer Jim Blew, among the founding and current board members, helps to keep that dream alive.

Chapter 11, The Phoenix, describes the evolution of Rocky Mount.
John Von Rohr took on a monumental task when he signed up with
Rocky Mount Charter School in North Carolina. The local Chamber of
Commerce worked with an EMO to start the school. But that did not
prevent common start-up problems with facilities, finances, staffing, district hassles, principal turnover, and disagreements over the school's
course of study. Added to the headaches were the community's fears
that the school might skim the best students, and the charter founders's
fears that public schools would off-load their worst problems. The real
test, however, came when Hurricane Floyd destroyed the school in
1999. The school was rebuilt from scratch in a true community effort. It
continues to thrive.

Chapter 12, Planting Life Practices, conveys the development of East
Bay Conservation Corps. Richard Lodish took a sabbatical from his job
as administrator at the prestigious Sidwell Friends School in Washington, D.C., to become the founding head of the East Bay Conservation
Corps effort. He was intrigued by East Bay's mission to prepare students
for their lifelong roles as citizens. This is accomplished through four
programs: the EBCC Charter School, Project YES, AmeriCorps, and
the Institute for Citizenship Education and Teacher Preparation.
Lodish's journey took him back to his roots as an elementary school
teacher in inner-city Cleveland, where he worked with at-risk youth and
their parents. This time, however, with EBCC backing him in areas such
as revenue projections, fund raising, and employee benefits, he and his
colleagues have been able to guide students, teachers, and parents toward the goal of interactive and independent learning—and enabling
young people "to help and respect each other," as one of his kindergarten students succinctly put it.

Chapter 13, Owning Wobegon, presents the report of Minnesota
New Country School. Doug Thomas created a unique learning environment that became one of the nation's most celebrated charter
schools, one designed from the ground up to do things differently. It
has no courses, no bells, and no principal. Students each have their own
computer work station. The curriculum fuses high technology with self-
directed scholarship in a project-based learning mode. The school

developed EdVisions Cooperative, a teacher ownership and professionalism model copied in several other schools. It is now the subject of a book about teacher ownership. After meeting initial resistance from school boards, Minnesota New Country School has succeeded in terms of standardized measures as well as student and parent satisfaction surveys.

Chapter 14, No Cats, describes Tomorrow's Builders YouthBuild Charter School. It took nearly three years to overcome district objections and obtain approval for the school, which was envisioned as part of the mission of Emerson Park Development Corporation to revitalize the neighborhood of East St. Louis, Illinois. The school's initial application was repeatedly denied at both the local and state levels in a decidedly non-charter-friendly state. The charter was finally approved for a school that would allow at-risk 16- to 21-year-olds to obtain high school diplomas or GEDs. The school also provided construction trade training, counseling, and leadership development, as well as job acquisition, placement, and retention skills. The revitalization of the Emerson Park neighborhood is underway.

Chapter 15, Darkness before Dawn, chronicles the development of ABES, the Arts-Based Elementary School, which began in 1996 as a concept to deliver a curriculum emphasizing the arts. An opportunity arose to partner with the local school district in opening an arts-based magnet as a charter school. This offered the benefits of the district's extensive resources, especially in finding a suitable location. In order to make the partnership work, it had to be approved by the ABES board, teachers, and family members in the school site's enrollment zone. State charter legislation had to be amended. All hurdles were overcome except family approval. ABES founders did not give up, however, and found a champion in the local school superintendent, who allowed them to lease several classrooms in an underutilized junior high. Eventually, ABES relocated to a larger facility. It now has an enrollment of 180 students, with a waiting list for every class.

Part 3, A Future View, extracts issues of leadership emphasized in each story as well as the ubiquitous leadership themes common across sites. Chapter 16, A Call for Leaders of New Jobs, distills themes, contrasting charter school leaders with school principals in traditional public schools. The tasks and roles involved in creating charter schools are fundamentally different from those of a typical public school principal, requiring more entrepreneurial and tenacious leadership. Fortunately, people with these talents and skills are being drawn to charter schools, from within and outside the formal educational administration profession.

NOTES

1. Overview of Charter Schools (2003). Retrieved November 15, 2003, from http://www.uscharterschools.org/pub/uscs_docs/o/index.htm

2. Overview of Charter Schools (2003).

3. State Profiles (2003). Retrieved November 15, 2003, from http://www.uscharterschools.org/cs/sp/query/q/1595

4. Hill, P. T., and Lake, R. (2002).

5. Good, T., and Braden, J. S. (2000).

6. Gill, B. P., Timpane, M., Ross, K., and Brewer, D. J. (2001).

7. Nordquist, J. (2000).

8. See Finn, C. E., Manno, B. V., Bierlein, L. A., and Vanourek, G. (1997).

9. Bulkley, K.E., and Wohlstetter, P. (2003).

10. See http://www.cacharterschools.org for more information on the Charter School Development Center at California State University at Sacramento. For a listing of resource centers in each state, see http://www.uscharterschools.org/pub/uscs-docs/sp/index.html.

11. See http://www.abs-services.com/ and http://www.exed.net for more information about these organizations.

12. See Hendrie, C. (2003).

13. See http://www.charterfriends.org/ for more information on the Charter Friends National Network.

14. See http://www.ncsc.info/ for more information on the National Charter School Clearinghouse.

15. See http://www.USCharterschools.org/pub/uscs-docs/sp/indexz.html.

16. See http://www.edisonschools.com/ for more information on the Edison Schools, Inc.

I

A BIRD'S-EYE VIEW

1

NEW ISSUES IN AN OLD INDUSTRY

At the same time charter schools were getting their start, three broader trends were rolling forward in U.S. education: (1) increased awareness of the benefits of schooling, raising the stakes for education;[1] (2) growing inequality among household incomes, substantially greater in the United States compared to other industrialized countries, increasing risk factors for the less well-to-do; and (3) government's growing inability to fund increases in K–12 education, causing both governments and households to pursue non-public supplementary support. These three trends provide the context for launching government-supported (but no longer totally funded) charter schools. Government assistance in the form of enabling legislation provided increased opportunities for local groups to create and help fund schools to meet local needs. While broad policy issues are being debated at state and federal levels, localities grapple with concrete issues of choice, accountability, and performance—issues that make or break each new charter school initiative. The tipping point is in the hands, heads, and hearts of charter school leaders whose stories appear in subsequent chapters. They are among those who have tried and, so far, succeeded.

HIGHER STAKES WITH FEWER CHIPS

What do we know about charter schools? Plenty—if judged by the over 400 studies and reports listed on the United States Charter Schools website.[2] All have been conducted and written since the first charter school law passed in 1991. But the sheer volume of reports does not yield consensus about whether charter schools loom as a promising innovation or are doomed as another damaging and expensive distraction. It may be too soon to tell. But the consequences of being wrong carry a higher price now, especially for children poorly served by existing public schools. Charter schools are arising in a knowledge-based economy. It is a time when a good education matters more, and universal access to *quality* schooling is declining. The stakes are raised for all children—especially those now underserved by conventional programs. Today's students have more to win if their education prepares them for a rapidly changing set of challenges, and a lot to lose if it fails. Just as they begin to get more schooling choices, today's children are faced with increased consequences (positive and negative) of those decisions.

As the world evolves toward the "information age" or "knowledge society," the value of human capital—what's between our ears—escalates. Both for individuals and for societies, the more knowledge acquired, the

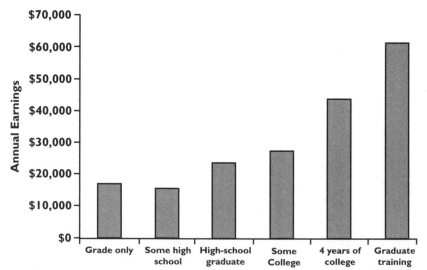

Figure 1.1.   Annual Earnings of U.S. Workers by Education, 1998. Source: U.S. Bureau of the Census, Current Population Survey.

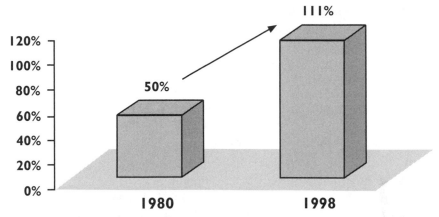

Figure 1.2. Widening Pay Gap Between High School and College Graduates, 1980 and 1998. Source: U.S. Census Bureau and ML Growth Stock Research.

more financial rewards reaped. The more you learn, the more you earn (see figure 1.1), and more and more (see figure 1.2).

Even if our ability to measure this relatively new form of human capital is rudimentary, its potential impact is massive in scope and scale. For many decades, many assumed that education and earnings were positively correlated. Less well known is that the connection is becoming even more pronounced. Education has become the best way to climb upward to a better financial life. The bad news is that the ladder has some broken or missing rungs, especially for children in large urban systems. Those consistently and pervasively near the bottom of the learning hierarchy are falling farther and farther behind.

We know that the quality of schooling has a large influence on student achievement, on a par with home and family factors.[3] It is also evident that we have not improved the quality of services available to urban and rural youth on parity with their suburban counterparts. In fact, underserved youth still put up with poorly trained teachers, outdated textbooks, fewer advanced placement courses, and crumbling and overcrowded buildings.[4]

In the future, the primary providers of education services will continue to be agents of local, state, and federal government. More than four out of five children currently attend publicly financed and operated schools, most of which are organized to provide necessary services within a geographically specified attendance area. Yet, government's ability to provide significant increases in support for schooling is constrained by its lack of political ability to raise tax revenues. It is also unable to shift significant proportions of tax dollars to education from competing government services such as health, infrastructure, criminal justice, transportation, and environment. Each takes a sizable bite.

Furthermore, governments no longer enjoy traditional hegemony over businesses and households. Among the 100 largest "economies" in the world, multinational corporations now outnumber nations.[5] The wealth of the 200 richest individuals (households) now equals the combined income of 41% of the world's population.[6]

Government bodies, especially state-funded school districts, now compete with each other to provide education services, even to those living outside their formal jurisdictions. Individuals (households) increasingly move across governmental boundaries to find a better quality of life, much like the free flow of financial capital in search of more productive investments. With the growing social value of a more highly educated citizenry, governments and households find mutual ground in collaborating on educational matters. Private individuals, through a variety of means, are shouldering more responsibilities for schooling their children. To retain educated households, governments are taking note and looking for ways to facilitate—not oppose—the process. Charter schools—along with growth in home schooling, private and public voucher schemes, educationally designed toys and games, and privately funded tutoring services—are coming of age.

The changing roles of governments and households over the last three decades are illustrated in increases in home schooling. Somewhere between 2.5% and 4% of today's school-age students are educated at home.[7] This represents a significant upward shift from previous decades. In 1980, home schooling was illegal in 30 states. By 1993, it had been made legal in all 50.[8] This migration from public to private schooling both reduces demands on publicly funded schools and decreases the likelihood of losing a tax-paying household. Charter schools, though different in form from home schooling, reflect the same changing relationships between governments and households. They represent a trend of increased consumer spending for educational goods and services, aided and abetted by necessary changes in legislation.

While part of the increased demand for better schooling is the result of growth in private (household) purchases, such arrangements are necessarily limited by a family's discretionary income. With more and more parents recognizing the link between school performance and future earnings, families with means are investing in their children's education. The quantity and variety of privately funded tutoring, mentoring, virtual schooling, and after-school and child development programs are growing rapidly, as are learning-oriented games, books, software, and websites. This trend handicaps still further youth from low-income households, who are already underserved by the public schooling system.

Exploding inequalities in private income and wealth, especially in countries like the United States, exacerbate the disparity between rich and poor, since children from low-income families receive less material (as opposed to social and emotional) support from their parents. Limited support for learning at home increases their relative disadvantage.

Charter schools are more a product of these forces than a cause, as are many contemporary public education initiatives such as performance-based accountability and home schooling. The stakes are increasing, and individual households and governments are starting to place their bets on a variety of new measures to get more from education. Charter schools are simply one of those wagers. What sets them apart from other initiatives?

SECOND CHOICE: CHARTERS AT THE FAULT LINE?

The growing concern about access to quality schooling among underserved populations has created two loose confederations with opposing views. The battle pits those who are an integral part of the education establishment (teacher groups, school boards, chief state school officers, school administrators, affiliated associations, and legislators) championing "professional education reform" against coalitions of parents, business leaders, conservative think tanks, and urban ethnic and faith-based groups favoring "radical education reform."[9] The first approach attempts to change the system from within; the other attempts to redo the system from outside. Both compete for the support of the non-aligned "public." One side promises improvements in the "one best system," while the other pursues "demand- and market-based" systems of choice.

Although these two groups differ on most major policy options, such as vouchers for private schools, they have come to an uneasy détente on charter schools. Charter schools exist at the nexus where small-scale advocacy largely outside the public system meets a cautious, reluctant, partial acceptance from inside. Charters represent an acceptable second choice juxtaposed against the perceived unacceptable first choices of two opposing alternatives: status quo vs. vouchers.

Consensus between the warring camps grows out of their slightly different perceptions. Radical reformers see charter schools as an alternative to the way public schools are currently created, organized, and operated—including more choices in schooling provision and consumption. Professional reformers, from their perspective, view charter schools as a logical extension of changes they have been pursuing all along—including greater school-based autonomy and accountability.

The devil is in the details. Many efforts to acquire charters have been rebuffed initially before ultimate approval. Theoretical principles behind charter schools are straightforward, even simple, but their ultimate impact in the real world is complex and profound. In states that have passed charter school legislation, a community dissatisfied with currently available services may submit an application to the appropriate authorizing agency requesting authority to operate its own school. In the application, "founders" propose schooling services and promise outcomes to the charter "authorizers." In return for the right to run the school and receive state per-pupil aid freed from some regulations, founders agree to shoulder the responsibility for delivering schooling that enough parents find preferable to their other options. If the founders do not deliver, authorizers may withdraw funding and put the charter school out of business. This benign exchange, however, masks the ideological differences, fears, bureaucratic ineptitudes, and political battles that accompany many, if not most, charter creation efforts.

Most reports on the characteristics of charter schools—number, average size, focus—fail to reveal the nature and intensity of battles waged pro and con. Since the early 1990s, over 40 states across the country have authorized legislation creating nearly 3,000 charter schools.[10] About two-thirds of these are new institutions. The bulk of the other third are converted public or private schools (in states where permitted). All charter schools are public in the sense that state governments authorize their operation and provide financial support and oversight. In so doing, state governments have declared that they are no longer responsible for operating *all* public schools or for providing universal funding and technical assistance. In many instances, operating support for charter schools is less than that provided to regular public schools. With start-up charter schools, there is usually little financial support for school facilities. These shortfalls are currently being supplemented privately and voluntarily.

The growth of charter schools depends in no small part on financial and managerial support from nongovernmental organizations (NGOs), both nonprofit and for-profit.[11] The vast majority of charter schools, especially start-ups, are themselves nonprofit corporations, typically 501(c)3. Many of these have grown out of the efforts of other nonprofit civic, cultural, faith-based, corporate, and community organizations.[12] These "partners" have provided money, buildings, expertise, political connections, and other resources necessary to run a school.

For-profit businesses have played at least two different roles in charter school creation and operation. One is similar to that of nonprofits, extending resources and leadership to help start and run the school. The other role is a "whole school management business enterprise" or "educational management organization" that contracts with founders to operate the school. Whether as donor or as contractor, for-profit businesses provide financial and human capital otherwise unavailable to the fledgling charter initiative.

To both enthusiasts and opponents, charter schools represent several significant departures from convention. To name just a few, they separate funding from operation, exchange funding for accountability, involve private providers (nonprofit and for profit), leverage public money with non-public money, and replace the "comprehensive" with a more focused model of schooling. Seen from a broader context of history and other nonschooling initiatives, however, the emergence and growth of charter schools may not represent a radical revolution. Instead it may be an incremental, inevitable next stage in the continuing evolution and devolution of public K–12 schooling and the more pronounced departure of total governmental support.

Do partnerships undergirding charter schools portend a new definition of public responsibility and promise new kinds of schooling consonant with 21st-century urban America's needs and demands? Or, alternatively, are they precursors of a form of privatization unresponsive to the educational welfare of underserved children? Answers to these questions are important but as yet unclear. That's why charter schools, as the second choice of the two major competing interest groups, serve as a battleground for playing out a tug-of-war between ideologies in American education. Like most political fights, the outcome will be determined in the middle of the political fault line, not at the extremes.

BATTLES OVER WHAT WE KNOW

A large body of data does not automatically produce consensus. Often studies and surveys are cited to support existing and entrenched beliefs. Those contradicting prevailing assumptions and myths are explained away. The battle over the theory of charter schools is now being fought over how to interpret the accumulating studies, stories, and statistics. Beliefs and unresolved issues are remarkably resilient after a decade of post hoc research.

Consider two examples of ideological battles—one con and one pro—not yet put to rest through research: "charter schools cream off the best students,"[13] and "charter schools provide a source of innovation in schooling."[14] Early fears of charter schools poaching more able students from traditional public schools have not proven out. However, the argument has not subsided. Rather it has shifted in two ways. First, it has drifted from crude proxies of "more able"—for example, achievement levels, race, class, family status—to more subtle, more complex, and more difficult to document concepts such as "more able due to a more supportive family." Second, the student comparison group has shifted from nearby traditional public schools to the average of all children in the state. Opponents tend to believe that charter schools provide unequal opportunities taken advantage of by families that, *by virtue of the fact that they have chosen charter schools*, are "better" than those that have not. Proponents, on the other hand, tend to believe that charter schools provide alternatives to families for whom traditional choices associated with residential location or expensive private schools are largely unavailable.[15] Coveted charter school seats not yet available should be reserved for those not well served by the traditional public school system *by virtue of the fact that they are willing to choose charter schools*. Opponents continue to compare charter school students (current and potential) with "those less fortunate who are left behind," whereas advocates continue to compare those same students with "those more fortunate who have already locked in superior choices" in traditional public schools. Both sides are partly correct.

Consider another argument where data have not resolved differences in beliefs: charter schools will foster innovative practices leading to significant improvements in student academic achievement. According to opponents, there is little that can be claimed to be innovative in most charter schools. Students are largely organized in grade-level classrooms, staffed by teachers in schools that operate on traditional daily, weekly, and yearly schedules. There do exist, however, some radically innovative "non-seat-time" (distance learning) initiatives. These have been a target of vigorous opposition on the basis of purported "poor quality." Proponents, on the other hand, argue that charter schools, by virtue of extensive growth and waiting lists, are providing services and environments heretofore unavailable. For many parents, these innovations include special curricular emphases, safer, more personal environments, and a culture that places greater value on school work. Opponents argue that these are hardly true innovations, while proponents in rebuttal argue that *for these charter school students they* do *represent major innovations*. Again, both sides are partly right.

Increasingly we are seeing a more realistic picture of charter schools and, at last, developing some tentative generalizations based on actual practice. Often these illuminate and sometimes reconfigure generalizations drawn from theory. However, we don't think grounded generalizations will come solely from studies, because they will not necessarily resolve prevailing contradictions of competing beliefs.

After reviewing a goodly portion of what has been published on charter schools and talking with many who play a role in their creation and operation, we've identified five dueling sets of beliefs that most likely will not be resolved soon. Each of the leaders whose stories are featured in subsequent chapters strikes us as being governed by one side, and not the other, of the contested beliefs described below. These beliefs, more than what research reports in general, guide their actions.

Belief in Escape of the Public Schools,
not Escape from the Public Schools

Do charters represent sanctioned gutting of public schools in favor of uncivic private interests, or do they symbolize the highest ideals of public education? Opponents see charter schools as a legalized form of escape from public schooling. With the exception of a very small number of states where only existing public schools can become charters, most are incorporated as private, largely nonprofit organizations. Even though states generally provide less per-pupil support for students, when facilities costs are factored in,[16] opponents still see charters as "siphoning" and "diverting" financial support from local school districts.

Proponents, on the other hand, believe state financial aid should support the education of *children* rather than the operation of *school districts*. Logically, therefore, money should follow the child wherever he or she is being educated. Those in charter schools are public school kids who have chosen to leave district-managed public schools. To charter proponents, "public" describes who pays, not who provides the service.

Charter opponents and proponents differ over interpretations of the quality of student flows. Opponents fear that "better" students (those who are brighter, easier to teach, and higher achieving and who have more supportive family backgrounds and fewer handicapping conditions) will flock to charter schools, leaving disproportionately difficult pupils in traditional schools. Charter schools are said to "'scrape off' the most talented public school students," or "implicitly or explicitly discriminate against minority or poor children," or "discourage the inclusion of . . . students with special needs."[17] It is also argued that "charter schools will leave behind not only low-income and minority students, but also low-achieving students and those with physical or learning disabilities, 'skimming the cream' of high academic performers from the public schools."[18]

Advocates, on the other hand, argue that charter schools are required (upon pain of removal of financial support) to admit students racially and academically representative of the populations from which they are drawn. They maintain applicants represent, by definition, those not being adequately served by available traditional options. Studies have usually focused on one or more selected differences between traditional and charter enrollments, such as race, income, ability, and learning disabilities. These studies are usually limited to subsets of districts or states and are necessarily constrained by definitions of what constitutes traditional comparison groups.

Despite great variability, there is little evidence that charter schools are skimming successful students from public schools, failing to educate special education students, or ignoring minorities. Half of U.S. charter pupils belong to minority groups; the figure is one-third in conventional schools, and 34–41% of charter school children come from low-income families.[19]

In Washington, D.C., 80% of charter school students and 85% of public school students are black; 16% of charter school students and 9% of public school students are Hispanic; 1% of charter school students and 4% of public school students are white; 13% of charter school students and 7% of public school students are limited-English students.[20]

Belief in Feeling Better about School and Achieving at Higher Levels

Opponents argue that the primary justification for charter schools is improved academic performance. Based on that lone criterion, charter school students have not performed any better than those in traditional public schools.[21] Proponents counter with several arguments: (1) it is too soon to tell, because it takes several years for learning impacts to take effect; (2) charter schools are admitting those *not* doing as well as their counterparts and should not be expected to achieve at higher levels; and (3) other factors, such as safety or security, are just as important as student achievement.

Studies differ based on what is measured, how measurements are made, and which populations are being compared. A recent RAND study formally acknowledges the conditional nature of most comparative studies. RAND found that California's charters perform almost as well as their traditional counterparts. After controlling for the fact that charters enroll poorer and academically troubled students, there is only a marginal difference, if any, between test scores.[22]

Studies confirm the most significant effects are attitudinal—relatively positive *opinions* about charters compared to previous experiences in traditional public schools. A Pacific Research Institute opinion survey of parents in 100 California charter schools measured academic success and found 66% of parents were very satisfied. Most parents (94%) were somewhat or very satisfied with their child's placement and perceived that their child was doing better than at the previous public school.[23]

The Hudson Study, like the Pacific Research Institute survey, used opinion surveys to measure academic performance. Analyzing responses from 17 schools across 10 states over a two-year period, the authors concluded that: (1) the number of students doing "excellent" or "good" work rose 23.4% for African Americans and 21.8% for Hispanics after enrolling in charter schools; (2) students and parents, of all ages, races, genders, English proficiency, special needs, and family incomes, report that students are doing better; and (3) among students previously performing "poorly" (as judged by their parents), nearly half are now doing "excellent" or "above average" work.[24]

What constitutes "success"? Whose measures count? To what extent do studies lead to consensus or merely reinforce differences in beliefs and values? At the operational level, charter schools carry on with the conviction that they provide a better learning environment than conventional public schools, and that feeling better about the program, safety, proximity, schedule, and other elements are necessary precursors to the possibility of achieving more.

Belief in Social Cohesion over Geographic Segmentation

Opponents and proponents hold fundamentally different beliefs about the role charter schools play in the social fabric of communities. The mission of the century-old public "common school" was to provide a shared experience for all children in a geographic jurisdiction, thereby creating an equal opportunity for civic and economic advancement. The common school was championed as a socializing as well as educational vehicle.

Opponents argue that creating schools around special interests jeopardizes the fundamental purpose of public schools. No longer will the local neighborhood public school serve as a common platform for a community's involvement in education. Charter schools, by their very nature, encourage specialized, often elitist, interests not endorsed by the community as a whole. A study of 17 charter schools zeroed in on the fact that, technically, students can be denied enrollment based on whether parents can meet a school's volunteer requirements.[25] The study raised this as a concern even though no data were cited to show how or whether any students had been denied enrollment based on a parent's willingness to volunteer. The point made was that they *could*.

Proponents propose four rebuttals. (1) The local neighborhood school varies greatly, depending on its residential community. Today no "common" school socializing experience exists *across schools and districts*. (2) By virtue of thematic focus, charter schools are able to attract like-minded parents, students, teachers, and administrators, and perforce can form a more socially cohesive community. (3) The fact that charter schools have more autonomy to shape programs suggests they will be more responsive to local community desires than a traditional public school governed by a distant board of education and the state. (4) Many parents value opportunities for more participation in the schooling of their children and feel relatively excluded from traditional public schools.

Belief in New and Different Schooling in Ways That Matter

Proponents believe that charter schools, freed from homogenizing regulations, can provide a wide array of innovative practices. Opponents believe that, except in a few areas, charter schools have not lived up to this promise. Furthermore, "different" can open the door to *even lower* quality. Proponents, in rebuttal, argue that charter schools have to be different enough, in ways that matter enough, to attract parents and students. In addition, the inherent conservatism of school-district authorizers inherently limits the scope and scale of permitted innovation.

Differences abound, but are charter schools innovative? Charter school leaders have more varied backgrounds than their traditional counterparts.[26] Governance structures are more diverse than in district-run schools, and administrators are more prone to share decision-making with teachers and parents. (In a few instances, teachers actually own schools as a cooperative enterprise.) The teacher workforce is more varied along several dimensions, depending on individual state charter requirements. In 21 states and Puerto Rico, all charter school teachers have to be certified. In 10 states, at least a portion of the teaching force requires certification. In five states and the District of Columbia, credentialing is left to local control.[27] The number of states requiring certification has gradually increased as a result of pressure from both the AFT and NEA, longtime advocates of teacher credentialing. More than half of U.S. charter schools require certified staff, and 72% of these teachers are credentialed.[28] Even when the decision is left to local discretion, the majority of charter schools hire certified teachers. The fact that charter school leaders make the hiring decisions, not school-district personnel offices, may lead to a different breed of teachers being hired, but there is little objective evidence of this.

When schools dismissed certification as a hiring requirement, they chose individuals with either practical work experience or a degree in the desired area of study. In fact, 70% of noncredentialed charter school teachers came with either five years of work experience or a degree in the appropriate field.[29] Most stated they would not work in education if a credential were required. In this way, charter schools were "tapping into sources of instructional horsepower not attracted to more conventional schools."[30]

Although most charter schools hire credentialed teachers by choice or law, many use nonclassroom positions as a means to bypass credentialing requirements: "charter school operators and often parents enjoyed the flexibility they have to hire outside instructors to teach noncore, vocational or enrichment classes."[31] Employing more part-time personnel, charters have been able to hire noncredentialed staff with valuable outside experience who are less expensive, non-union personnel.

While charter schools are often not innovative, it is not entirely their fault. Authorizing petitions often confront skepticism, negativity, or explicit hostility from the body that must approve a group seeking to challenge the status quo.[32] Charter schools are expected to innovate, but at the same time, media coverage and political attention focus on high-stakes standardized tests. This creates pressure to stick with conservative, proven approaches.[33] When states mandate standards and standardized tests, charter schools are pushed from innovation toward more traditional, research-based practices. Given the inherent conflict between petitioners and authorizing school boards, innovation is seldom encouraged and often penalized.

Belief in Getting More out of a Dollar
While Having Less to Spend

The consensus about relative spending suggests that charters receive less public financial support than their traditional counterparts. Different reasons are cited. A recent RAND study concluded: "charter schools, particularly start-up schools, report receiving less public funding per student than do conventional public schools," a difference explained in part by a lower rate of participation in categorical programs such as the state's transportation funding program and the federal Title I program.[34] In addition, until recently, most start-ups received virtually no funding for facilities and relatively little for initial start-up costs.

According to a four-year, large-scale U.S. Department of Education study, the most frequent barriers faced in initial stages were lack of start-up resources (49%), operating funds (37%), and adequate facilities (32%).[35] Charter schools also do not have the capital available to traditional schools and in many cases cannot receive categorical or bond monies. Without sufficient funds, start-up schools struggle to get loans necessary to lease or purchase facilities. When charter schools lack mechanisms to access bond or new-construction money, the space problem is complicated even further. Yet, charter school leaders believe they can deliver superior services. In many cases, charters partner with established community organizations to provide programs, capital, and space to launch operations.

SKIRMISHES ON THE GROUND: THE WORM'S-EYE VIEW

Rather than trying to "settle what we know from research to date," we sought to take a more grounded approach—from the perspective of charter school founders in the thick of things. How does a worm's-eye view differ from or complement competing beliefs surrounding charter schools developed from analysts above the fray? Our interest is to acknowledge the presence of these broader generalizations and issues, but then to listen carefully to a sampling of individuals from various walks of life who have devoted a substantial part of their life to launching and operating charter schools.

The examples we report embody many of the theoretical issues raised: the education stakes for (underserved) students are higher than ever; charter schools are public in the best sense of the term; there can never be a substitute for doing better, but feeling better is a good place to begin; charter schools help create social cohesion in a community; getting the job done for kids and parents trumps both innovation and conformity; and doing more with fewer resources is both a curse and blessing inherent in developing a charter school.

We sought to concentrate on the individual stories of people who create and grow charter schools. Our hope is to reveal *their* versions of the issues, complexities, and realities. New forces and circumstances have fostered the legalization of charter schools. But as another public school reform effort, how distinct are they really? Are the *leadership issues* faced by charter school creators really different from those faced by leaders in public schools? Are schools any more unusual to change than most organizations?

NOTES

1. Professor Gary Becker, Nobel Laureate economist who pioneered in the study of human capital, estimates that the financial value of the average American is somewhere between $500,000 and $5,000,000. Assuming the low end of this range, the value of human, social, and other non-financial capital in our country is roughly $207 trillion (in 2002 dollars) or about three times greater than the more traditionally measured forms of financial capital ($49 trillion). See Knowledge Universe (2004).

2. See Center for Education Reform (2003).

3. For a current, comprehensive summary of the degree to which home and school factors affect student achievement, see Barton, P. (2003).

4. Betts, J. R., Kim, R. S., and Danenberg, A. (2000).

5. Gabel, M., and Bruner, H. (2002).

6. Milken Institute (2002).

7. Based on the National Center for Educational Statistics study on home schooling conducted in 2001. Available at: http://nces.ed.gov/pubsearch/pubsinfo.asp?pubid=2001033.

8. National Center for Educational Statistics study on home schooling, 2001.

9. Hentschke, G. (1997).

10. To capture the latest developments on charter school numbers, state legislation, and the like, see http://www.uscharterschools.org.

11. Wells, A. S., et al. (1999).

12. Wohlstetter, P., Malloy, C. L., Hentschke, G., and Smith, J. (in press), and Wohlstetter, P., Malloy, C. L., Smith, J., and Hentschke, G. (in press).

13. Gill, B. P., Timpane, M., Ross, K., and Brewer, D. J. (2001).

14. Hill, P., and Lake, R. (2002). See also Horn, J., and Miron, G. (2000).

15. Gill, B. P., Timpane, M., Ross, K., and Brewer, D. J. (2001).

16. Gill, B. P., Timpane, M., Ross, K., and Brewer, D. J. (2001).

17. Metcalf, K. K., Theobald, N. D., and Gonzalez, G. (2003).

18. Gill B. P., Timpane, M., Ross, K., and Brewer D. J. (2001).

19. Nelson, B., et al. (2000).

20. Henig, J. R., Moser, M., Holyoke, T. T., and Lacireno-Paquet, N. (1999).

21. See Zimmer, R., et al. (2003). See also Loveless, T. (2002); and Miron, G., and Nelson, C. (2001).

22. See Zimmer, R., et al. (2003).

23. Riley, P. (2000).

24. Finn, C. E., Manno, B. V., Bierlein, L. A., and Vanourek, G. (1997).

25. Wells, A. S., et al. (1999).

26. Bulkley, K., and Fisler, J. (2002).

27. Education Commission of the States (2001).

28. Riley, P. (2000).

29. Riley, P. (2000).

30. Riley, P. (2000).

31. Wells, A. S., et al. (1999).

32. Hill, P. T., and Lake, R. (2002).

33. Hill, P. T., and Lake, R. (2002).

34. Zimmer, R., et al. (2003).

35. Nelson, B., et al. (2000).

2

MUDDLING THROUGH
ENDURING ISSUES

Creating new charter schools has become a full-fledged national education movement.[1] It is hard to find current professional publications that do not feature some aspect of launching a new effort. The initiatives also provide colorful grist for local and national media stories.[2] The movement is fueled by a widely touted, rampant dissatisfaction with the performance of America's public schools.[3] This is true especially at state or national levels, where policy-makers have made educational reform a top priority. Governors are staking their reputations on making schools better.[4] The president of the United States proposed and Congress passed the aggressive No Child Left Behind legislation, which is based on the premise that every student should have a fighting chance to succeed despite the current system's uneven playing field; it also puts some teeth into ensuring that school districts and schools take the mandate seriously.[5] Scores on standardized tests are the universal measure of proof. Charter schools, and their passionate advocates and detractors, are in the epicenter of all of this foment.

None of this contemporary concern and action, however, is new. It is, instead, a novel twist on an old story. For many years, school improvement efforts have been aggressive frontal attacks, usually sponsored by federal or state governments.[6] Private foundations have also added their influence in the form of direction and enticements.[7] Whether the primary motivation was carrot or stick, the results have usually been puny, particularly when weighed against the scope of the campaign and the expenditure of financial resources. Enter charter schools as an end run. Rather than trying to reform timeworn, entrenched patterns, they begin anew—a fresh start toward better schools devoid of historical or bureaucratic baggage. Traditional public schools are too much a captive of their current "markets" and require a separate structure with different rules in order to have a chance to improve.[8] At least, that's the strategy.

SUPPORT FOR CHARTER SCHOOL STRATEGY

The charter strategy has support in the organizational change literature. Burton Clark observed years ago that significant change requires one of three conditions.[9] The first is crisis. But that condition, articulated by a national panel of educators in 1983, had little long-term impact on initiatives to transform the nation's schools. The clarion call of *A Nation at Risk* captured ample attention at first. But the American public didn't seem as concerned as the blue ribbon panel about the dismal status quo portrayed in the report. This is not a new discrepancy between national and local opinions. Almost invariably, people will nod their heads in agreement that American education needs help. But then they report satisfaction with their local schools.[10]

The second condition favoring change, according to Clark, is evolutionary openness to innovation. Even business organizations wrestle with how to improve outmoded patterns and ways. The track record of corporate mergers and acquisitions is a prime example. Well over half fail to meet their intended objectives.[11] Schools, by their nature, are not open to change—for good reasons. For one, parents are supportive of innovation as long as it doesn't make things different for their kids or unfamiliar to them. Very few would argue that most public schools actively seek out or readily adopt new programs and practices. Most often, it is wiser to keep things pretty much as they are.

The third condition fostering an introduction of more promising methods is the creation of a new institution. This promise of starting afresh is the wind beneath the wings of charter schools. If you can start from scratch, it may improve the odds of success. The beginning anew strategy has been tested favorably in the business world. Saturn Motors is a good example. For years executives at General Motors labored to improve their company's performance. Put simply, it was widely known for its reputation of producing lousy cars. But the organization seemed to have an unlimited, perverse capacity to absorb or derail any attempt to make things better. Tired of unsuccessfully banging against a stone wall, executives tried a different approach. They created a new organization called Saturn.

Saturn was designed and launched by a committee of 100 employees and managers representing a cross section of roles and levels. The Gang of One Hundred, as it came to be known, spent a year searching the world for the best examples of how to organize people to build an exemplary car. The group then distilled what it learned into a revolutionary approach to automobile manufacturing. Almost a mirror image of a traditional GM plant, Saturn soon confirmed the wisdom behind its creation. Almost immediately, cars rolling off the assembly line were top quality.[12] This and a new, more customer-friendly approach to sales soon captured a highly satisfied and intensely loyal group of customers.[13] Despite the predictable ups and downs of a new enterprise, employees (mostly from old GM) are satisfied and committed. They are proud of the car they produce. While the jury is still out on the company's long-term profitability, Saturn demonstrates what a new start-up can do.

Can charter schools emulate Saturn's success? That remains open to question. In the 1970s a similar initiative in education was launched to maneuver around conventional public schools. It was labeled the alternative schools movement. Funded by both private and public funds, these innovative schools were launched with two ends in mind: (1) to provide a more challenging and humane learning environment and (2) to model more successful options for public schools to emulate. As an alternative school pioneer remarked: "Our mission is to build a Volkswagen to compete with Cadillacs, so stodgy cars with fins will change." The spirit and optimism of the movement proved hard to maintain, even though their expressed ends were largely met. Very few of these noble experiments survived. Some collapsed under the sheer weight of unresolved issues. They evaporated without leaving any tangible footprints in the snow. Others retreated to the traditional sanctuary they tried to escape. They became traditional schools in alternative clothing. Like most educational innovations, they began with a bang and ended with a whimper. Schools that survived discovered some basic characteristics of schools as organizations and some enduring principles of effective leadership.[14]

SCHOOLS AS ORGANIZATIONS

Schools have a lot more in common with other organizations than most people think. But public schools also have some special features that set them apart. They are highly vulnerable to external political and social pressures. Goals are typically vague and often conflicting. Core technologies are uncertain and open to speculation from laypeople as well as professionals. Results are hard to measure. As a result, schools do not fit the mold of technical or product-oriented enterprises. They are more like churches than hospitals or businesses. Faith and belief play an important role in determining how well schools measure up. To be deemed successful, they must conform to prevailing expectations and myths.

This brings us to a curious and paradoxical time in our history. As detailed in the previous chapter, national leaders, governors, and other policy-makers universally champion education as a primary national (and state and local) interest. Almost always they agree that higher standards and more rigorous measures are the key to better performance.[15] To improve schools, it is argued, we have to make them run more like results-oriented businesses. What they often overlook is that people don't choose a hospital based on its mortality/morbidity statistics. Nor do they ask for a salvation rate before joining a church. Such choices are made more on the basis of belief and faith than on technical proof.

Today's educators must therefore walk a tightrope between providing results and bolstering confidence through less tangible, more symbolic ways. Otherwise, they walk blindly down a false business-oriented, rationally based path, overlooking the unique features of educational organizations that make them special. In responding to the current political rhetoric, they overlook a more fundamental and enduring purpose of schooling. Most successful alternative school leaders figured this out and worked hard at cultivating a shared mythology that instilled a deep sense of loyalty and commitment among all constituents. An alternative school head was told by a local businessman: "If I ran my business like you're running the school, they would fire me." The school head responded: "But if I tried to run this school like you manage your business, we would fail." This important lesson is not lost on today's private school leaders. It will provide a crucial test for emerging charter schools as they make their way.

THE ESSENCE OF LEADERSHIP

The importance of leadership in any endeavor is endorsed unequivocally across the board. But exactly what leadership looks like in practice is open to debate. The first problem in capturing the essence of leadership is confusing it with management. Both are important. Managers focus on clarity, control, and accountability. Leaders embrace passion, purpose, and inspiration. Successful organizations have a blend of both that fits the current situation. In times of stability and scarcity, we look to managers; in times of chaos and uncertainty, we summon leaders.

The second problem is the emphasis we put on leadership action without recognizing the importance of reflection. Former Chief of Naval Operations Admiral Trost put it this way: "The first thing any leader must do is to figure out what is going on." Sizing up a situation is a crucial skill and requires leaders who have a comprehensive framework for making sense in the topsy-turvy life in organizations.

Bolman and Deal (2003) have identified four lenses or frames leaders rely on to figure out what is going on in situations. Their approach is somewhat akin to the Windows program on a computer. It allows you to open multiple frames on the screen and work on several things simultaneously. In trying to capture reality, leaders have four windows or choices. The *human resource* frame centers attention on human needs and sees problems arising when basic needs are unmet. The *structural* perspective emphasizes the importance of goals, roles, and authority predicting problems when the structure is either too tight or too loose. The *political* approach assumes a world of scarce resources where different interests compete, relying on power to get their way. The *symbolic* frame pictures a nebulous world in which people depend on symbols to bestow meaning, hope, and faith. Using cognitive mind-sets to predict managerial or leadership effectiveness, the structural frame dominates management; the symbolic frame stands out as the stuff of leadership, closely followed by political adroitness. Attention to human needs figures in both.

Like most organizations, charter schools need sound management to survive and thrive. The challenge will be even more daunting than for existing public schools because structural arrangements begin with a blank slate rather than following a standard formula. While this presents some appealing opportunities, it also poses some obvious dangers. But beyond good management, charter schools crave inspired leadership. New institutions, by their nature, are tender and unpredictable. Peaks and valleys are to be expected, and leaders are needed to relish the joys and to help others through the anguish. As charter schools evolve, effective leaders will find the right path by muddling through and plowing ahead rather than by planning and controlling what comes to pass. As they muddle along, some predictable challenges will undoubtedly make themselves known. How they meet and engage these expected trials will determine whether the charter school movement flourishes or flops.

CHARTER SCHOOL CHALLENGES

It is premature to assume that a new start and a clean slate will promote a smooth launch for charter schools. In fact, the exact opposite may be a more apt assumption. Certainly, a number of potential and formidable barriers will arise to choke their progress. Some of these challenges will originate outside the school; others will arise from within. A number of these challenges are discussed in the sections that follow.

Meeting Diverse Expectations

As noted, schools are judged as much on how they appear as on what they actually do. As charter schools pursue their unique form of education, they will still be held accountable for conforming to time-honored historical precedents. Credentialed teachers, classrooms, curricula, and other features are part of the partly conscious mythical accreditation package schools will need to reflect.[16] Some parents will want the charter to pursue more radical educational opportunities. But other constituencies—local governments, community residents, unions, and state agencies—may be looking for conventional signs of solid performance, and failing that, at least "solid process." Believing is seeing, not the other way around. Because they are supposed to be better, charter schools will ultimately be judged on what is seen.

Achieving Results

Whatever unique instructional route charter schools choose to take, paradoxically, they will still be held accountable for results on standardized tests. Whether or not existing test batteries adequately measure primary goals is irrelevant. Many of the noble purposes charters undertake are not easily quantifiable. This will make it difficult to prove their unique worth. In many instances, the standardized test bar will be set higher for charters than for other public schools.

Dealing with District Bureaucracy

In theory, charter schools are set free of constraining bureaucratic rules and policies. But they are still funded by public funds and housed in traditional districts. There is a political version of the Golden Rule that argues: "Whoever has the gold makes the rules." Charters still depend on higher echelons for some resources. In the corporate world, such dependence has been a source of constant friction for Saturn Motors. It will be as daunting a challenge for charter schools. In addition, charters must reckon with the reality that others in the district will, at some level, want them to fail. The "screw Saturn" mentality in General Motors stemmed from the hope that Saturn's failure would be a reaffirmation of the "Old World" practices of GM.

But the sources of trouble for charter schools will originate as much from within as from without. Human organizations are complex enterprises. People bring to any situation prejudices, quirks, and a host of other personal baggage. As they intermingle, all of the well-known issues roil in a complicated vortex of daily messes. To assume that these everyday problems will vanish because a charter school is starting fresh with a shared mission is foolhardy.

Establishing Effective Leadership

Most people who champion a new charter school will have an unlimited supply of passion and energy and an abundance of heart and soul. But whether they will have the know-how to deal effectively with political strife and inspire others with the same fire and sense of purpose is up for grabs. Those drawn to leadership positions are usually strong in two areas: they have good people skills, and they have an ability to analyze things rationally. But most of the internal (as well as external) messes they will confront will be politically charged and culturally based. The political and symbolic skills needed to survive and thrive will usually have to be learned on the job in the school of hard knocks. Some prior preparation and ongoing leadership development may help. But for charter schools to succeed, a healthy dose of symbolic and political leadership will be essential.

Creating a Workable System

In most public schools, a system of rules, responsibilities, and authority is in place. It may be dysfunctional, but at least it's there. Routine may sometimes feel boring and stifling, but it is often preferred to ambiguity and confusion. Many years ago, a research study reached a striking conclusion. It compared teacher morale in two urban districts—one highly bureaucratic, the other very participative. The initial hypothesis was that teachers' morale would be higher where given a chance to shape decisions. The opposite panned out. The explanation: teachers knew where they stood and whom they needed to lobby to get things done.[17] In charter schools, the system or structure will need to be negotiated while the operation is moving into high gear. This is akin to trying to fix an airplane in flight. Principals need legitimate authority, as do teachers, to elicit compliance. Rules help students (and everyone else) know where they stand and what will happen if they run amok. Rules make explicit what people are supposed to do and the expected rewards or sanctions for doing well or falling short. One of the most daunting challenges charter schools face is creating a system that works.

Creating a Shared Score

People carry cultural scripts formed through prior experiences. Think of them as mental tapes or CDs playing private scores. In new situations, on a semi-conscious level, these private scores shape what people do. When Marvin Runyon launched newly formed Nissan of America, he knew he had a rare opportunity. He had funding and symbolic credibility from a Japanese corporation, combined with his own leadership notions shaped by many years at Ford. His mission was not unlike that of a charter school—funding assured, playing field wide open, and unlimited potential. But shortly after the company's launching, as Runyon walked through the brand-new manufacturing plant, he noticed behavior he had observed at Ford and heard about in Chevrolet, Chrysler, and Nissan. His articulated vision was being overshadowed by the private scores people brought with them from previous experiences. Prototypical public school scores are deeply ingrained, not only in parents and outsiders, but also in principals, teachers, and students. Perhaps the most formidable challenge of charter schools is developing a unified song sheet, a score that melds diverse voices into a unified chorus. Without a new and shared story, charter schools will either revert to traditional practices—or fail.

Avoiding Staff Burnout

Everyone in a newly formed charter school is full of energy and excitement. For many, it's a dream come true—a chance to give birth to an enterprise with a purpose and a real commitment to teaching and learning. But energy and enthusiasm can erode quickly in the face of everyday bumps and disasters. When acute problems arise, people often compensate by spending more time. The added time commitment steals energy and emotion from family, friends, and outside pursuits. This dissipates energy to deal with problems at work. And so the cycle spirals downward.

The launching of People Express in the late 1970s was heralded as a major revolution in air travel. And for a time it was. Employees rotated through functions. Participation was a way of life. People voluntarily spent time at work. The spirit of being on the ground floor of something big was contagious. Suddenly the signs of burnout became evident—depression, divorces, and other individual pathologies. These stresses were coupled with other system and growth issues, and a noble experiment fell on its own sword. People Express, too early in its young career, became a casualty of desired quality and commitment exacting its unintended toll.

Confronting Conflict Head On

Conflict is a normal byproduct of cooperation. In any human endeavor, resources are scarce. Individuals and groups scrap for their share, using power to get their way. This prevailing dynamic ensures that conflict is part of everyday life. The modal response to conflict in most organizations is to ignore or smooth over rifts and then go underground or behind the scenes to get even. In a newly formed enterprise, conflict intensifies. If left unattended, it can undermine even the most noble of efforts. This is why Saturn Motors mandated training in conflict management for everyone before the assembly line started to roll. At Saturn, people learned to confront conflict head on and face to face, following principles of compromise and negotiation. Charter schools must deal openly with conflict early, or they will pay a steep price later.

FOREWARNED IS FOREARMED

The leaders of the 1970s alternative schools, like the founders of People Express, were deeply committed and highly motivated. They wanted to create environments where teachers could teach and students could learn. For a time, they succeeded. But their noble experiments soon faltered, and many failed because their zeal was not matched with needed management and leadership talent. They launched a voyage without anticipating storms that lay ahead. They were surprised and caught off guard when things did not work as planned.

This chapter has distilled what we know about what lies ahead in a general sense. We have drawn lessons from history, the literature, and contemporary experiments in the world of business. But the best lessons about what to do and what to avoid in running a charter school will be found in the experiences of those who are actively wrestling now with everyday realities. Their stories follow.

NOTES

1. The number of charter schools in the United States grew from just two in 1992 to over 2,300 in 2001. See Hentschke, G., Oschman, S., and Snell, L. (2003).

2. See, for example, http://www.cnn.com/US/9812/03/charter.schools/index.html and http://www.cnn.com/2000/ALLPOLITICS/stories/05/04/education.debate/index.html.

3. The 35th Annual Phi Delta Kappan/Gallup Poll of the Public's Attitude Toward the Public Schools, published in September 2003, reports that only 26% of the population would give public schools in the nation as a whole a grade of A or B.

4. See, for example, Chaddock, G. (1999).

5. For information on the No Child Left Behind legislation, see http://www.ed.gov/nclb/landing.jhtml.

6. See, for example, Tirozzi, G., and Uro, G. (1997), which reviews national policy initiatives that have supported local efforts for school improvement.

7. Some private foundations that support public schools include the Carnegie Corporation, Bill and Melinda Gates Foundation, Broad Foundation, KnowledgeWorks Foundation, National Endowment for the Humanities, Stuart Foundation, and Stupski Family Foundation District Alliance Program. See http://www.schoolredesign.net/srn/server.php?idx=864 for information on these and other foundations.

8. See, for example, Clayton Christenson, *Innovator's Dilemma* (2003). According to Christenson's model, innovative new products (in this case, charter schools) start out by cutting into the low end of an established market, carving out a niche that established organizations (in this case, school districts) would overlook as too small to consider. Eventually these small segments grow and overlap the territory of established organizations from below. The established organizations in this view typically ignore the innovators until it is too late, because they are too focused on their established markets (in this case, traditional public schools).

9. Clark, B. (1975).

10. The 35th Annual Phi Delta Kappan/Gallup Poll of the Public's Attitude Toward the Public Schools, published in September 2003, reports that 26% of

the population would give public schools in the nation as a whole a grade of A or B, but when asked about the public school that their own oldest child attends, 68% would give that school a grade of A or B.

11. See "Mergers: Let's Talk Turkeys" (2000).

12. See Deal, T. E., and Jenkins, W. A. (1994).

13. See testimonials from enthusiastic Saturn owners at http://www.saturn .com/aboutus2/news/ownerstories.jsp?nav=1210.

14. See Deal, T. E. (1975).

15. See U.S. Department of Education (2004).

16. See Meyer, J., and Rowan, B. (1983).

17. See Moeller, J. (1968).

II

A WORM'S–EYE VIEW

3

GUARDING THE MISSION

Kathleen O'Sullivan, Odyssey Charter School

O*dyssey Charter School, an independent public school chartered by the Los Angeles County Board of Education, is located in Pasadena and serves a diverse community of 240 K–8 students who learn best by doing. Kathleen O'Sullivan, the founder and a member of the governing board, piloted Odyssey through its first years of operation as the executive director and has worked with a multitude of organizations—federal, state, local, and private—during the past six years to bring her dream to a working reality. O'Sullivan is a highly skilled communicator, trainer, and facilitator who identifies a problem, works to solve it, and moves on to the next challenge. Over the past 10 years, she has developed expertise in workforce preparation, particularly with at-risk youth. She has over 25 years of business experience in public, private, and nonprofit settings in the areas of recruitment, employee development, marketing and sales, program development, fund raising, and grant writing, and she draws on her professional and personal experiences as a student, wife, mother, foster parent, and grandparent to create and sustain the vision of Odyssey. O'Sullivan and her husband, Michael, an architect, live in South Pasadena.*

Odyssey Charter School is located in Pasadena, California. At the outset of our third year of operation, I am proud to say Odyssey's success is a result of sometimes heroic efforts by many, while weathering the challenges and opportunities that await any new and innovative venture, admittedly by just hanging on one minute longer in many cases.

To understand Odyssey's vision is to understand how and why it was birthed. Unlike many charter school developers, my background is not that of a formal educator, nor did I intend to reform education from the perspective of academia. On the contrary, my motivation for venturing into this uncharted territory was driven by a passion that grew out of my 25 years of experience in the corporate, nonprofit, and public sectors, working for others and for myself, much of which involved training and development. By nature, I am an entrepreneur. I delight in finding innovative solutions that will make a difference, then empowering others to take ownership and grow the vision and the capacity for fulfilling it. Over the years, my work has resulted in successful and innovative programs that have been able to stand on their own as I have moved on.

As a result of my experience and observations in the workplace, and perhaps a bit of providence, I made a decision about 10 years ago to take my career in a new direction. I became immersed in the arena of workforce preparation and workforce development. I was determined to find creative ways to help at-risk youth prepare themselves for the world of work, and to assist adults who were trying to get off welfare and into the workplace. This was my most challenging and rewarding work. Most discouraging was my work with experienced and successful individuals who were suddenly and unexpectedly facing a career transition because their jobs no longer existed.

I found common ground among all these individuals, even though they seemingly had little in common. Regardless of their level of education, training, or experience, these individuals were rarely equipped with the skills that would help them transfer whatever knowledge and skills they had from one environment to another, whether it was from one subject to another in school, from school to the community, or from one job to another in the workplace. All had acquired knowledge but were ill equipped to apply that knowledge in a meaningful way, or transfer that knowledge into another context.

In addition, many of these individuals were lacking the all-important "soft skills" needed to become responsible citizens and successful in the workplace—skills that help individuals succeed, whether they are the janitor or the CEO, inexperienced or experienced, at-risk or highly educated. They include such things as personal qualities, critical thinking skills, people skills, the ability to manage information and resources effectively, and an understanding of how systems work. These are all highly valued in the workplace, as well as essential to relationships, and yet they are given little attention in our educational system. Not surprisingly, those who seem naturally to possess these soft skills often succeed in spite of their education, training, or previous experience. Those who are lacking in these soft skills often fail, even if they are highly educated and well trained in job-specific skills.

This may account for why so many young adults find entry into the "real world" so difficult, and why many experienced and respected professionals are at a total loss when faced with having to make a shift into a new career. Schools today are focused, if not obsessed, with measuring how much knowledge has been gained, often at the expense of helping students learn how to learn and to discern when it might be appropriate to unlearn something. With such a narrow focus, we undermine our ability to create lifelong learners and skillful thinkers. I became more and more convinced that we *must* figure out a way for our educational system, from kindergarten on up, to incorporate opportunities to develop these soft skills in a purposeful manner.

"Sadly, for my children and many others (including myself), school became boring, uninspiring, and all about compliance."

My direct experience with the educational system has been both as a student and as a parent. I have been blessed with children (natural, foster, and adopted) who are bright, naturally precocious, curious, and very active. Like many children, growing up they were doers, and "why" seemed their favorite word. I'm sure my parents would voice the same about me, too. For children who continually challenge every assumption possible, school is rarely a safe, nurturing place. Worse, all too often these students are misunderstood and even mislabeled. They are no small challenge for the parent or for the traditional school system, public and private alike. Sadly, for my children and many others (including myself), school became boring, uninspiring, and all about compliance.

There was one exception for me as a student that was to forever change my view of education. At the age of 16, I had the opportunity and privilege of performing with *Up With People* and becoming a student in their newly formed high school. I joined 100 students from around the world in the adventure of a lifetime. We traveled full-time, performing an inspiring two-hour musical wherever we went. Sixteen teachers traveled with us, mostly by bus, sometimes by train. The towns we visited throughout North America and the families and fellow students we stayed with during that year became our classroom. It challenged everything I knew about education and about people. All of us struggled for at least three months to figure out how to function in this classroom without walls, with the opportunity and responsibility of designing our own learning projects. I stayed on an extra year after graduation to do advance public relations. It called upon every possible resource I had, and then some. It provided advanced training in how to live and work with people who are different from me, and how not to give in to uncertainty and adversity, something I would call upon throughout my life. It was terrifying, enlightening, and extremely rewarding. I wouldn't trade those experiences for anything!

The idea to create Odyssey Charter School was first conceived in the spring of 1998. I had started a private consulting business, Purposeful Training Systems, LLC, in the beginning of 1997 and had just completed writing *Ready for Success*™, a workforce preparation curriculum designed for at-risk students and welfare-to-work clients. My business partner, who had been an educator for over 30 years, was working with me to find creative ways to introduce this curriculum to the marketplace. We decided to attend an international conference on innovation to get some fresh ideas. One of the workshops we participated in was "Effective Intelligence." The presenters, Jerry D. Rhodes and his colleague Ian Wigston, gave a dynamic presentation on this research-based cognitive process, which addressed the soft skills that I believed were essential to prepare our youth for life and work in the 21st century. Effective Intelligence proponents assert that thinking is a strategic skill that drives all other aspects of attitude, skill, and knowledge. They say that thinking is the most "transferable" competence with direct and indirect benefits to *every* activity. My partner and I were both so excited that we made a proposal to Jerry and Ian that we work together to adapt Effective Intelligence for K–12 education. Jerry and Ian were both based in the United Kingdom, so we agreed to meet them in Washington, D.C., shortly thereafter to consider the possibilities.

About the same time, we heard about pending California legislation that would be more favorable to start-up charter schools. George Bernard Shaw, the British playwright and social reformer, is quoted as saying, "The people who get on in this world are the people who get up and look for the circumstances they want, and, if they can't find them, make them." We were fascinated and intrigued by the possibility of starting a school from scratch. We soon found ourselves in the United Kingdom, working with Jerry and Ian to become licensed and accredited to use Effective Intelligence to design and implement a charter school. Naturally, the vision for the school, its target population, the mission statement, and the educational program grew out of our experiences—personally and professionally.

In writing the charter, the first thing we considered was the target population. My experiences with the *Up with People* high school gave me a true appreciation for Confucius's saying: "I hear and I forget. I see and I remember. I do and I understand." While most agree that all students benefit by doing, there are students for whom it is absolutely essential to their success. Odyssey is designed specifically to serve these students, whose learning styles are not well suited for a conventional classroom that is focused on paper-pencil activities, lectures, textbooks, and standardized tests. Students who are bored, unmotivated, and underachieving need a more engaging, "hands-on" learning environment that respects different ways of demonstrating their knowledge and abilities and isn't easily intimidated by their curiosity and creativity. An environment where, according to Plutarch, "The mind is not a vessel to be filled but a fire to be kindled."

One mission of Odyssey is to partner teachers, students, parents, and business and community volunteers to develop leaders and innovators for the knowledge-based global community in the 21st century. Another mission is to be responsive to the demands of the ever-changing, high-performance workplace. I was struck by an article in *Time* magazine in 1993, "The Tempting of America," in which Lance Morrow was quoted as saying, "America has entered the age of the contingent or temporary worker, of the consultant and subcontractor, of the just-in-time workforce—fluid, flexible, disposable. This is the future. Its message is this: You are on your own. For good (sometimes) and ill (often), the workers of the future will constantly have to sell their skills, invent new relationships with employers who must, themselves, change and adapt constantly in order to survive in a ruthless global market." It is a stark reminder that the ability to cope with change and the ability to learn and unlearn may be the only job security on the horizon for our youth.

The design of Odyssey's educational program was heavily influenced by the work of Jean Piaget (1896–1980). Piaget contends that "The principal goal of education in the schools should be creating men and women who are capable of doing new things, not simply repeating what other generations have done; men and women who are creative, inventive and discoverers, who can be critical and verify, and not accept, everything they are offered." Odyssey is committed to facilitating life-long learning by skillful thinkers. The school's learning environment supports a *thinking-focused* program designed to develop timeless, transferable skills within three interdependent learning components: character development, academic excellence, and future focus.

Keeping in mind our target population, we include in the learning environment a multiage setting designed to be student centered—focusing on what students need to succeed, engaging everyone as teachers and learners. Project-based learning opportunities provide a means for students to *take charge of their own learning* by actively planning, researching, and developing in-depth studies of topics of personal interest. Teachers and students evaluate learning on an ongoing basis through a variety of methods that honor different learning styles. A positive climate in the classroom is facilitated through peace education, conflict resolution, and peer mediation to build relationships and resolve conflicts. Parents are viewed as partners; Odyssey encourages and values parents' participation in their children's learning, at home and school.

By providing tools designed to improve the thinking performance of everyone in its learning community, Odyssey seeks to effect significant and fundamental change throughout the school, acknowledging that real change always requires a real paradigm shift in the way we think, the way we teach, and the way we learn. The most distinctive and compelling characteristic of the school design is the powerful combination of Effective Intelligence and the MicroSociety® Program. Odyssey was awarded a $150,000 grant to assist in customizing Effective Intelligence for K–12 education. MicroSociety® is a national school reform model that transforms classrooms by providing a real-world context for academic learning. It also provides endless opportunities for developing critical-thinking skills. Students collaborate with parents, business volunteers, and teachers to create functioning small communities. Students have jobs that help them learn to run businesses, apply technology, develop government and social agencies, and create cultural and arts organizations. Over time, students become immersed in the realities of a free-market economy, including the details of taxes, property concerns, income issues, and politics. MicroSociety® enables teachers to answer two persistent questions students ask: "Why do I need to know this?" and "How do I fit in?"

THE CHARTER

As a change agent who consistently challenges assumptions about what's possible and consistently steps outside the box, I have been faced with numerous obstacles, land mines, and outright assaults throughout my life. My venture into the charter school arena has been no exception. The draft of Odyssey's charter was completed in August 1998, and we began the dialogue with the local school district with high hopes that the local school board would support and approve it. I had been involved in the recent reaccreditation process for the local high school over the previous year and thought I had gained some valuable insight into the unmet needs of students and the ways in which a charter school might address them. Over the next seven months, there seemed to be productive meetings with district staff to address their questions and concerns about the charter. We thought they were good faith negotiations. There were many refinements and revisions to the charter. During the review process, a critical decision was made to locate the school outside the district boundaries in response to concerns that were raised about the possibility that students from outside the district boundaries would be enrolled. However, we selected a site that was still close enough to effectively serve the students in the district who were interested in enrolling.

"Over the next seven months, there seemed to be productive meetings with district staff to address their questions and concerns about the charter. We thought they were good faith negotiations."

During this time, we also began our community outreach. I recently came across a quote from Ellen Frankfort that says, "Choice has always been a privilege of those who could afford to pay for it." This is especially true in the realm of education and is a particularly relevant issue as charter schools enter the market. Parents are conditioned when it comes to education. We had to introduce the community to the concept of school choice via "independent" public charter schools. We had to educate parents about what a charter school is and that a charter school is a *public, tuition-free* school *open to all* students. We learned that helping parents evaluate their choices, particularly those parents who historically have not had a choice, was more difficult than anticipated. All that being said, when the required charter petition was presented to the local school district, it contained far more signatures than the law required.

We held numerous mandatory parent orientation meetings to assist parents in determining whether Odyssey would be a good match for their children. We did not have a school to show parents, but we shared with them our vision and the distinctive characteristics of the school. My business partner engaged parents in an activity specifically designed to demonstrate the differences between a traditional classroom and what Odyssey intended to offer. At the conclusion of the orientation, parents were asked to carefully consider whether this would be a good fit for their children and whether they would be willing to be part of a start-up school, understanding there would be many expected and unexpected challenges. We later discovered that our efforts were subject to the limitations of words and the difficulty associated with helping others fully grasp something new and unfamiliar.

We formally submitted our charter petition to the local school board in March 1999. While we certainly anticipated questions, we were not prepared for the intense resistance and, in some cases, hostility. Of particular concern was the perceived liability for special education students and the decision to locate the school outside the district boundaries. There was an unrelenting flurry of legal intervention on both sides; however, no amount of explanation, even by attorneys, could overcome their fears. The charter was denied.

"We were thrilled. Odyssey became the first school in the state to be granted a charter by a county board after being denied by a local school district."

Over 100 parents had come to the final hearing to voice their support for the school. Having the charter denied was incredibly frustrating and disappointing after all that had been invested and the strong community support that had been displayed. We had a second chance, however. California's new charter school legislation had a provision allowing a charter that had been denied by a local school district to be presented to a county board of education for approval.

Once again, the charter went through more scrutiny, this time by county staff. There were more refinements and revisions, more legal interpretations and recommendations, and more refinements and revisions. Then, on May 25, 1999, the county board voted to approve Odyssey's charter. We were thrilled. Odyssey became the first school in the state to be granted a charter by a county board after being denied by a local school district. But there was no time to revel in our success; it was on to the next challenge.

THE OPENING STAGE

At a time when most education workers had already made commitments for the fall, Odyssey now had to secure a director of education, teachers, and support staff for a school that was anything but typical, where everyone would be a learner. Every employment ad ended with: "Only Learners Need Apply." Interviews were designed to discern whether an individual was a good match for the school. Lacking a school to show them, we were again dependent on words, ours and those of the applicants. When the selection process was completed, we were confident we had found a dynamic team to birth the school. Yet not until "the rubber met the road" would we really be able to evaluate whether our choices were a good match for Odyssey. We would discover that not all were.

In July, the state formally issued Odyssey its status as a public charter school. During this time, the legislature and the California Department of Education were struggling with a new charter school funding model. It presented challenges for all charter schools in the state; however, yet again, Odyssey would become the test case for how the state would apply this new model to a school chartered by a county board instead of a local school district. More tweaking of the legislation was required, and then everyone scrambled to figure out how to put it into action. Systemic change is never easy, especially when what is new doesn't fit into the existing system—by design. There were no easy or immediate answers.

Given the uncertainty of the funding situation, we sought to obtain private funding to ensure that the school could open in early September, as scheduled. We had no history as an organization, so it was nothing short of miraculous that a financial institution granted the school an unsecured $250,000 line of credit, based solely on the anticipated public funds that, although delayed, were expected to show up by February. The private funds came just in time for the school to open as planned.

We had been fortunate to secure a five-year lease for facilities on a church campus across the street from the local community college. We had exclusive use of a two-story education building. Staff and parents labored for three weeks before the school opened to deal with significant deferred maintenance issues and to make the building suitable for Odyssey's use. Everyone was relentless in his or her commitment to getting this done.

The "labor and delivery" process culminated when the school opened on September 7, 1999. Odyssey's 230 K–8 students, representing 167 families and coming from 12 different school districts within about a 15-mile radius, were diverse in every sense. Few knew one another before coming to Odyssey. About 100 other students were on a waiting list as a result of the school's lottery process. The staff of 18 included 10 teachers who had spent three weeks in August getting to know one another and preparing to open the school.

School furnishings were still arriving the first week of school. While teachers were busy creating a learning community within their classrooms, the administration and staff were dealing with the logistics of the drop-off and pick-up of students in a safe and timely manner, class schedules, recess and lunch breaks, and how to make the best use of limited playground and eating areas. Because the school had no cafeteria, parents were packing lunches every day.

"To everyone's surprise . . . a clear difference quickly emerged in educational philosophy and administrative style, and in short order my partner resigned."

By design my role had been more intensive during the design and development phase; my partner was to take a more active role once the school opened. However, somewhere between the charter being approved, the hiring of staff, our three-week training, and the school getting underway, my partner and I found ourselves strangely at odds on core issues. To everyone's surprise, as the reality of a nontraditional classroom and related school culture evolved, a clear difference quickly emerged in educational philosophy and administrative style, and in short order my partner resigned. I suddenly found myself in a position where I had to assume much more responsibility than anticipated. During this same time, our director of education had an unexpected health challenge and was out for six weeks. However, we had recently contracted with a consultant to assist us with our special education needs and she was able to step in during this crucial time. It seemed as if I was working 24/7.

THE ODYSSEY ADVENTURE

In choosing the name "Odyssey" for the school, we may have set a course consistent with its definition, "a long series of adventures filled

with notable experiences, hardships, etc." Over the next two years, like
Christopher Columbus, we came to the realization that it may in fact be
easier to discover a new world than to try to change the one that everyone knows so well. We gained firsthand knowledge that the difficulty is
not so much in developing new ideas as in escaping from the old ones.
Getting the OK to venture out where our independence and potential
success might be perceived as a threat, competition, or divisive was just
the beginning of our odyssey. There were many difficult decisions to be
made about how to set appropriate expectations, for ourselves and others, and the ultimate challenge of adequately preparing for a journey
that was moving us into more uncharted territory than we could have
imagined, with little lead-time and few start-up resources.

Over the years, I have come to realize that no amount of planning
or experience can ever fully equip you for a new venture. Like
Columbus, we left the familiarity of the shore on a new ship, with a
new crew and 167 families on board (including 230 children)—all of
whom had high hopes of a new world that would give them more
freedom and opportunity (and fix all their problems in record time).
We were learning to swim in the middle of the ocean, facing the natural perils of the sea and the indirect threats to our existence—efforts
to undermine charter legislation, erode funding, and withhold or delay needed resources.

During our first year, best-laid plans immediately came face to face
with the additional challenges associated with establishing a school culture from scratch, especially having opened with everything and everyone being new. This was especially true and understandable with the
middle school students. They came to Odyssey with considerable baggage from their previous school experiences, coupled with budding ado-
lescence, further amplified by being in a new school that not only lacked
a history and reputation to define its expectations but had an education
program reflecting a different philosophy. A quote from Pogo says it
well: "We are confronted with insurmountable opportunities." And we
genuinely were approaching the challenges with that attitude, doing all
we could to give change a chance. But change takes time and, more often than not, longer than some have the patience for. As a result, during
the school year we were faced with turnover in some of our middle
school staff and students.

"By the end of May, there was an attempted mutiny."

The first significant wave of discontent on our journey was in February 2000. In addition to our governing board, our initial governance structure included a 15-member advisory board; most were parents. This proved to be a major mistake. Although these parents were incredibly dedicated and gave way above and beyond expectations, what began as valuable help soon grew into a sense of entitlement. A number of parents began to encroach into areas that were not appropriate for parental involvement, and soon they were attempting to micromanage the school. This small, yet powerful contingent of parents (who were primarily Anglo and from a private school setting) made demands to get the "undesirables" (those who didn't look or act like them and, ironically, those who needed Odyssey the most) to conform to their expectations within three weeks, or they would be thrown overboard, so to speak. With the support of the governing board and staff, I followed our map (our charter), compass (the needs of our targeted students), and stars (our ultimate vision). Over the next three months, this stance resulted in waves of unrelenting attacks that at times became very personal and vicious.

By the end of May, there was an attempted mutiny initiated by seven families who enlisted the aid of those who had the power to end our journey (county staff, county board members, and local elected officials). We quickly scrambled to find our life preservers, naively thinking they were in the hundred or so families who signed a petition supporting the school, and in our thorough response to the complaints. But alas, it would take an exhausting six months of intense work, an unwavering resolve, amendments to our charter, and significant and costly legal intervention to preserve our school without compromising its vision.

During our first year, another significant wave came in the form of special education. While our director of education had 25 years of experience in meeting the needs of students with special needs, for practical reasons we had made a decision to outsource our special education services for at least the first year. Our commitment to our special education students was high; however, we were faced with unacceptable turnover in service providers, now beyond our control. As a result, our relationship with the contractor was strained at best. This took its toll on service delivery.

We also experienced difficulties educating parents on the full inclusion model to which we were so committed. In addition, parent expectations were probably unrealistic for a first-year, start-up school. They were further complicated by the fact that most came to Odyssey with a long history of needs not being met by their home district. Of course, Odyssey was expected to fix these problems without delay. We were also faced with a higher than normal percentage of students with a wide array of special education needs. Worse yet, we did not receive any special education funding until the spring. Fortunately, we were able to absorb these costs with our loan. No doubt, all of these challenges contributed to two parents filing for due process, unfortunately in a hostile manner. Even more problematic, driven by potential or perceived liability, we suddenly found everyone in the system taking sides rather than working together to resolve all the related issues. Once again, Odyssey was forced to seek what turned out to be costly legal intervention, but we were able to settle the cases responsibly.

"The challenge of finding a good match, whether in our staffing or in our students, is by far the most important struggle we have."

In the end, we certainly echoed Friedrich Nietzsche's words: "That which does not kill us makes us stronger." We went into our second year stronger and wiser. The challenge of finding a good match, whether in our staffing or in our students, is by far the most important struggle we have, in light of the innovative nature of our charter. We learned the hard way that parents always filter the information presented at our two-hour, mandatory orientations through their own understanding, previous experiences, hopes, and desires, and in some cases with their own agendas. As we prepared for our second year, we regrouped and worked harder, and I believe smarter, to recruit teachers and students who were up for the new challenges before us on the next leg of our journey. As a result of the sifting-out process at the end of our first year, we began the new term with about 70 new families and four new teachers. Nor surprisingly, it made a significant difference in the look and feel of our campus and our classrooms. We also made a decision to hire a full inclusion specialist and to contract out only special services (e.g., speech and language). This provided the stability our students needed and ensured that our special education services were in concert with the distinctive characteristics of our charter.

By January, we had reconfigured our governance structure, which resulted in one governing body. The governing board is a policy-level board and is truly a representative body. Stakeholders include three community members, the founder/executive director, one teacher and two parents (one K–4 representative and one grades 5–8 representative). This has proven to be a tremendous improvement and provides the support needed by the administration without encroaching on the day-to-day operations of the school.

By the spring, parents had finally recuperated from the previous challenges and were ready to put together a parent organization. They formed the Odyssey Parent Participation Group and established working committees to support various activities within the school, and they play an important role in the success of our school.

"There were remarkable turnarounds with students whom many would have gladly thrown overboard. It made everything we went through worthwhile."

Throughout our second year, we learned to enjoy our journey. We built the foundation for a strong community by taking important steps toward embracing our differences and resolving our conflicts in a productive and respectful manner. Periodically, those who had abandoned ship at the end of our first year continued to criticize and attempt to undermine our efforts. Fortunately, it was ineffective in the light of the critical mass of supportive parents, a team of professionals who were united in their mission, and county staff who seemed to recognize our commitment to continuous improvement.

During our first two years in operation, in the midst of and despite all the challenges, students were finding success and taking responsibility for their learning. There were remarkable turnarounds with students whom many would have gladly thrown overboard. It made everything we went through worthwhile.

The governing board graciously granted me a study leave at the end of the school year. The winds appeared calm; there seemed to be a fair sea before us—was that land on the horizon? As I reflected on our first two years, I felt blessed that we had come so far. We had a strong team, including our governing board, staff, parents, and students who were well equipped for the next leg of the journey. I invited our director of education, who was not only a valued colleague but had quickly become a good friend, to join me toward the end of the week to strategize preparations for the fall. That is when I learned she had been offered an opportunity to be part of a new special education school and hoped I would support her in that move. After I caught my breath, I realized that she and Odyssey were in a different stage of development, and perhaps our needs were now different.

It was almost July. How were we to find just the right educational leadership? As has happened so often in my life and the life of our school, providence set in. An individual immediately came to mind, but would she even consider a change, let alone on such short notice? As I began to reach out to others who might know of individuals who might be good candidates, her resumé appeared on the top of the stack. Within weeks she was on board. As an experienced educator who has been a leader in the field of progressive education, she brings the depth of knowledge and experience we need to enter the new world with the tools and resources needed to fulfill our vision.

We also had a change in our administrative support at the end of our second year. Our new office manager/registrar was learning the ins and outs of school operations. As the founder and executive director of the school, I had maintained my 24/7 role for over two years without a significant break. While I realized it wasn't healthy, I found it difficult to break the cycle. I was looking forward to entering the new school year with a strong leadership team that would help me shift into a new role. I was hopeful that these two new individuals would be capable of carrying the day-to-day operations and leadership at the school. The governing board was affirming that I needed to move back into the development mode. I envisioned becoming the ultimate "resource choreographer."

"The governing board was affirming that I needed to move back into the development mode. I envisioned becoming the ultimate 'resource choreographer.'"

What happened next not only forced the issue but was life changing and may have even been lifesaving for me. On the last day in July, we held a parent orientation meeting in the evening. It was late and I was tired. I was carrying things down the stairs to my office when I lost my footing, hit the concrete ground full force, and shattered my right heel. I spent the first six weeks in bed, three months in a wheelchair and crutches, and will be on crutches for several more months. While I would never wish this on anyone, it has shown me so much. I have certainly gained a whole new perspective on mobility issues. And I have finally been able to let go of the 24/7 role. My laptop, e-mail, and phone allow me to work from home, giving me time to regroup and prepare for my shifting role.

My new colleagues rose to the occasion in every way. They provide exceptional leadership and allow me to support and mentor them in their new roles. The real blessing for me personally and professionally has been to see the growth and maturing of the governing board, parents, staff, and students as they take ownership of the vision and make it more and more a reality every day. As I am becoming more mobile, I will be moving out in the community and am excited that my dream of becoming the "resource choreographer" will soon be realized.

In our third year, I believe we have finally made landfall. What challenges do we face as we embrace the new world? We have no doubt made many mistakes in our first two years, and we will make new ones as we seek to make this new world our own. Mahatma Gandhi was adamant in stating: "Freedom is not worth having if it does not include the freedom to make mistakes." California's charter school legislation offers Odyssey and others the freedom to innovate in exchange for greater accountability, and yet, with innovation, mistakes are a guaranteed part of the process. They are absolutely necessary if real and lasting change is to take place. We often find ourselves in a precarious position—under a high-powered microscope that zooms in on any and all mistakes, in a system that is historically "risk adverse." All too often, the system's reaction to something new and unfamiliar, especially when mistakes are being made, is to legislate it back into something that fits the standard paradigm. Learning how to survive in these waters and finding creative and constructive ways to work together for the benefit of the children will be essential to our very existence as we move forward.

GROWING GRASS ROOTS

Rev. Philip Lance, Camino Nuevo Charter School

Philip Lance, a co-founder of Camino Nuevo Charter Academy and chairman of the board of directors, is a nationally recognized leader in the field of community development. In addition to his responsibilities at the school, he serves as the president and executive director of Pueblo Nuevo Development, a nonprofit community development corporation dedicated to serving the residents of the MacArthur Park neighborhood, one of the poorest and most densely populated neighborhoods in Los Angeles. He has a bachelor's degree from Wheaton College in Illinois and a Master of Divinity degree from the General Theological Seminary, and he began his career as a minister in the Episcopal Church. Lance has extensive experience and training in community organizing, fund raising, and nonprofit management. While remaining hands-on with both Camino Nuevo and Pueblo Nuevo, he is constantly in search of new ideas and new projects. A school-linked health clinic opened in fall 2003, and a preschool and high school in fall 2004.

Several years ago I overheard a friend of mine introduce herself as a "producer." I tried to hide my shock and skepticism. My friend did not fit my mental image of a Hollywood producer. Since then, I have met several more very normal people, many of them relatively low income, who called themselves producers. In Los Angeles, being a producer is a role rather than an accomplishment. Producers don't have to have money or artistic talent. They use other people's. What they need is a good idea and strong sales skills to convince people to contribute their money and talent to making the idea a reality. In this sense of the word, you could say that I am the producer of Camino Nuevo Charter Academy. Although I produced a school, I wasn't an educator or a financier. I am a community developer. Creating a school was part of a larger strategy to renew a neighborhood.

Producing the school took about 28 months. It all began when I stepped down from the podium after winning an award and I met the runners-up, Kevin Swed and Jonathon Williams, co-founders of the Accelerated Charter School. This was in April 1998, and I had never heard of a charter school. I was getting an award from a business organization associated with the University of Southern California. The Entrepreneur of the Decade Award (Social Consciousness category) was for my work founding Pueblo Nuevo Enterprises, a worker-owned janitorial cooperative.

> **"In my acceptance speech I said that for-profit corporations . . . could do infinitely more for low-income neighborhoods than nonprofit corporations could. . . . Now I would say that the judges should have given the award to the accelerated school that went on to be named *Time* magazine's school of the year . . ."**

In my acceptance speech I said that for-profit corporations like my janitorial company could do infinitely more for low-income neighborhoods than nonprofit corporations could. Profit-making businesses have the potential to create tremendous wealth that can employ hundreds and even thousands of people. If the business is community-owned and controlled, the potential for sharing the wealth in a way that dramatically impacts a community is even greater. Now I would say that the judges should have given the award to the accelerated school that went on to be named *Time* magazine's school of the year in May 2001. Meanwhile my janitorial company was still struggling to pay a living wage to 45 janitors. More than half of the janitors were shareholders of the company, but they were still numbered among the tens of thousands of working poor in Los Angeles. Working long, hard hours day after day, year after year, does not necessarily mean that you make enough money to escape from poverty.

Although I didn't know it at the time, the seed for Camino Nuevo Charter Academy was planted that evening. As the executive director of a community development corporation, I was always looking for new ways to improve our neighborhood. Our mission is to serve the residents of the MacArthur Park neighborhood by creating self-reliant community-based organizations that offer opportunities for economic, educational, and spiritual empowerment. The charter school idea seemed to fit with this mission.

In the weeks following that encounter with the Accelerated Charter School founders, I learned more about charter schools. It occurred to me that they could make great community development vehicles. A charter school in our neighborhood would be a community-based organization that would be financially self-reliant through state funding based on average daily attendance. It would be empowering not only to the students but also to those of us who organized the school. It would give us influence over a larger neighborhood constituency of students and parents. And it would have the potential to strengthen our economic power.

I had been looking for another project to develop and was restless because of a failed effort to start a small swap-meet-style retail incubator in an adjacent warehouse. I wasn't happy when I didn't have something new cooking. In the past seven years, I had founded four organizations in the neighborhood, each one designed to meet a particular need. These included an Episcopal Church congregation (I am an ordained Episcopal minister), a charitable thrift store, a nonprofit community development corporation, and a worker-owned janitorial company.

The intention behind this smorgasbord of neighborhood organizations was to rebuild a blighted area of the city from the grass roots, beginning with a faith-based vision of community and developing businesses and business-like organizations that could attract resources and wealth. I wanted to avoid a social service model of community development whereby we became dependent on nonstop fund raising or government grants. Organizations that depend entirely on outside funding cannot create the "we are masters of our own destiny" kind of empowered community that I envisioned. Likewise, organizations that provide services through government grants typically become quasi-governmental bureaucracies that keep leaders and clients vulnerable to external political agendas, restrictions, regulations, and overwhelming reporting burdens.

I began my work in the neighborhood in January 1992. This was about four months before the civil disturbances that destroyed hundreds of businesses in the south Los Angeles, Pico Union, and MacArthur Park neighborhoods. The slow economy and burgeoning immigration from Central America during the late 1980s and early 1990s had created a labor glut that kept wages down and unemployment up. Racial tensions were high, and all of the other social problems that come with poverty were increasing.

The neighborhood where I decided to focus my efforts was one of the poorest and most densely populated areas of the city. Ten blocks west of the downtown high-rise business district, the MacArthur Park neighborhood was one of the city's front doors for refugees fleeing Mexican poverty and Central American war. The housing stock was mostly tiny apartment units in large, run-down buildings that were built decades before the city required open space and landscaping. Plummeting real estate prices meant that owners had no incentive to take care of their properties. A building with 50 units could easily have 100 children with no place to play except the hallways.

The large firms and corporations that occupied the office buildings along the Wilshire corridor abandoned the neighborhood because of safety fears and general blight. They left behind vacant shells of buildings. Some of the ground-floor spaces were leased to mom and pop businesses serving the local population, including "envios a Guatemala" (package shipping to Guatemala), immigration services, tax preparation services, Pentecostal churches, and botanicas (providing herbal, self-help remedies rooted in the folk religions of Latin America).

My community organizing effort began with a computerized list—courtesy of the Justice for Janitors union organizing campaign—of jani-

tors who lived in the MacArthur Park zip code area. Using an organizing strategy that I had learned from my years of working with the Industrial Areas Foundation (the organization founded by Saul Alinsky in
Chicago in the 1950s), I began to conduct one-on-one meetings with as
many of these janitors as possible. I called the janitors on the phone, told
them that I was an Episcopalian minister, and asked to meet them to
talk about the neighborhood. I met most of them in their home, but
some of them felt more comfortable coming to the local diocesan office
or meeting at El Pulgarcito (The Little Place) restaurant on the corner
of Wilshire and Westlake, where we ate pupusas and pan dulce.

The purpose of these interviews was to begin getting to know the
neighborhood and the residents—their interests, issues, hopes, and
dreams. I wanted to find potential leaders and potential followers for
my proposed congregational development plans. Finally, I wanted to
see what kind of grassroots support I could muster for founding a
church that would be a true liberating force in the neighborhood on
all levels.

By June 1992, I was meeting with a small group of people on Sunday
afternoons for a "mass in the grass" in MacArthur Park. Five months
later, we opened a thrift store staffed by volunteers from the congregation and supplied by donors from All Saints Church in Beverly Hills.
Profits from the thrift store were sufficient to rent an adjacent store that
we transformed into a chapel. In July 1993, we incorporated a nonprofit
community development corporation called Pueblo Nuevo Development (that became my full-time employer in 1998), and in March 1994
we incorporated Pueblo Nuevo Enterprises, the worker-owned janitorial corporation (for profit).

By 1998, when I discovered the charter school concept at the awards
banquet, I had been working in the neighborhood for six years. I had become more and more worried about the future of the children in our
neighborhood. For one thing, they weren't learning English well. One day
I was visiting with a mother from the congregation for pastoral reasons. I
was seated on the sofa of the one-room apartment with her four children
gathered around. A ladybug flew through the window and landed on
twelve-year-old Esmeralda's arm. I quoted the childhood verse that begins "Ladybug, ladybug, fly away home; your house is on fire and nobody's
home." She stared at me blankly. Her mother intervened, explaining that

Esmeralda didn't speak much English in spite of spending the past five years in the local school.

The problem was not only that the educational program wasn't working for many children. We also had a major crisis in the district with space for students. Construction of school facilities had not kept pace with the growing population of children. The district had taken two measures to cope: putting students on year-round, multi-track schedules in order to accommodate more students per school, and putting students on buses to remote neighborhoods that had less crowded schools.

"Her son had been threatened with expulsion for discipline problems, and she had never been to her son's school because she didn't have a car. . . . Her boss had granted her a two-hour leave from the sewing factory. . . . I didn't have the heart to tell her it was going to take at least four hours to get to the school and back on the bus."

One day while sitting in the reception area of the local elementary school (unsuccessfully trying to get a meeting with the principal), I witnessed a mother trying to determine how to get to the school where her six-year-old son was bused. Her son had been threatened with expulsion for discipline problems, and she had never been to her son's school because she didn't have a car. The office clerk was trying to explain which streets to take to get to the other school, and the mother was struggling to imagine which bus routes might take her there. Her boss had granted her a two-hour leave from the sewing factory where she worked. I didn't have the heart to tell her that it was going to take at least four hours to get to the school and back on the bus.

This incident happened not long after the awards banquet where I first heard about charter schools. I began telling my board members and staff about my interest in developing a charter school, and I set up meetings with the few educators that I knew, including the head of the Commission on Schools for the Episcopal Diocese of Los Angeles. She told me to talk to a man named Paul Cummins. After meeting with Paul, doors began to open.

Paul Cummins is the founder of the Crossroads School in Santa Monica, a private school that has won wide acclaim for its humane, joyful, and artistic approach to educating children. Paul is also the founder of several other educational institutions in Santa Monica, including the New Roads School, a younger cousin of Crossroads. Paul was intrigued by the possibility that a charter school could bring a Crossroads and New Roads quality of education to inner-city children who could not afford to pay tuition. By the end of our first meeting, he had agreed to help. At our second meeting, we decided to name the school Camino Nuevo, a parallel name to our respective organizations, New Roads and Pueblo Nuevo.

Paul brought credibility to our plan to start a charter school. His name recognition helped in the fund raising, and his experience with curriculum helped us to write the charter. He also knew how to imagine school facilities where others saw only neighborhood blight. When I showed him an empty mini-mall across the street from Pueblo Nuevo's thrift store, he assured me that it could be turned into a school. When the chairman of our board asked him how much the renovation would cost, he estimated $200,000. In the final accounting, he was off by $1 million. Our board chair agreed to support the property acquisition because he trusted Paul's renovation estimate. At that time, Pueblo Nuevo Development had $300 in the bank, and the biggest grant we ever got was $30,000 from the Ahmanson Foundation for a thrift store truck. If our board chair had known that the renovation would cost almost $1.2 million, he never would have given the green light.

Another critical component that Paul Cummins brought to the partnership was Bill Siart, a wealthy banker who had founded and led Excellent Education Development (EXED) to help develop and manage charter schools. By spring 1999, Paul Cummins, EXED, and I were raising money to buy and renovate the mini-mall and writing a charter petition to present to the Los Angeles Unified School District for a K–5 elementary school. We purchased the building in July 1999 for $650,000 cash. The charter was approved by the Board of Education in November 1999.

We spent the next eight months raising the $1.2 million needed for the renovation and preparing for opening in August 2000.

We were successful raising the money because Pueblo Nuevo had an eight-year track record serving the community with its church, thrift store, and janitorial company. Three foundations were impressed enough by this history and our vision for how a charter school could strengthen an impoverished neighborhood that they each gave $150,000 to the campaign. Two years later, two of these foundations gave $750,000 grants toward a middle school building campaign, and the third one gave $300,000.

The school opened in August 2000, immediately winning a number of architectural awards for its unique design. I breathed a sigh of relief, feeling that my job was done, but in some ways, the work of creating the school had only just begun. Fortunately, now we had a principal to share the burden. In fact, most of the burden was carried by the principal as I stepped into the background, serving as the chairman of the board of the nonprofit corporation that was incorporated to operate the school.

"All of the rental income serves to strengthen [Pueblo Nuevo Development's] 'bankability,' giving us the financing muscle to embark on new neighborhood development projects."

The partnership between Pueblo Nuevo Development and Camino Nuevo Charter Academy has grown into one that meets Pueblo Nuevo's objectives in many ways. For instance, the school is a tenant that pays $26,000 a month in rent to PND. Some of this rental income covers PND's mortgage on the property, while some of it supports PND's after-school program and wellness center. All of the rental income serves to strengthen PND's "bankability," giving us the financing muscle to embark on new neighborhood development projects.

5

NEW KID ON THE BLOCK

Yvonne Chan, Vaughn Next Century Learning Center

Under the leadership of Dr. Yvonne Chan, Vaughn Street Elementary School in Los Angeles became Vaughn Next Century Learning Center, the nation's first independent, urban, conversion charter school. Chan and Vaughn Next Century have gone on to push the idea of school reform to its limit, creating inspired solutions to many endemic urban school problems. She has led a transformation that has seen dramatic increases in student achievement and attendance, a sharp reduction in crime, and the creation of a Family Center to provide for the needs of the school's primarily low-income, minority families. Additionally, Chan has been instrumental in mustering the support and resources needed to expand the school from its original elementary grades to a Pre-K–12 learning center. Vaughn families have become involved in their students' education as well as in the larger community, thanks to the efforts of Chan and the Vaughn staff. Vaughn was named a California Distinguished School in 1995, a National Blue Ribbon School by the U.S. Department of Education in 1996. It has been visited by Hillary Clinton, U.S. legislators, and dignitaries from around the world. Chan, who immigrated alone to the United States from Hong Kong at age 17, has worked since 1968 in various regular education, special education, and administrative capacities within the Los Angeles Unified School District.

On March 6, 1999, 17-year-old Francisco was shot to death in front of his home, apparently the victim of gang rivalry; he was a block from his elementary school. His younger brother Eddie, a fourth-grader at the school, now named Vaughn Next Century Learning Center, is a member of the student council and is determined to go to college. The brothers led a different life because their school offered them different types of opportunities.

Vaughn is a neighborhood public school located in Pacoima, a designated "Empowerment Zone" in the city of Los Angeles, due to its extreme poverty and high-crime status. Since 1951, Vaughn Street Elementary was cited as one of the worst schools in the Los Angeles Unified School District. Single-digit test scores and poor attendance were a pattern. It served 1,050 K–6 students: 94.9% Hispanic, 5% African American, 0.1% Asian; 80.5% were Spanish-speaking English learners; 97.4% received free or reduced-price lunch.

"Francisco was shot to death in front of his home . . . ; he was a block from his elementary school."

Francisco attended Vaughn beginning in kindergarten. He was always in classrooms with 32–35 students. The school provided 163 instructional days on a three-track schedule due to overcrowding. Francisco was bused briefly to another school in 1991 for four months because of a court-ordered desegregation plan. Francisco had special needs that were not identified until grade 3. Vaughn had a psychologist only one day per week; counseling and after-school tutoring were not available. As soon as he was identified as a severely learning-disabled student, he was bused to another district school for special education services. Vaughn did not offer a special day-class program, due to lack of classroom space and personnel. In order for Francisco to return to Vaughn, his neighborhood school, his parents had to waive the right to intensive special education services beginning in grade 4. Chronic asthma prevented him from maintaining regular attendance. He did not qualify for public health care, and Vaughn had a school nurse only one day per week.

During Francisco's entire education at Vaughn, he was taught by only one fully credentialed teacher. All his other teachers were on emergency permits. Vaughn was a "hard-to-staff" inner-city school. Each year, the school lost 30% of its 39 teachers. Every week, Francisco's classroom was vandalized. New computers were stolen before they were unpacked. Student suspension rose to 12%, and fights between Hispanic and African American students occurred daily. When Francisco transferred to the neighborhood middle school, he had not passed the bilingual redesignation test and was still reading in Spanish with limited skills in English.

Vaughn converted to an independent charter school in 1993. Francisco's brother Eddie started at Vaughn Next Century Learning Center at age three in 1994. Prior to entering kindergarten, Eddie had two years of preschool education at Vaughn, which provides space to the sponsoring district and the Los Angeles County Office of Education to operate the State Preschool and the Federal Head Start programs. The class size at Vaughn is kept at 20 students in all grades. An extended school year provides Eddie with a full 200 days of instruction as well as daily after-school academic and enrichment activities until 6:00 p.m. Overcrowding is no longer a problem; Vaughn has eliminated the multitrack schedule by building an additional 56 classrooms since the charter school conversion.

"Vaughn, which failed Francisco miserably, provides Eddie with a world-class education. ...The student demographics have not changed, but the adults at Vaughn have."

Though Eddie was also identified as a learning-disabled student, he received intervention as early as kindergarten. Services are provided in an inclusive setting that includes co-teaching by general and special education teachers, speech therapy, peer tutoring, after-school tutoring, family counseling, and attendance and motivation activities. Eddie successfully exited from the special education program in grade 3. When Eddie has health care needs, Vaughn's site-based clinic operated by the Los Angeles County Health Department provides immunization, medication, medical tests, and various primary care services.

Along with his friends, Eddie enjoys surfing the Internet during class to conduct research, write reports, and e-mail overseas penpals in China. Eddie's mother is taking a GED class at Vaughn offered by the district Adult Education Division. Her classroom is right next door to Eddie's. She usually waves to her son after her class. On her way to the Vaughn Family Center, where she volunteers child care services, she keeps an eye on the new construction site. She knows that Eddie, after completing grade 5 at Vaughn, will continue his middle school and high school education at this Little School That Could.

Vaughn, which failed Francisco miserably, provides Eddie with a world-class education. Vaughn Next Century Learning Center is located at the same site, serving 1,300 students from special education infants to grade 5: 95.3% Hispanic, 4.6% African American, 0.1% Asian; 76.5% are Spanish-speaking English learners; 97.6% receive free or reduced-price lunch. The student demographics have not changed, but the adults at Vaughn have.

OUT OF THE BOX: WE COULD DO NO WORSE

Vaughn Street Elementary was a typical large, urban public school im-pacted by multiple social stresses. I was assigned to Vaughn in May 1990 amid 24 teacher grievances, two lawsuits, ongoing intergroup disputes, and three death threats directed toward the principal. Vaughn was the third public school where I assumed leadership. My main role was to promote racial-ethnic harmony and improve campus safety. Vaughn needed a battlefield sergeant, not an instructional leader. Student achievement was never on the radar screen of anyone, including the parents. Who had time for teaching and learning? Besides, there were no consequences for failing kids.

Staff morale was low, especially during the 1992–93 school year, when all district staff members were notified of a 10% pay cut, which followed a 3% pay cut from the year before. Waiver applications for increased personnel and fiscal autonomy were rejected by the school district and the teacher's union. A group of teachers began to investigate other means to achieve more flexibility in the operation of our school. Parents of special education students wanted to return their children to the neighborhood school. Instead of the 3Rs, our days were filled with the 3Bs: bus duty, budget constraints, and "But, you can't!"

In November 1992, our school council sent 12 of us to Sacramento for training conducted by Senator Gary Hart and his staff. We were thoroughly enlightened. Though scared by lawyers and district staff, 86% of the teachers voted to start the charter application process. We believed that we could do no worse. On July 1, 1993, we became the first independent, urban conversion charter school not only in the state of California but in the nation.

"When no government funds flowed to us in July . . . I mortgaged my house. All staff agreed not to be paid until August."

We had no clue of the hard journey ahead. Skills needed to educate students were never a problem; the problems centered on legal and fiscal liability issues. When no government funds flowed to us in July, when our year-round school began, I mortgaged my house. All staff agreed not to be paid until August. When local banks refused to set up accounts due to our lack of legal status, we had to manage with our small donation account until the IRS recognized our existence. When the labor unions demanded their monthly dues even when the employees received no paycheck, I took out personal savings to pay all dues. When no reputable insurance companies submitted bids for our liability, workers' comp, and health care, we had to accept a lower-rated firm at high premium costs. When the free or reduced-price meal program was threatened, we flew to the nation's capital to beg for approval just one day before school opened.

BUILDING A POWERFUL COALITION

When very few applicants responded to our 11 open teaching positions, Vaughn started classes with seven emergency-permit teachers and four long-term substitutes. When the assistant principal, the plant manager, and seven other classified employees left, we did not fill these positions, because everyone was willing to pick up the slack. Gradually, a coalition developed that included media and legislators, businesses and foundations, universities and organizations.

"We became media savvy immediately. We were a failing inner-city school striving to be independent and accountable. The press portrayed our struggles as a battle between David and Goliath."

Media and Legislators

We became media savvy immediately. We were a failing, inner-city school striving to be independent and accountable. The press portrayed our struggles with the large Los Angeles Unified School District as a battle between David and Goliath. The *Daily News* and *Los Angeles News* published almost weekly stories as we developed our charter, gained our teacher votes, and battled through the approval process and all the subsequent problems with funding. Even the *Sacramento Bee* tried to defend the defenseless. We were invited to radio talk shows. Television channels joined in the advocacy. We were spotlighted in local news, in a segment by Diane Sawyer on *Prime Time*, on *Good Morning America* and national and local PBS stations, and in magazines such as *Time*, *Business Week*, and *Newsweek*.

Our legislative representatives lent us their ears. The first person who came to our rescue was our assemblyman, Richard Katz. He made it clear to the school district that Vaughn was to receive its fair share of the state's education dollars. He or his staff represented us in meetings with the USDA for food services for our students, with the U.S. Department of Education regarding Title I funds, with the Department of the State Architect regarding our new construction, and with district lawyers regarding our right to buy and own land.

I became an instant national spokesperson on the charter school movement. I served as a keynote speaker and have testified at state hearings in more than 32 states, including Alaska and Hawaii. In addition, I participated in a small focus group discussion with President Bill

Clinton, Vice President Al Gore, Secretary of Education Richard W. Riley, and leaders of the Democratic and Republican parties. A congressional hearing on school reform was held at Vaughn in 1997. Legislators who wanted to sponsor a charter school bill as well as candidates running for local offices visited us. In 1997, Hillary Clinton's visit confirmed that Vaughn was a village fully capable of raising its children.

Businesses and Foundations

Various chambers of commerce and their board members rallied behind our struggles. They wrote letters and op-ed pieces. Their lawyer and accountant members helped us pro bono. The San Fernando Chamber was trying to arrange a loan for us. The League of Women Voters spoke on our behalf in front of the Board of Education. The Valley Industry and Commerce Association adopted official policies in support of us.

Foundations watched our slow but steady efforts in improving the lives of the children and their families. Mayor Richard Riordan donated more than 100 computers and software. The McGraw-Hill Company shipped us obsolete books. Other foundations, including RJR Nabisco, Schwartz Family, Community Technology, Kaiser, and Unihealth, recognized our capacity and funded our grant proposals.

One of our greatest coaches was the Los Angeles Education Partnership. This intermediary helped us create the Family Center and school-linked services. It prompted us to think about the need for a Pre-K–12 urban learning center that would provide comprehensive, community-based programs and services.

Universities and Organizations

Researchers were fascinated with our process. Vaughn participated in various free evaluative studies and long-term case study research. Studies were completed by the Consortium of Policy Research in Education, WestEd, the California Charter Development Center, the National School Reform Center, the Milken Family Foundation, Federal and State After-school Program, and the Nutrition Network. Universities also sent students to conduct observations and to complete master's theses and doctoral dissertations. Professors invited us as class speakers, and they brought classes to Vaughn for on-site visits. Visitors came from Japan, Korea, China, Argentina, Mexico, Chile, New Zealand, and England.

"For 40 years ... we were to answer to accountability measures established by the state and the district. Now when external accountability knocks, we don't have to answer. In fact, we're seldom home!"

BUILDING AN INTERNAL ACCOUNTABILITY SYSTEM

The key to our success lies in our ability to build an internal accountability system. For 40 years, as an existing public school, we were to answer to accountability measures established by the state and the district. Now when external accountability knocks, we don't have to answer. In fact, we're seldom home! After the conversion into an independent charter school in 1993, we began to design an internal accountability system that we own and must answer to.

Leadership Accountability: Shared Governance and Responsibilities

Vaughn has three working committees with full decision-making authority: the Instruction Committee, the Business Committee, and the Partnership Committee. Each committee consists of 20 members, 50% staff and 50% parents and community members. All teachers must serve during alternate years. This structure aligns directly with our internal accountability model. This is done to ensure a bottom-up and maximum-inclusion design. This structure also allows us to develop greater organizational capacity, longevity of leadership, equalization of power, and responsibility. (See table 5.1.)

Stable governance supports the goals of the charter; our administrative team has remained intact since the beginning of charter conversion

Table 5.1. Vaughn Governance Structure

Curriculum and Instruction Committee	Business and Operations Committee	Partnership Committee
Curriculum	Personnel	Parents and families
Instructional delivery	Evaluation	Community and organizations
Class organization	Compensation	Universities and businesses
Instructional teaming	Fiscal and facilities	Joint venture
Professional development		
Technology		
Materials, tools, and supplies		

in 1993. This is my 11th year at Vaughn. No promotion can lure me away, and I will not retire until our new high school is built. As many as 26 of the 39 teachers who led the charter school conversion in 1993 are still with us. The entire administrative team remains intact.

Teacher Accountability and Professional Growth

We have devised a review and assistance system to help each teacher reach high teaching standards. Areas we stress include lesson planning, classroom management, literacy, language development, special education students in inclusive settings, integration of technology as a teaching and learning tool, mathematics, science, social studies, and arts. We have developed specific rubrics or standards for teachers (especially beginning teachers) for each area. Systematic staff development that follows is based on observable needs. We have been able to help teachers move up these developmental levels that positively impact student learning. In addition, an elaborate teacher compensation system is linked to demonstrated knowledge and skills. Thus, we have a teacher accountability system that links teaching skills to instructional supervision, to assistance and ongoing evaluation, to precise staff development, and to incentives.

Parent Accountability and Family Capacity

Though 69% of our parents do not hold a high school diploma, most of them rise to the occasion when we help each other in building capacity. Our on-site Family Center is a one-stop shop that provides families with basic needs, drop-in counseling, prenatal care, family literacy, a parent exchange service bank, adult education classes, job referrals, and services provided in collaboration with agencies.

"The families and school sign a compact each year. Each family is involved for 30 hours per year in their children's education, for example, by attending parent training ... or even singing in their church choir."

The families and school sign a compact each year. Each family is involved for 30 hours per year in their children's education, for example, by attending parent training or evening parent forums, taking their children to the public library during vacation, providing child care for another family's sick child, preparing materials at home, participating in neighborhood watch, cleaning up the community, or even singing in their church choir.

As many as 30 parent-educators participate in a Career Ladder and Advanced English-Proficiency Program. Parents may supervise students on the playground, prepare and serve foods in the cafeteria, assist with clerical tasks, or help handicapped students as a one-on-one aide.

Educational Accountability

In order to carefully and accurately monitor our progress, we measure student achievement using multiple measures and ongoing assessments. Our measurement instruments and practices include:

1. California Standardized Assessment Program using Stanford 9.
2. California Professional Development Institute at UCLA, RESULTS Project Assessment, administered three times a year. The project includes a comprehensive, research-based battery of criterion-referenced, diagnostic tests in every skill area of language arts and English language development aligned with state standards. The subtests are given in August, February, and June of each year. Data must be input by teachers and electronically transmitted to UCLA for processing and analysis.

Table 5.2. Academic Performance Index for 1998–2000

1998–1999		1999–2000	
API	443	API	494
State Rank	1	State Rank	2
Comparison School Rank	5	Comparison School Rank	9
1999–2000 Growth Target	18	2000–2001 Growth Target	15

3. Title I multiple measures using SAT 9, student report card rubrics, and writing samples.
4. Los Angeles Unified School District English Learner Profile, with state standards for English language development and redesignation criteria.
5. Our progress is ranked by the state using the Academic Performance Index. (Results for the past two years are shown in table 5.2.)

We construct a safety net around students with special needs to ensure the success of all. Proactive activities to end social promotion include a state preschool program beginning at age three, small-group early literacy development, full-day kindergarten, three intersessions (winter warm-up, spring sting, and summer sizzle), tutoring, and cross-grade teaming. Extended learning opportunities for as many as 600 students include a variety of closely supervised after-school activities daily until 6:00 p.m. Since we serve 119 identified special education students and 844 English learners, we have placed extra efforts in developing and implementing effective process and instruction to meet their needs. These efforts include systematic identification, highly structured service delivery, ongoing monitoring, and follow-up.

Fiscal Accountability

Vaughn has historically been fiscally and operationally sound. We have established sound fiscal standards to ensure financial stability. These standards include:

1. Establish consistent internal control by using effective budgetary and accounting procedures.
2. Complete interim budget projections to make sure that the school is financially sound.

3. Maintain adequate reserve and cash flow of $2,000,000 in the Los Angeles County Treasury.
4. Review all contracts carefully prior to entering into agreement with vendors and providers.
5. Maintain comprehensive liability insurance coverage, $15,000,000 per occurrence.
6. Prepay necessary contracts, liability insurance premiums, and employee health benefit insurance.

For every dollar spent, we consider the students first. A yearly budget is prepared and tentatively adopted each May for the following school year. The Business Committee utilizes a bidding process when needed, tracks its expenditures using computerized programs, reallocates funds, and makes adjustments. We follow systematic accounting practices, with all revenues and expenditures accounted for at all times. All errors are reconciled within a week. Final accounting reports are audited by an independent CPA. The State Controller's recent four-month comprehensive audit found that we are accountable in all aspects audited.

We continue to make investments through the Los Angeles County Treasury. Currently, we enjoy a cash flow of $4.5 million as well as $2 million in a CD. PaineWebber manages our investment portfolio of $1.2 million. The California Teachers' Credit Union, where we have deposited $500,000, is managing the health benefit expenses of our retirees.

SOLVING THE URBAN SCHOOLING PROBLEMS

Charter school status has given us the opportunity to solve many pressing urban school problems that impact student achievement. These problems include overcrowding and limits to the learning environment, teacher shortage and quality, special education's unfunded mandates, lack of quality preschool, child care and expanded learning opportunities, poor health and nutrition, high-stakes testing, ineffective pre-K–12 education, and the inability of a poor community to support its youths and schools.

Overcrowding and the Learning Environment

Vaughn was the first multi-track year-round school in the northern part of Los Angeles. We operated on a three-track schedule for more than 20 years. Two-thirds of our students (680) were at school while one track (340) stayed home. Siblings were separated; students' language needs were ignored due to scheduling problems and teacher assignment preferences. Our neighborhood does not have theaters, malls, or a library. It is filled with liquor stores and motels. We also transported 260 students out to other schools due to overcrowding. Teachers had no workroom. There was no space for a computer lab, tutoring, intersession, parent education, or student enrichment. We ended the school year on June 30 and began the new school year on July 1. The district and the state couldn't do anything to help us resolve overcrowding, the lack of an optimal learning environment, or our scheduling nightmare.

Our charter school status has changed all that. We have made the following improvements since charter conversion:

1993: 22 teaching stations, on a 60/20 multi-track calendar (year of charter conversion).

1994: Installed six portables and reduced class size to 27 in all grades.

1995: Built Panda Pavilion ($1.2 million) with 14 new classrooms; installed eight portables; eliminated multi-track schedule; reduced class size to 20 in grades K–3.

1999: Built Panda Village ($3.2 million), with new community library, clinic, museum, multimedia lab, science center, professional development center, and 10 demonstration classrooms; reduced class size to 20 in every grade. Vaughn now has 78 teaching stations.

2000: Purchased 2.5 acres across from the school for a 600-seat primary center to house preschool, kindergarten, and grade 1 students. The main campus will then enroll grades 6, 7, 8 (expand one grade per year). Anticipated completion date for the PandaLand Primary Center was set for July 2002 (estimated $8 million).

2001: Purchased 3 acres four blocks away for a small 500-student high school academy (Panda Academy) with the focus on training future teachers beginning in grade 9. Anticipated completion date is July 2005 (estimated $10 million).

By 2005, Vaughn will provide 2,500 students with an optimal and personal learning environment on four campuses located within a 10-block radius, with approximately 600 students on each campus.

Our capacity building began in 1994. After the first year of the charter school conversion, we realized a $1.2 million surplus from a $4.5 million budget. As a principal of a traditional public school, I had no clue how much it would cost to run my school. The district paid for everything, and the system could not control waste and abuse. Our new internal accountability system demands effective deployment of human and fiscal resources. Savings came from reduced costs in administration, special education, food services, insurance premiums, substitutes, utilities, maintenance, and general purchases. Joint ventures with organizations in delivering health and mental health care added to our savings, as did parent volunteer hours.

"With $600,000 of our savings, we turned a crack house into a school house with 14 classrooms in less than 10 months."

With $600,000 of our savings, we turned a crack house into a school house with 14 classrooms in less than 10 months. We awarded the project to a local contractor. The bid specified the requirement of hiring at least 70% of the labor locally, giving preference to our parents who are in the construction trades, including reformed gang members living in the neighborhood as apprentices, and using district high school students in a career-to-work program (Federal Perkins) to build the cabinets. Not only is this a cost-saving strategy, but we have provided jobs in the community and training to at-risk youths. Our students stared with pride at their parents doing electrical work and at their siblings doing the plastering. Vandalism and theft are nonexistent at Vaughn.

In 1996, California began its class size reduction program. The state provided $650 for each student (K–3) in a class with a pupil-to-teacher ratio of 20:1 and $40,000 for each classroom built or leased for the purpose of class size reduction. With such a substantial reimbursement from the state, we paid off our first building within one year. Through shrewd reinvestment and timely land purchases, we went on to build the second building and have paid it off. We still have $4.5 million in our building fund.

We have solved the overcrowding problem. We can accommodate 1,350 students with a class size of 20 in each class. Busing is reduced to 14 students. We are the only school in Los Angeles to eliminate the multi-track calendar and offer 200 school days per year. There are rooms for three computer labs, a teacher resource center, a site-based clinic and counseling center, a large multipurpose room for fine arts, a piano studio, a museum, a large science lab, a large library with 17 books per student, a special education infant room, three resource rooms, and space for child care, parent education, and community activities during school hours.

We are now able to provide space for district training, including school nurse CPR training, special education workshops, beginning teacher seminars, and early childhood make-and-take workshops at no cost to the district. Two universities hold their credential classes at Vaughn: UCLA and CSUN. A small rental lease is paid, and our beginning teachers may take some of these mandatory credentialing classes tuition free. Community organizations and governmental entities including the Department of Justice are now housed at Vaughn. It is now a village bigger than Hillary Clinton had envisioned.

We contract with the district for routine repair by paying 2% of our base revenues. By helping the district pass a citywide bond fund (Proposition BB) and agreeing to provide a small percentage of match dollars, we have received $1.4 million worth of network infrastructure upgrade, E-rate support, modernization of the main office, and various technology and safety projects. In collaboration with Fenton Avenue Charter School and the district, we applied for and received $3.8 million from the Federal Qualified Zone Academy Bond, an interest-free loan with a 12-year term. We used the funds for modernization, repair, and equipment purchase. In the meantime, the bond funds are accruing interest.

Teacher Shortage and Teacher Quality

Without union contract constraints and district personnel policies, we are able to assertively recruit and retain qualified teachers. We now have 69 teachers, 14 with a master's degree, 19% on emergency permit, and

38 certified bilingual teachers. The turnover rate is 7–8% each year. Tools are provided for every teacher to succeed.

Teaching Environment and School Culture   Our teachers form teams of three teachers responsible for 60 students. Each team consists of an experienced teacher with 10 or more years of teaching experience. He or she is partnered with a teacher with three to five years of experience and one emergency-credentialed, beginning teacher. Each team establishes team goals. The focused, targeted collaboration includes frequent communication, weekly planning, a search for common solutions, mutual support, and help to reach collective goals.

Our teachers can share full-time positions in various ways, including a four-day work week, one-semester assignment, and a six- to 10-week positive switch between a general and a special education teacher. Every two grade levels have a resource specialist and an instructional coordinator. This structure strengthens the schoolwide teamwork.

Paraprofessionals with a teaching career goal are provided with a flexible work schedule and sufficient compensation so they can complete their studies in a timely manner. Each year, two or three qualified paraprofessionals are selected to fill vacant teacher positions. Often, the experienced teachers who train them become their team leaders. Our preschool and Head Start teachers are guaranteed elementary teaching positions upon completion of elementary certification requirements. Teachers have ample opportunities to rotate to other grade levels and subjects within our pre-K–12 structure. In addition, teachers with specific expertise such as special education, technology, or English language development can teach university courses at Vaughn. Both UCLA and the California State University–Northridge schedule eight different credential classes on campus in the evening and during weekends.

Teacher Training and Professional Growth   Our teachers have developed a set of teaching standards related to lesson planning, classroom management, and various subject areas that are linked to the students' learning standards. Levels of performance in each area are clearly described using a four-point scale with descriptive rubrics (for details, visit our website: www.vaughn.k12.ca.us).

We replaced the state teacher evaluation system with our Peer Assistance and Review System that takes place four times per year. Our teachers reflect on their own performance and rate themselves using the established teaching standards and scoring rubrics. Selected peer reviewers observe their colleagues and provide feedback as well as assistance. Instructional coordinators also conduct classroom visits and confer with teachers on an ongoing basis. Beginning teachers are assigned one-to-one mentors. Elected grade-level chairpersons are responsible for ensuring that teachers understand and focus on grade-level standards. The director of instruction and I conduct weekly visits, monitor progress of beginning teachers, and focus on school-wide goals.

Based on an individual teacher's performance review, teachers are provided with differentiated training. Training opportunities include small-group workshops, individualized conferencing, observing another teacher, participating in seminars, conducting research, using technology, and pairing with a teacher buddy. We generally spend 5% of our base revenue in staff development (approximately $200,000 per year).

Teachers must base teaching decisions on solid data rather than on assumptions. Data help us monitor and assess student performance. The governor's Professional Development Institute provided results-focused programs for 70,000 teachers this year. We captured the opportunity, and all our teachers participated in UCLA's Focusing on Results training at no cost to us. Our teachers were paid by the Institute to attend.

> **"In addition to base pay and extra compensation for certification and advanced degrees, teachers receive skills and knowledge pay, contingency-based awards, schoolwide student achievement bonuses, expertise compensation, gainsharing, and other benefits."**

Teacher Compensation The single-salary pay plan does not support standards-based instruction and does not work for Vaughn. In an effort to recruit and retain quality teachers, we developed a performance pay plan. In addition to base pay and extra compensation for certification and advanced degrees, teachers receive skills and knowledge pay, contingency-based awards, schoolwide student achievement bonuses, expertise compensation, gainsharing, and other benefits.

Skills and knowledge pay. Level 1 skills include literacy, language arts, mathematics, working with special education students in an inclusive setting, classroom management, and lesson planning. A score of 2.5 or higher in the performance review earns $4,500. An overall score of 3.0 in other subject matters (social studies, science, arts, English language learning, physical education) earns another $5,300. Any fully credentialed teacher whose average in all of the areas is 3.5 or higher earns an additional $4,500. The maximum in bonuses that a teacher can earn by getting top scores on every part of the knowledge and skills review is $14,300.

Contingency-based awards. Teachers can earn a total of $2,000 a year for achieving certain goals in the areas of student attendance, discipline, parental involvement, and working in teams.

Schoolwide student achievement bonuses. All teachers and administrators get an annual bonus of $1,500 if the school as a whole meets the Academic Performance Index (API) goal set by the state, regardless of how much the state provides. Noncertificated staff and part-time staff members also earn a prorated amount.

Expertise compensation. Teachers in a leadership role, including grade-level chair, committee chair, peer reviewer, mentor, and faculty representative, receive additional stipends. A teacher who sponsors after-school clubs, student government, or field learning or who teaches intersession is compensated $3,500 to $4,000.

Gainsharing. Unused sick days continue to accrue, and $250 is provided for every 10 unused days as an attendance award. A separate investment account with more than $1,000,000 is set up to guarantee these bonuses. Teachers share the accrued interest as a form of stock option. The amount is estimated at $1,000 per year per teacher. Based on payroll records (excluding expertise pay), a first-year fully credentialed teacher earns $46,000. A first-year emergency-credentialed teacher earns $39,000. A teacher with 10 years of teaching experience and average scores of 3.0 earns $63,850.

Added benefits. To provide a further sense of security, we have purchased a long-term disability insurance policy for every teacher which provides 60% of their full pay till age 65. In addition, we have set up an account with $500,000 in the Los Angeles Teachers' Credit Union to guarantee health benefits after retirement. We are in the process of developing further benefits for teachers, including college and child care subsidies, and cash reimbursement for out-of-pocket purchases for classroom use.

Not only have we solved the teacher shortage problem, but we have built a highly qualified, cohesive, and dedicated teaching corps. Most recently we accepted veteran teachers who resigned from the district to transfer to Vaughn. This team led Vaughn to win the California Distinguished Schools Award in 1996 and the National Blue Ribbon Schools Award in 1997. As many as 154 of us went to Washington, D.C., to accept the award in 1997. In 2001, as many as 84 teachers and support staff went to China, with all expenses paid. We spent 11 days together, teaching at three schools in Beijing and Shanghai. There's a huge sense of pride and accomplishment.

Special Education and Unfunded Mandates

Every district in the nation is seeking better ways to meet the mandates of the Individuals with Disabilities Education Act (IDEA). Public schools must serve special education students effectively without huge encroachment costs to general education. As a traditional public school, Vaughn was totally out of compliance while costing the district huge encroachment costs. As an independent charter school, we are fully responsible for all the special education students attending Vaughn.

We are implementing a unique inclusion program staffed with three certified special education resource specialists, three special education assistants, and a team of seven support personnel. We make accurate identifications, forge close collaborations between the general education and the special education teachers, and maintain positive relationships with parents. Our inclusion program serves 87 identified special education students (mild and severe). They are meeting their IEP goals in a timely manner in an inclusive learning environment.

We entered into a revenue-neutral agreement with the district. Vaughn receives all the funds for special education and is committed to serve all identified special education students living in the pre-charter geographic boundary. For low-incident students whom we can't serve, we contract with the district and pay for the costs. We make every effort to keep our special education students at Vaughn by providing our teachers and families with the needed support. We are meeting all IDEA provisions with success with minimum excess costs.

Access to Preschool Education and Quality Child Care

Children in our community need an early start, but our parents can't afford the costs. There is no licensed child care center in our neighborhood other than a district-operated Children's Center that has a multiyear waiting list. A state Desegregation Program provided only 90 spaces for four-year-olds four days per week and 2.5 hours per day. The majority of our students stayed home with no early childhood education opportunities.

In 1998, we read about the universal preschool strategy discussed by the State Department of Education and the expansion of state preschool in poor neighborhoods. The Los Angeles Unified School District received an expansion grant but was short of space. With our flexibility as a charter school, we collaborated with the district by converting the desegregation-funded classes to a licensed preschool with eight state preschool sessions, four in the morning serving 80 students and four in the afternoon serving another 80 students, five days per week, three hours per day. We can even enroll three-year-olds in the afternoon, many of whom are students with some identified disabilities. The school district passes the grant funds to us and withholds 4% for administrative costs.

When we learned that the Los Angeles County Office of Education was administering the expansion of the federal Head Start program, we made use of the opportunity to further strengthen our preschool program. The new initiative focuses on locating the program in elementary school sites where the articulation with formal schooling can take place. We are the first elementary site with such a wrap-around program, using our charter school flexibility. We now have four sessions of Head Start serving the same afternoon state preschool children till 6:00 p.m. These younger and developmentally delayed children now receive 6.5 hours of daily instruction and language development. We now serve as the model site for a unique, universal preschool education program.

Lack of Expanded Learning Opportunities

Prior to charter conversion, we kept our playground open as a voluntary, permissive after-school child care program from 2:25 to 4:25 daily. We had two playground workers for as many as 400 students on certain days. There were no organized sports or clubs. Our charter school status now allows us to apply as a local educational agency (LEA) for competitive after-school grants. In 1999, we won the Federal 21st-Century Community Learning Center Grant, the State Safe School and Neighborhood Grant, and the city-funded LA BEST Program. All three revenue sources now support a well-organized after-school program for as many as 600 students, with daily tutoring, homework support, sports, and 16 interest clubs.

As an LEA, we applied for the state Early Literacy and Accelerated English Learning Grant, which provides intensive intersession instruction to ELD students. We have been funding 20 extra instructional days for three years, and now the state is funding what we started.

Lack of Health Care and Nutrition

Due to poverty and lack of documentation, many of our students do not receive adequate health care. We built a little on-site clinic and convinced the Los Angeles County Health Department to provide primary care services to all Vaughn students and their siblings up to age 18. A team of nurse practitioners, a doctor, and medical assistants are on-site daily, providing immunizations, CHDP, blood and urine tests, health education, medication, treatment for communicable diseases, and referral to the nearby UCLA/Olive View Hospital for critical care. The program is funded by a federal match grant to the county for its dollar-for-dollar expenditures on health care in Empowerment Zone communities. The focus is to offer primary care at school sites and reduce costs for emergency care at county-operated hospitals. Vaughn provides the facilities and in-kind costs for utilities, maintenance, a part-time school nurse, and a health advocate. After six months of infrastructure building and operation, the Unihealth Foundation agreed to assume our in-kind costs.

Often, the school meals are the only meals our students receive throughout the day. In an effort to provide more nutritious meals and more choices of healthful foods within the same USDA Child Nutrition budget, we took over the operation from the district beginning in 1994. Since 95% of our students qualify for free or reduced-price meals, we take advantage of a new policy offered by the USDA. Students apply once every four years, as a base year. During the subsequent years, paperwork is kept to a minimum. This universal feeding program eliminates the loss of valuable instructional time while trimming costs. All students are provided three free meals daily: breakfast, lunch, and a late snack. They have five choices of entrees, fruits, and vegetables.

Last year, we were admitted to the Nutrition Network as a separate public entity. The Network, through the State Department of Health, provides match grants for nutrition education, health awareness projects, and community outreach efforts. Our in-kind budget spent on health- and nutrition-related programs leverages approximately $25,000 per year from the Network. More important, our students and their families now receive additional health and nutrition services.

High-Stakes Testing and Sanctions

In 1996, our standardized test scores dipped because of the inclusion of all special education students as well as English learners with low English proficiency levels. Such departure from the norm resulted in many negative comments regarding our academic accountability. But in 1997, our test scores improved. Later, the state of California passed Proposition 227 and required that all English learners take the SAT 9. We were ahead of the curve.

> **"As a charter school, we are in a fish bowl. When an anonymous phone call . . . alleged cheating, we were on the front page . . . for months. . . . At the end of five months, we were exonerated."**

As a charter school, we are in a fish bowl. When an anonymous phone call to the district office alleged cheating, we were on the front page of both local newspapers for months. Four teachers were investigated by the district. We called in a team from McGraw-Hill and the UCLA Assessment Center to readminister another standardized test (Terra Nova) to cross-validate our student achievement. At the end of five months, additional expenses, and investigative sessions, we were exonerated.

We must develop and implement alternative and multiple assessments so we won't be subjected to SAT 9 testing only and the subsequent sanctions when applied. For two years, we administered an additional standardized pre- and post-testing (Terra Nova) in addition to the SAT 9. External proctors from UCLA were assigned to each class, and data were analyzed by McGraw-Hill. In addition, three times per year, we administer block testing on reading and math and collect writing samples. Each student has a portfolio of work that goes from teacher to teacher throughout the student's educational years at Vaughn.

Beginning in 2000–2001, as the entire district focuses on Open Court and Success for All, we have the autonomy to participate in the Governor's Initiative on standards and assessment. We began to transition to a comprehensive instructional and assessment system (Focus on Results) managed by the UCLA Professional Development Center at no cost to us.

We met our 1999–2000 API goal and received a monetary award from the state. Instead of issuing $591.32 to each full-time staff member, we offered $1,500 each as part of the guarantee of our performance pay program. To continue the incentive even when the state discontinues the award, we will provide every teacher with $2,000 each year if together we meet the future API goals.

Lack of Community Resources

Urban schools compete for limited community resources. Low-income communities have a hard time supporting their members and children. We utilize our charter autonomy and flexibility to help build a healthier and even wealthier community. For instance, we forged a partnership with a neighborhood for-profit dump site to build a community library on our campus to illustrate social injustice. Our site-based clinic provides health care, and our counseling center staffed with outsourced personnel from nonprofit agencies helps many families deal with various social realities. Our Family Center provides a one-stop shop for social services, including food and clothing, housing assistance, employment referrals, taxi coupons, and prenatal care. Adult classes are on-site during the day and evening, and we have a Media Center for computer training.

We bought as many dilapidated buildings and crack houses as possible. By building new schools, we beautify the community and provide many jobs. Property values in the neighborhood have gone up. UCLA and California State University–Northridge established a Professional Development Center and offer teacher credentialing classes during the week and on weekends. Our future Business Co-Op operated by the parents will add economic development to our neighborhood. Little by little, our community begins to look like a learning village, with Vaughn as its anchor.

> **"We witnessed our 14-year-old former students becoming pregnant and our 15-year-olds joining gangs. We decided to . . . provide a seamless pre-K–12 education at Vaughn. . . . Since two universities are already on campus, Vaughn can easily develop into a pre-K–16 learning center."**

Disconnected Pre-K–12 Education

We are saddened whenever our graduates, especially those with special education needs, do not succeed in the large neighborhood middle and high schools. There is little articulation between elementary, middle, and high school levels. Every school stays in its box and maintains its turf. In fact, there is frequent finger pointing among the three levels. We witnessed our 14-year-old former students becoming pregnant and our 15-year-olds joining gangs. We decided to build a middle school and a high school to provide a seamless pre-K–12 education at Vaughn. Our instructional program will be well articulated throughout the grades, all under one leadership team, with a collective mission and vision. The four campuses (primary center, elementary, middle school, and high school academy), with 600 students in each, will be within walking distance of each other. High school students can mentor the middle school students, who in turn can tutor the elementary peers who will assist the preschool teachers. It is our goal to usher every graduate to a postsecondary education. Vaughn will have ample internal human capital to make sure that every child succeeds. Since two universities are already on campus, Vaughn can easily develop into a Pre-K–16 learning center when opportunities allow.

Our consistent strategy is to redeploy our human and fiscal resources to meet the needs of our students as we research the educational and political trends that match our programs. Then, in a timely manner, we lobby or compete for the resources targeted for these programs. We have never failed, not once. Even if we don't implement certain programs, other organizations will be knocking at our door.

THE AMERICAN URBAN SCHOOL DREAM

In 1993, we were given a license to dream. The dream is not about power, wealth, and status; it is about opportunities to solve urban schooling problems that we have faced for over 40 years. It's the American Urban School Dream. For eight long years, we pursued this dream with all our passion, energy, enthusiasm, teamwork, and newly learned skills. We are now a successful full-service, community-based public charter school that turned mission impossible into mission possible.

> ## "Our relationship with the [school district] was very difficult during the first three years. . . . We consistently challenged their existing practices."

Our relationship with the Los Angeles Unified School District was very difficult during the first three years of charter conversion. We consistently challenged their existing practices and pushed reform to its limits. After we built capacity and proved our worth, the district adopted new policies that we have set in place, including the USDA Universal Child Nutrition Program, per-pupil budgeting, special education inclusion, the Qualified Zone Academy Bond Project, and various activities to end social promotion. In addition, the district has contracted with Vaughn for state preschool, modernization of existing school buildings, special education services, and beginning teacher training. Vaughn was also asked to provide guidance to the District Accountability Team regarding performance-based evaluation. Most recently, I participated in the district committee to adopt criteria for the selection of the new superintendent. When Vaughn speaks, the district listens!

6

A COMPANY SCHOOL

Michael Lynott, Ryder System Charter School

In 1998, *Michael T. Lynott, assistant general counsel for Miami-based Ryder System, Inc., an international, $5 billion, integrated logistics and transportation services company, became involved with the formation of Florida's first workplace charter school when Ryder decided to open a school on company land. Although his area of expertise was real estate law, he soon became familiar with the intricacies of opening a charter school, and he was responsible for forming a nonprofit corporation to seek a charter, negotiating contracts between Ryder and external parties, reviewing and gathering information for the charter application, and working with consultants to apply for zoning permits necessary to open a school on industrial land. All of this was in addition to his regular duties as in-house council for Ryder. After much hard work and negotiation with various agencies, including the local school district and zoning commission, Lynott was successful in helping Ryder open its charter school for the 1999–2000 school year. Lynott joined Ryder in 1995. He provides legal counsel to the company's asset management group and focuses primarily on the company's real estate, environmental, and purchasing issues. Before that, he was a partner in the real estate department of the law firm of Mershon, Sawyer, Johnston, Dunwody and Cole, which he joined in 1985.*

The history of the Ryder System Charter School begins in the summer of 1997, when a charter school industry consultant approached Ryder senior management to promote the idea of Ryder opening a charter school. Ryder was seen as an appropriate "target" for this type of project because it had a long history of charitable and community involvement in south Florida and because it had previously opened a day-care center for the preschool children of its employees on land owned by Ryder adjacent to its headquarters in Miami-Dade County, Florida. After these initial meetings with the consultant, senior management endorsed the charter school idea and determined to open a school. It was viewed as a significant employee benefit that could be used to recruit and retain employees, and it was also considered a natural extension of the preschool day-care center. In addition, the school would provide positive community benefits in an area where school overcrowding was a serious problem.

"What's a charter school and why are you asking me to get involved?"

My involvement with the school started in January 1998, when I was asked by Ryder's director of corporate services, Glenn Schneider, to attend a meeting about a proposal for a charter school. My first reaction was, "What's a charter school and why are you asking me to get involved?" I was Ryder's in-house real estate lawyer and had worked extensively with Glenn on selling and developing the vacant land that surrounded Ryder's headquarters. One of Glenn's many duties was overseeing Ryder's headquarters building and its surrounding campus. I told Glenn that I didn't know anything about charter schools (he admitted that he didn't either) but that I would attend the meeting with him to see how I could help. From the time of this first meeting in early 1998 until the day the school opened in August 1999, Glenn and I learned an awful lot about the problems and issues connected with building and opening a charter school.

I don't know whether our experience with creating the school could be considered typical, and I wouldn't say that the rest of this story could be used as a blueprint for others on how to open a school. I would definitely say that anyone considering the idea needs to be prepared to deal with many different types of issues, and that Glenn and I were constantly surprised by the number and types of problems and challenges that arose during the process. In fact, one of the interesting side effects of my reviewing my files to refresh my memory for this story was that I was reminded of certain problems which at the time seemed insurmountable but which were quickly forgotten once I became caught up in the rush of day-to-day things that needed to be done in order to open the school. For example, my notes indicated that the original proposal for the school contemplated a K–2 facility with 200 students. The school that is up and running today is a K–5 school with just under 500 students.

"The consultant notified [us] ... that they were no longer interested in pursuing this project because of the site plan issues. ... Using 'site limitations' as the excuse was an easy and nonconfrontational way for the consultant to bow out gracefully."

As I mentioned earlier, I became involved in the school project because of my background as a real estate lawyer. In fact, the first several project meetings that I attended focused mainly on issues such as the site plan for the school, roadway access to the school, the size of the parcel of land needed to construct the school, how long it would take to construct the school, zoning and permitting issues, etc. These were all subjects that, as a real estate lawyer, I understood and felt very comfortable handling. During these meetings in January and February 1998, it was determined that the best place to locate the school was on a parcel of land adjacent to Ryder's existing day-care center. There was, however, the slight problem that Ryder had recently contracted to sell this parcel of land to a local real estate development company that planned to build an office complex on the property. Because Ryder had a long-standing relationship with this developer, Glenn Schneider was tasked with approaching the developer about getting back about an acre and a half of the eight acres that Ryder had contracted to sell. When the developer understood why Ryder was making this request, it agreed to release the necessary parcel for the school site. In one of the many ironic twists in this history, this same developer would later play a role in the construction of the school.

Once the parcel was secured, the consulting firm that had approached Ryder about this charter school project began to prepare preliminary drawings for a school facility. Almost immediately there were problems with this process because the designers felt that the parcel was too small, street access would be a problem, and there was no room for parking or play areas. Glenn and I were somewhat dismayed by this news because the same firm that was raising these issues was the firm that advised us that the school would only require a 1.5-acre site for the school facility. We advised the designers that because Ryder owned the adjacent day-care center site, Ryder could consider sharing parking areas, playgrounds, and access ways to help mitigate the site issues. At the same time, we also told the designers that they really needed to work with the parcel that was available, since it was extremely unlikely that the developer would give back any more of the land that Ryder had contracted to sell. We also advised that it was unlikely that the developer would grant the school parking or other access rights over their office project, since this would negatively impact their ability to develop and sell their office project. After a lot of discussion about various alternatives, the consultant notified Ryder in March 1998 that they were no longer interested in pursuing this project because of the site plan issues. My own suspicion is that there were other factors behind the decision to not move forward with the plan. Using "site limitations" as the excuse was an easy and non-confrontational way for the consultant to bow out gracefully.

"Having a group with all of these different competencies was critical to the project's success. Without the assistance of all these players, there is no way the school could have been . . . ready."

This news temporarily put the project on hold. However, because Ryder management had determined that Ryder was going to open a school, Glenn Schneider was asked to speak with other charter school management and consulting companies to see whether they would be interested in helping Ryder build and operate a school and whether it could be done on the designated site. Over the next few months, Glenn met with several different companies about the project, and in early May 1998, Ryder selected Charter Schools USA of Ft. Lauderdale, Florida, as the company that would assist Ryder with opening a charter school. CSUSA had experience with charter schools and had opened and was operating several in Broward County when they first met with Ryder. In addition, CSUSA was particularly appealing to Ryder because they brought a holistic approach to the project. Although they had never opened a school "from scratch," they had partnered with an architectural firm that had designed many schools in the state of Florida, with an investment banker to advise on financing the construction of schools, and with a real estate development company to manage and oversee the construction of schools. This real estate developer was the same company from which Ryder had retrieved its land for the school. Although Glenn and I did not realize it at the time, having a group with all of these different competencies was critical to the project's success. Without the assistance of all these players, there is no way the school could have been designed, constructed, and ready for occupancy in August 1999.

In June 1998, representatives of all these different companies began having meetings at Ryder's headquarters to discuss the project. The biggest issue facing this group was the timing. Ryder wanted the school open for the 1999 school year, which meant that it would have to be ready in mid-August 1999, barely 14 months later. Everyone agreed that it could be done, and also agreed that it would take a major commitment from each party to succeed. The party with the biggest commitment to make was Ryder, since it would be required to advance all of the funds necessary to get this project rolling without any guarantee that the school board would approve its application for a charter, that there would be enough parent and student interest, and that all of the required zoning and permitting issues could be overcome. Glenn Schneider, as the Ryder project "owner," had to obtain senior management approval to proceed in the face of all these uncertainties. Glenn had his discussions and was given the green light to proceed.

Ryder and the external parties (CSUSA and its partners) signed a letter of intent that guaranteed the external parties would be paid for the work they were being asked to undertake. Glenn decided that he would draw on Ryder's internal resources and asked various other Ryder employees to get involved in the project. This group was very deliberately chosen for the expertise that they could bring to the table, and Glenn involved people from Ryder's facility management, communications/public relations, finance, treasury, and human resources departments. Glenn also decided that with so many people having responsibilities for different aspects of the project and with so many different things proceeding on parallel paths, regular group meetings were essential if this project was going to succeed. Starting in July 1998, representatives of all the external parties and all of the Ryder internal people agreed to meet on a monthly basis to update each other on their respective progress. These monthly meetings proved to be extremely important, and I am convinced that the school could not have opened without these team meetings.

"There was a sense that we were working on something important for the company and for the local community . . . that we were doing something that had not been done before . . . [that] Ryder's planned 'charter school in the workplace' was to be the first of its kind in the nation."

A number of "take-away" assignments came out of these team meetings. At the conclusion of the first meeting, I was charged with (1) forming a not-for-profit Florida corporation (which was a legal requirement to apply for the charter from the local school district), (2) negotiating and finalizing the letter of intent between the external parties and Ryder, (3) reviewing the form of the application for the charter and gathering information required to submit the same, (4) assisting the land use/zoning consultants with assembling the information required to submit applications for the zoning variances that would be necessary to construct a school in an area zoned for industrial and office use, and (5) generally assisting Glenn with all of the other issues that needed to be addressed internally and externally. This was all in addition to my regular duties as an in-house lawyer for Ryder, which normally kept me busy enough for my liking! Notwithstanding the amount of work involved, the entire team was energized because there was a sense that we were working on something important for the company and for the local community, and the realization that we were doing something that had not been done before. Ryder's planned "charter school in the workplace" was to be the first of its kind in the nation, and on September 10, 1998, Ryder held a formal press conference at its headquarters to announce the plan to its employees and the public.

"By involving these key people early and making everyone aware of the . . . potential obstacles . . . [we] hoped to get their 'buy-in.'"

Ryder public relations people put a great deal of time and effort into planning this event. Members of the local and national press were invited to attend the press conference, along with local school district board members and other local politicians. Tony Burns, Ryder's CEO at that time, made the formal announcement about the school. It is important to remember that, at the time, all Ryder had was an artist's conception of what the school would look like on a vacant piece of land across the street from its headquarters. There was no zoning approval to build a school, no one under contract to build a school, no contract with any company to run the school, nor any charter from the school district to authorize the opening of a school. The people invited to attend the press conference were deliberately chosen because they were the same people whose help and votes would be required to obtain the zoning approvals, building permits, charter contract, etc. By targeting and involving these key people early and making everyone aware of the timing and other potential obstacles that the project faced, the project team hoped to get their "buy-in" and achieve some measure of support and goodwill for the project.

Ryder's formal announcement of the project caused the pace to quicken, since Ryder did not want to miss its deadline. In addition to moving full speed ahead with the architectural design of a school for 500 students and obtaining all of the necessary permits to construct the same, work began in earnest on the charter application. Because CSUSA had been through this application process before, they took the lead on the first draft that was to be submitted to the school district. Once the first draft was completed, it was circulated to all of the Ryder people involved in the project for review and comment. The application was submitted to the Miami-Dade County school board on September 11, 1998. CSUSA was able to get the school board's commitment that they would vote on the application at their November 18, 1998, meeting. This was a significant development because it was important for everyone involved to know as early as possible whether this application would be approved. If the application was not approved, there would be no need to move ahead with all of the other related zoning, planning, and construction approvals for the school (and the attendant costs).

In fall 1998, while all of the external parties were working on their respective aspects of the project, the internal Ryder group was focused on selecting the first board of directors for the not-for-profit Florida corporation that had been formed to apply for the charter. This group, too, was selected for the specific expertise that each person could bring to the board, and there was significant overlap between this group of board members and the internal project team that had already been chosen to assist with getting the school open. Once the board was formed and roles were assigned, this group began having its own meetings to deal with the charter application process. This board was created at precisely the right time, because shortly after the charter application was submitted, the feedback from the school district was not positive. The district's process for reviewing the charter application began with the district's Technical Assistance Team meeting to discuss the application. The team was composed of representatives from 18 different departments within the school district (e.g., legal, finance, transportation, health and safety, academics), each of which was required to review and comment on the charter application.

"I was surprised at the depth of the opposition (and, in some cases, open hostility) to the application and did not understand why they were opposed to something so positive."

After several initial meetings between this team and CSUSA, I was asked to attend the next meeting to hear the concerns of the school district's team. As soon as the meeting started, it was immediately apparent that the team had real concerns about certain portions of the application. Certain team representatives let it be known that they would not approve the application unless serious modifications were made. I was surprised at the depth of the opposition (and, in some cases, open hostility) to the application and did not understand why they were opposed to something so positive. However, as the meeting progressed, I learned that the district's team was upset that this was the first time someone from Ryder had attended one of the meetings about the application. In their view, Ryder was not truly engaged in this process but had simply turned it over to an outside management company. In addition, this was the first time that a charter school applicant had retained a school management company, and there was some apprehension on the part of the school district's team because of this complication. For all of these reasons, it was very important to clear the air on both sides so that everyone involved could get down to the business of the actual application rather than the perceptions about why the application was being submitted in a certain way.

It also became apparent that one of the main reasons for this lack of trust between the parties was that there were simple communications failures. It turned out that CSUSA had in fact not invited anyone from Ryder to attend the early meetings because they felt it was not necessary. CSUSA believed that they had been retained by Ryder to handle this application process because they were the experts in this area. They also believed that there were many other noncharter application issues that Ryder needed to be focusing on and that they were making things easier by handling the application process alone. During my first meeting with the school district's team, I emphasized that Ryder was very engaged in the project but that operating a school was not one of Ryder's core competencies, and for this reason Ryder had to depend upon outside expertise to get this school off the ground. Once these and other similar factors came to light, each side was able to gain a better understanding of who was doing what and why, and real progress was made on the application. After several more meetings and many revisions to the original document, the application was approved by the Miami-Dade County school board at its November 18, 1998, public meeting. Ryder and the school district could now start negotiating a charter contract.

Simultaneously with the application negotiations, the project team was proceeding with the preparation of the site plan and facility layout, the plans and specs for the construction of the school, and most important, zoning approval for the school, without which the school could not be built. The local zoning process required that there be a public hearing on the application so that all interested parties could be heard. This hearing was scheduled for December 15, 1998. The external people working on this project for Ryder were relatively confident that they would obtain the necessary approvals. However, because of the space limitations with the proposed school site, they were always very cautious whenever they were asked about the prospects for success. Everyone seemed to agree that the site was too small to accommodate a school for 500 students. In addition, because of traffic patterns in the streets surrounding the school, there were real concerns about curb cuts and access to the site, traffic flow, parking, and safety.

Notwithstanding the space limitations and related issues, on the day before the public hearing, Ryder was advised that the county's zoning staff had approved the plans for the school and would support approval at the public hearing. This was great news for the project team, and everyone went home the night before the scheduled public hearing relieved that this matter seemed resolved. However, the next morning, Ryder's zoning consultant was advised that the zoning staff would be voting against the school's application on the basis that the proposed school was located within the flight path of a runway to the Miami International Airport. Upon hearing this information, the group responsible for obtaining the zoning approval did some quick investigation and discovered that in addition to Ryder's day-care center (which had been permitted about five years earlier), several Miami-Dade County schools were also within the same flight path, not to mention the thousands of people living and working in this area. Despite not having the endorsement of the county's zoning staff, the local zoning board did approve the application. But, as usual, there were conditions attached.

Several of the local zoning council's conditions for the approval were somewhat unusual, but the Ryder group that presented the application before the zoning council did agree to them. One condition was that the school give preference to residents of the area that was subject to the zoning council's jurisdiction (the Doral area of West Miami). At the hearing, I explained to the council that the law (and the charter application previously submitted to and approved by the school district) did not permit Ryder to grant any preference for admission to the school based on a geographic area. Nevertheless, the council insisted that this condition be inserted into their final zoning approval. Another condition demanded by the zoning council was that a resident of the Doral area (to be appointed by the council) must always serve as a member of the school's advisory committee. This school advisory committee was an organization mentioned in the school's charter application. It was to consist of parents, teachers, and community representatives whose role was to advise the board of directors of the school on issues of importance at the school.

Both of these seemingly non-zoning-related demands were driven by the fact that the Doral area had experienced rapid population growth over the previous five to seven years and school overcrowding was a serious problem. The local zoning council was actually a great proponent of Ryder's school, but they wanted to be sure that the school would have seats available for local students to help alleviate overcrowding. This subject of access to the school was an important issue for both the zoning council and the school district, and it would surface again. Both of the conditions were included in the final zoning approval and were incorporated into the final charter agreement between the school and the Miami-Dade County school board.

The next significant set of problems involved the negotiation of the actual charter contract between the school and the local school board. Predictably, the district wanted to use their standard form. I maintained that the proposed form was much too long and did not take into consideration that this was the first charter school in the workplace, which meant that the standard form did not work. The school district's representatives seemed genuinely surprised that Ryder wanted to make changes to their charter contract. As negotiations progressed, four big issues separated the parties. The first had to do with the personal liability of the board of directors of the school. The district's form contract contained language stating that if the school was shut down or terminated, the board of directors of the school would be individually and personally liable for the school's debts. I told the school district representatives that they would never find anyone willing to serve on the school's board if there was any chance that these people could be held personally liable for the school's debts. I also pointed out that Florida's charter school law required all charter applicants to form a not-for-profit corporation to apply for the charter, and that it was inconsistent to require people to form a corporation and then ask them to be personally liable. One of the main reasons that people form corporations is to shield themselves from personal liability. Despite all of these arguments, the school district was unwilling to change their standard language. Ryder was forced to contact the State of Florida's Department of Education lawyers, who advised the school district that the school was correct and the personal liability language should be deleted.

A second major issue involved admissions to the school. The local school board was very concerned that Ryder's intention was to have a small "elite" school at the Ryder headquarters that would be open only to the children of Ryder employees. Ryder pointed out that this was never its intention and that the school had been designed to accommodate significantly more students than the Ryder employee base could deliver. The third issue was that the school district wanted Ryder to provide transportation to any student within Miami-Dade County who wanted to attend the school. Ryder countered that this was out of the question. The expense associated with providing busing for all students would make the entire project cost prohibitive. Ryder also pointed out that as a charter school in the workplace, the original conception for the school was that Ryder employees would transport their own children to and from the school when they came and went to work each day. This impasse was broken when Ryder agreed that it would provide transportation to students living within a very limited area in the vicinity of the school. This was truly a win–win for all involved because the defined transportation area was equivalent to the boundary of the Doral zoning council's jurisdiction. The vast majority of potential students residing within this area were not children of Ryder employees, and thus the school would be serving the local community by transporting Doral area students to a new school and helping to alleviate the local overcrowding problem.

The final big issue separating the parties was how the construction of the school would be financed. Ryder originally proposed to donate the land on which the school was to be constructed to the not-for-profit corporation formed to hold the charter. This corporation could then mortgage the land to obtain a loan to fund some of the cost of constructing the school building. The funds to be received from the state for operating the school could then be used to repay the mortgage loan. The school district objected to this proposed arrangement; they were concerned about state funds being used to construct a public school building on privately owned land. After many meetings and much negotiation, this problem was solved when Ryder agreed that it would lease the land to the not-for-profit corporation formed to hold the charter. The end result was that Ryder would be required to advance the funds for the construction of the school; however, these advances would be repaid from the lease payments made by the not-for-profit corporation to Ryder. The school board actually preferred that Ryder use this lease arrangement.

When all of these issues were resolved, the charter contract was submitted for approval by the Miami-Dade County school board, which approved the contract at its March 17, 1999, meeting. The charter was for a five-year term, and this length of time was also a first in Florida. At this point, all approvals necessary for the project were received. The focus then shifted to the actual construction process and whether the school would be ready on time. The school district had made it clear that if the school did not receive a certificate of occupancy to open in time for the start of the district's school year, they would not approve its opening until the following school year. Missing this deadline would have been a serious financial and public relations problem for the school and Ryder, so all efforts were made to be sure the job was completed on time. In fact, the contracts that were signed with the architects, construction company, and construction management company all contained provisions granting incentives to finish early and penalties for delays.

Many other issues arose and were dealt with before the school was ready to open. However, all of the deadlines were met and Florida's governor, Jeb Bush, was present at the grand opening of the school in August 1999. The Ryder Elementary Charter School was officially opened for 300 K–3 students for the 1999–2000 school year.

"[It is important to have] a positive attitude when faced with unexpected challenges ... to create a team with the right skills and ... to include people outside the education field ... with legal, financial, facilities/real estate, public relations, and human resources experience."

As I mentioned early in this story, my intention was not to provide a blueprint for how to open a charter school. Rather, I have attempted to give the reader a feel for the types of issues that can arise and the way that these issues were dealt with in our particular case. The advice that I can give from my experience with the school is that anyone planning to open a charter school must have realistic expectations and must be prepared to negotiate and compromise. Having a positive attitude when faced with unexpected challenges is also important. It is equally important to create a team with the right skills for the project, and this team needs to include people outside the education field. If possible, the team should include people with legal, financial, facilities/real estate, public relations, and human resources experience. Finally, the team must communicate well, and regularly scheduled project status meetings should help foster this type of communication. Even with the right attributes and team members, it still won't be easy, but seeing the end result on the school's opening day will make all of the effort worthwhile.

7

CLAWING YOUR WAY

Joe Lucente, Fenton Avenue Charter School

On *January 1, 1994, Fenton Avenue Elementary School became California's 30th charter school and one of the few that are totally autonomous. Fenton Avenue Charter School, one of the largest public elementary charter schools in the nation, is a nationally recognized model of a conversion charter school. Joe Lucente, co-director of Fenton Avenue Charter School, has been a teacher and administrator with the Los Angeles Unified School District for 20 of the past 30 years and has helped guide the school along a most successful path. The school was a 1997 California Distinguished School awardee, and Lucente was one of five charter school directors from across the nation invited to the White House in August 1998 for a conference sponsored by First Lady Hilary Rodham Clinton and the Department of Education for new D.C. charter schools. Lucente was born to immigrant Italian American parents in Renton, Washington. He has lived, gone to school, and worked in Los Angeles most of his life. His employment background includes being an administrative officer in the United States Air Force, three-plus years in management positions with the Los Angeles* Herald-Examiner, *and 32 years in education (two of them abroad).*

In August 1987, I was one of two assistant principals at a large, year-round elementary school in Pacoima, California. Pacoima is very much the inner city of the San Fernando Valley, with a predominantly minority population at very low socioeconomic levels. I was working under the tutelage of a very competent and knowledgeable principal, and I was very happy, but I was learning as fast and as much as possible because I knew my time was coming. Due to an acute shortage of administrators in the Los Angeles Unified School District, capable assistant principals were being promoted after two years of experience. I was now a veteran of 20 months with a name well-known in LAUSD because of two older sisters who were longtime successful LAUSD administrators. I didn't have to wait long! I was summoned to the region superintendent's office on a Friday afternoon in mid-August. As my principal put it, the good news was that I was being given a principalship. The bad news was that it was a very "difficult" assignment, about two miles east of my current school. Undaunted by my principal's bad news, I set out to meet my new challenge.

"I was told that Fenton was a school totally out of control, and that I was to be the fifth principal of the school in six years."

The one-and-a-half-hour meeting that followed with the superintendent and region administrator bordered on the bizarre. The majority of the time was spent describing what the superintendent called a "hell-hole" known as Fenton Avenue Elementary School—my new assignment! I listened in disbelief. I thought they must be exaggerating to make a point. I was told that Fenton was a school totally out of control, and that I was to be the fifth principal of the school in six years:

- Number one left after nine years during which the school's demographics changed from predominantly African American to predominately Hispanic.
- Number two died after 18 months.
- Number three asked to leave after one year that was punctuated by numerous death threats from a parent!

- Number four sat in his office an entire year with the door closed and a large "No Admittance" sign on it. He relinquished control of the school to a fifth-grade teacher new to our district.
- Number five was lucky me!

Fenton was rife with racial problems, theft, vandalism, high student and staff absenteeism, frequent fights among students, staff, parents, and community members, single-digit test scores, financial mismanagement, and every other sign of a totally dysfunctional school! I was informed it was one of the two worst schools in the San Fernando Valley. (To understand the magnitude of that statement, one must realize that if the San Fernando Valley were a school district, it would be the seventh largest in the nation. It is also of note that the other of the two worst schools was Vaughn Street Elementary School.) To make matters worse, the region administrator who recommended me for the position informed me that I was her last hope because her last several promotees had failed. "You must succeed. I'm counting on you, Joe!" were her exact words.

The entire weekend I thought about what I had heard. What had I gotten myself into?!? I wondered if I could succeed. To this point in my life, I had taken my business degree and self-confidence and succeeded in many challenges with no prior experience: as an Air Force administrative officer, as a business manager in several different businesses, as a teacher, a newspaper production supervisor, a real state broker, and an assistant principal. Would being principal of Fenton be my Waterloo?

Fenton is hard to find without directions. After being lost for a half-hour, I finally arrived at my new school. My briefing at the region office never included any information about the actual school site itself, so I was pleasantly surprised by the campus: a square city block with multiple bungalow-type classrooms and more than 70 mature trees. Although desperately in need of maintenance, it appeared to be a "good looking" school. Originally built to house 350 students, it now had 950.

My indoctrination at the region office was not exaggerated. If anything, they had softened the blow! It was certainly going to be the greatest challenge of my adult life! Undaunted by teachers and parents who would brush me off with "I'll talk to you if you're still here in six months," I spent the next two years smiling, shaking hands, putting out "fires" everywhere, and eliminating the incredible number of inequities that permeated the organization. One thing I discovered was that all African American teacher assistants had six-hour positions while all Hispanic T.A.'s had only three-hour assignments although 60% of the students were Spanish-speaking Hispanics.

We made the campus safe and secure by adding gates, fencing, and lights. We reroofed and painted the entire school. The long line of staff who wanted to leave Fenton were shown the door. With no volunteer replacements, anyone who appeared willing to accept the challenge of working at Fenton was hired. At least they were willing to be there! For the first two years, I did not have an assistant principal. When one was assigned in 1990, it was like receiving reinforcements in battle!

"I assumed charter schools were just another paper reform movement. . . . Then I heard . . . that although the school district got $4,100 per student from the state, less than $2,900 reached our schools."

In 1991, a slumping economy, LAUSD's shortsightedness, and the teachers' union practice of putting children second resulted in a 10% pay cut for all LAUSD employees. Other changes increased the norm for assistant principals. This resulted in a domino-effect bumping of personnel. Fenton's assistant principal was bumped back to a coordinator's position and a new A.P. was assigned. I was not pleased! This action, however, has had the greatest positive impact on my professional life and on the lives of the members of the Fenton community. Our new A.P., Irene Sumida, proved to be the shot in the arm we all needed: brilliant, caring, unparalleled in instructional knowledge and ability, organized, goal-oriented, hard-working, unflappable, and a wonderful human being! Working side by side we accomplished much. It just wasn't enough! Although Fenton was hardly the "hell-hole" of five years ago, there were some undeniable facts:

- We were not impacting student achievement; standardized test scores were still in the single digits.

- Staff morale was low after the pay cut and years of "having things done to you."
- Most of our leadership team had made the decision to leave the district or even the state.
- My hands were raw from being slapped by those above me each time I circumvented the system to get something accomplished.

We were a group of educators who wanted to make a difference but were very close to abandoning Fenton, and I did not think I could handle another five years as an LAUSD principal in order to reach early retirement. Bearing all the responsibility but without any authority to make substantive changes was no way to manage. Our monthly principals' meetings had degenerated into "bitch sessions with lunch." Dr. Yvonne Chan, a fellow principal, had been talking about her school leaving the district and becoming a charter school. I assumed charter schools were just another paper reform movement akin to moving the deck chairs around on the *Titanic*. Then I heard from our representative to a negotiating team that although the school district got $4,100 per student from the state, less than $2,900 reached our schools. I began listening to Yvonne and investigating the charter school concept.

I firmly believed that control of the decision-making process was not enough. You had to have control of the money and enough to make substantive changes. Yvonne and I teamed up and began asking questions about the money. Surprisingly, we could not get firm numbers from anyone we queried at the state and local level. We ended up wading through LAUSD's prior year's financial statements—all three inches! We, too, were unable to extrapolate firm numbers. We were able to identify a range. We believed our students would generate between $4,300 and $4,800 each. Armed with this information, Yvonne and I went back to our schools and pushed on.

I costed out our current operation to determine current expenditure levels by LAUSD. I then created on paper "Joe's Dream School": reducing class size from 32 to 25, six additional teachers, a full-time counselor and psychologist, a full-time Family Center director, new textbooks, reversal of the pay cut. When I costed out my "Dream School," much to my surprise, I found that it was fiscally doable at the lower number of $4,300 per student. Armed with this information, I began discussing converting to a charter school with our leadership team. We explored the concept daily for about 10 days. With one exception, we agreed we would all stay at Fenton if we could become a charter school. (The one exception had already signed a contract with a district in Maryland, where he taught for one year, only to return to Fenton as our dean of students.)

We presented the idea to the staff at a faculty meeting and suggested they think about it. For two weeks, teachers met in small and large groups at various times throughout the day. We occasionally reassembled as a staff to ask questions and share ideas. At the end of the two weeks, over 95% of our teachers voted to commence writing a charter. California's Charter School Law at that time required that a charter be signed by 50% or more of the teachers at the school. We divided into 11 writing teams and wrote our charter, attempting to create the perfect educational environment for the entire school community. We kept the few things that LAUSD did well, and we changed all the many things we disliked. We were going to empower a totally disenfranchised school community!

> ## "The road to 'charterdom' was a rocky one. . . . We fought it out on the front page of our local newspaper, in the board room, and at the negotiating table, and we utilized political and business allies . . . to get every cent our students deserved."

The road to "charterdom" was a rocky one. The state superintendent of schools interpreted the law that said "The State Superintendent of Public Instruction shall apportion the charter school entitlements" to mean that he would continue business as usual and let the sponsoring district give the charter schools their funds. This set up an immediate adversarial relationship with the district. They were just attempting to create "paper" per-pupil budgets for schools who volunteered for their institutionalized reform effort. They certainly didn't want to give charter schools more than these schools. Many uncomfortable situations arose. We fought it out on the front page of our local newspaper, in the board room, at the negotiating table, and we utilized political and business allies in an effort to get every cent our students deserved. We could not begin operating on July 1, 1993, because LAUSD interpreted the 60 days they had by law to act on our charter as 60 working days. So we began operation as an independent charter school on January 1, 1994.

"We could no longer blame district staff, board rules, the union contract, or any outside entity for any condition that existed at our school."

It is truly amazing what can be accomplished when impediments—real or perceived—are eliminated. As a charter school, the finger-pointing ceased. We could no longer blame district staff, board rules, the union contract, or any outside entity for any condition that existed at our school. We were truly in charge of our destiny! Attitudes changed and so did behaviors. We were now both the employer and the employee. We underwent a metamorphosis. For example, schools are normally hotbeds for worker's compensation claims, and one Thursday morning, one of our kindergarten teachers fell in our parking lot and broke her ankle. She was a member of our Budget and Facilities Council. On Monday morning she was in a wheelchair teaching in her classroom. When I asked her why she was doing this, she replied, "I don't want our worker's compensation insurance rates to go up."

In 1997, 10 years after I was assigned to the "hell-hole," Fenton Avenue Charter School was named a California Distinguished School. We, however, were not finished. Success is a journey, not a destination. We accomplished much, but much is still to be done. The recent senseless deaths of two of our ex-students in a gang-related shooting but a half block from our school punctuate that charge.

Nonetheless, our accomplishments are quite incredible. Our students have demonstrated significant gains on performance indicators and standardized tests in each of the past nine years. Their educational environment is unparalleled at any elementary school anywhere. When visiting Fenton in 1996, State Superintendent of Public Instruction Delaine

Eastin stated, "I want to make sure education is a joy for every kid in California the way it is at Fenton Avenue Charter School." In June 1998, the most comprehensive case study of a charter school to date commissioned by LAUSD and conducted by WestEd concluded the following:

"Relative to schools with similar demographic characteristics, Fenton has moved from the bottom to the top in rank in performance."

"The change in school rank as compared to all other elementary schools with test data in the District . . . shows a large improvement . . . and an increase in rank."

"The data suggest strong evidence that the longer students stay at Fenton, the more likely they are to improve performance than students at comparison schools."

"We immediately recognized the idiocy of a principal as both instructional leader and business manager. Thus, we have co-directors."

Visitors from around the nation and several other countries ask, "What specifically are you doing differently?" My response is "Everything!" First of all, we immediately recognized the idiocy of a principal as both instructional leader and business manager. Thus, we have co-directors. My partner, Director of Instruction Irene Sumida, focuses on the most important function of the school while I concentrate on the financial management—bringing and sustaining resources to support instruction. We are in the most important business there is—the education of our youth. Nonetheless, it is a business and should be approached as such. When we expend our public dollars, we always try to get as much "cluck for the buck"—better, faster, cheaper.

As a school business, we must recruit outstanding teachers, or candidates who can be trained to be outstanding teachers. Without outstanding teachers, no school can be successful. To be most successful, even the best teacher needs the appropriate support and resources. Our teachers have the most sophisticated tools available. With a computer to student ratio of 1 to 1.5, our classrooms are the most technologically advanced of any elementary school anywhere in the world. This was achieved as the result of the leadership of a visionary teacher and is sustained through astute budgeting, business partners, multiyear contracts, and effective use of the E-Rate Program and the Qualified Zone Academy Bond Program.

As one of the largest public elementary charter schools in the nation (1,460, soon to be 1,600 when our current construction project is completed), we are faced with many challenges. As we deal with each, our guiding principle is: "Do what is in the best interest of our students." We help our students in many ways. Over 400 of them have computers at home, donated by business partners. Over 400 parents and community members are on campus each week, volunteering or learning themselves. Day and night adult literacy, ESL, citizenship, parenting, computer, and leadership classes are conducted in our Family Center. We also strive to work collaboratively as partners with all members of our school community. Everyone has a voice in what happens at our school.

Even our sponsoring district has been the recipient of our successes, though reluctantly. We have modeled true per-pupil budgeting, fee-for-service, and customer-oriented operations. We have generated millions of dollars in additional annual resources for them by demonstrating their way is not necessarily the best way.

What does it take to become a successful charter school? The Fenton Avenue Charter School experience would indicate the following:

- strong and consistent leadership
- outstanding teachers and staff
- parents as partners
- business and political partners
- a willingness to continually challenge the status quo
- lots of hard work
- the development of internal instructional and business expertise
- a "can do" attitude
- always putting children first!

8

A FAST TRACK IN HARLEM

Judith Price, Sisulu Children's Academy

The Sisulu Children's Academy, the first charter school in the state of New York, is situated within the Center for Community Enrichment in New York City. Judith Price, a native New Yorker educated at the Richman Country School and City College of New York School of Business Administration, is an active business developer who has spent more than 35 years in senior management positions of major corporations and nonprofit organizations. She specialized in commercial international transportation and has extensively traveled and worked abroad, principally in European markets. Her business involvement has also included sole proprietorship and six-state distribution of imported products. Price's civic and community interests have included business development in government-funded youth enterprises (through the Departments of Commerce and Labor), career development and technical assistance with a host of local, regional, and national organizations such as the Urban League Black Executive Exchange Program, Louise Wise Services, directorships in Big Brothers, New York YWCA, ICBO, OIC, and a three-year gubernatorial appointment to the New York State Economic Development Board. She is the comptroller of Canaan Baptist Church of Christ, a senior partner of the Trade Source Group Ltd., a director of Greenhope Services for Women; past chairperson of the Board of

Trustees of Canaan, founder of the Resource Center, and president of the Center for Community Enrichment, Inc. Her current business development is focused on youth empowerment; she has developed several incubator businesses with students ages 14 through 18 covering retail packaging services and computer training.

In our densely populated urban neighborhoods, there has been a physical ache that "something must be done about our schools." All of the fond (mostly accurate) memories of how our public schools served us so well in the distant past seemed to be a fantasy. How did all of this disappointment and failure happen to us? When will this pain start to go away?

"Two of our most noteworthy clergymen ... put their valuable credentials on the line and supported the passage of charter school legislation."

When fast-track charter school creation was under consideration by the state legislature in Albany in 1998, two of our most noteworthy clergymen—the Rev. Dr. Wyatt Tee Walker (Canaan Baptist Church in Harlem) and former congressman, the Rev. Dr. Floyd Flake (Allen A.M.E. Cathedral in Queens)—put their valuable credentials on the line and supported the passage of charter school legislation. Overnight, people arrived in our communities, canvassing the neighborhoods for likely institutional candidates who would (or could) sponsor a charter school application. Simultaneously, community organizations began putting their ideas together to become viable candidates for a charter school. Our Canaan church was no exception. With an impressive array of teachers, social workers, school administrators, and other working professionals in the congregation, it was reasonable to assume this effort could succeed.

Time is so deceptive. The lead time looked promising, but seemingly overnight the time was up. The legislation passed, and the statewide race was on to obtain approval to open new public charter schools immediately. The dotted i's and crossed t's are always confusing and cumbersome reading for most folks. But in this case it was very clear that the legislation provided no capital funds to assist in creating space where this educational experience could take place. Our charter schools are public schools. However, public real estate and public bricks and mortar were not a part of the legislated vision. Space. A space was needed that would be a safe, stable environment for the children, and that would nurture students, teachers, and community alike. Where were the resources to come from? What form would this pioneering effort take?

Others had launched similar schools in other states. They took the form of advisors, consultants, not-for-profit resource centers, and a newer element: the for-profit educational management organizations (EMOs). As they emerged, the reality firmed up that they would nudge this new public school charter market toward a very fast start-up by September 1999. Charter school applications abounded in New York State to be considered by charter grantors: the trustees of SUNY and the Board of Regents. Each had the granting privilege of 50 charters. When April 1999 rolled around, we found ourselves face to face with an offer to become the site of the first charter school in New York State.

"We found ourselves seated at the table with our representation intact *as a church* but contemplating the operation of a *public school.*"

Religious institutions of all denominations have long been accustomed to establishing schools in the primary through high school grades. These schools have been operated as religious schools without public-sector funds, in keeping with the doctrine of separation of church and state. Now we found ourselves seated at the table with our representation intact *as a church* but contemplating the operation of a *public school*. This was certainly new and challenging, and we were talking with all new people, not of our community and also not of our ethnic culture. Without even a blink of the eye, we were talking, listening, learning, and activating proposals—all at the same time!

The corporate parties formed up quickly. One was Canaan Baptist Church, a local church with international stature, a property owner, a community development institution, and a charter school advocate. The second was Steven Klinsky, a successful, powerhouse businessman, a founder of a for-profit educational management company, a sponsor of a successful after-school program in Brooklyn, and a charter school advocate. Each party sat down from the very first day with a "shirtsleeves" attitude. It was painfully clear that the short time left to start a new venture was the first hurdle to get past. This was April, and the only physical reality of having a new charter school in Harlem by September was the building we were sitting in: the Center for Community Enrichment at West 115th Street.

Wyatt Tee Walker, senior pastor of Canaan, always on the cutting edge of civil rights and humanity issues, had partnered with the Rev. Dr. Floyd Flake, former congressman, to make charter schools the new *real* opportunity for our students. Under his leadership, the Canaan congregation had sacrificed to build a $3 million, multipurpose, four-story building right next to our church. We spoke of many possibilities for this building.

When I was a child we played a little hand game that had a singsong ditty as we clasped our fingers together: *Here's the church! Here's the steeple! Open the door—and there's the people!* This new building was very much like that childhood ditty. The church (Canaan) stood foursquare in the community, accomplishing all sorts of feats and miracles for the neighborhood. Our efforts included housing, senior advocacy, drug abuse intervention, social action support, and hypertension screening. A steeple of protection covered all of us. The open door in the charter school scenario would be this brand-new building with a new sense of destiny, open to all the public and a place for community activities!

The Planning Committee had to be immediately available to accomplish this in such a short time. The EMO, Victory Schools, was attracted to this quality space, reinforced by the noteworthy profile of Dr. Walker and Canaan's decades-long history of public service. Their five-member management team, in addition to Steve Klinsky, included a senior partner and associate of an impressive law firm, an advance acquisition team specialist, and senior management executives of the EMO. Our team consisted of Dr. Walker, Minnie Goka, a retired veteran New York City school system principal, and myself, comptroller of the church and president of the church's economic development corporation. Although seemingly outnumbered, we had faith and confidence we would *not be outclassed*. This was a turf issue, for bricks and mortar and, more important, for our community's children and their families.

SETTING THE AGENDA

It was kind of scary. Could we correctly calculate the risks of being a pioneer, especially given the controversial issues of politics, labor (school unions), educational curriculum, operation (bureaucracies), and public relations (community control)? The actual charter application had been fully drafted already by the EMO and had been missing only the "where" it would happen. Also significant to the application was the choice of *the actual person* who would be the named applicant for the charter and who would also become a trustee. So we arrived at a crucial spot right away as to which persons on the Canaan team would balance the board of trustees and also provide important recommendations for an acceptable and credible charter school applicant.

In church we are given to saying that we are not "lucky," we are "blessed." This was evident as the Canaan team was able to quickly identify likely persons worthy of consideration as the applicant. Our choice was a young mother, raised and married in our church, who was acquiring her doctoral degree and already working in the educational profession. We proposed; she accepted.

In building the roster of trustees, the obvious lead choice was Dr. Walker, but his outstanding record as a theologian and pastor of Canaan and his leadership in the lobbying effort caused the EMO group to pause on his selection. Mindful of the separation of church and the public school, they did not want it to appear that an eminent churchman would rule the trustees. We disagreed, considering their fears unfounded, as we had an abundance of experience with locally and federally funded projects. Dr. Walker rose to the occasion; he deemed getting the school on board as the priority. Consideration for representative board service passed to Minnie Goka and myself as natural selections for trusteeship. Also included for recruitment were one of our district councilmen and the executive director of a successful children's service agency in Harlem. All trustees would be under scrutiny, as the charter school statute requires scheduled trustee meetings to be open to the general public.

Of course the management team had their recommendations as well, and we began the process of invitation and review. This was yet another hurdle to conquer if we were to have start-up in September. Remember, this was the earliest discussion among people who never did a single thing together before! All of this was just a fast walk; then we speeded up to a full run!

The challenges at first were physical rather than intellectual. Every day was a fitness test. Just scheduling meetings to everyone's busy calendars was magical. We knew we would have to sweat every detail, as there was no time for doubling back to fix things. School opening day was set in stone for September 8, and all plans had to be activated by August 1. Here we were at the end of April with a plate full of challenges:

- Develop overall working model of the partnership between Canaan and the EMO concerning primary issues of shared space, lease, building code compliance.
- Submit charter school property use to Canaan's official board and, subject to approval, present the plan for adoption by the church's congregation.
- Prepare for application follow-up and site visit of SUNY trustees relative to charter grant.
- Identify correlating professional teams for each party for legal, architectural, and political comments.
- Enumerate the concerns of community activists, proponents, and opponents of charter school operation.
- Identify the method of recruitment and retention of all school academic personnel.
- Understand thoroughly the curriculum to be offered.
- Discuss openly the ethnic issues, addressing serious issues of professional and job opportunities offered to our community.
- Identify financial issues of EMO's advanced start-up costs, capitation rates, salaries, leasehold improvements.
- Understand how school lotteries work for student selection.
- Identify general marketing issues prior to school opening.

OUR SPACE—SPACE!—SPACE!!

We didn't know at the time what a lasting, sensitive, and basic problem space would be. First of all, when our church built this new state-of-the-art space, the concept was to serve our many diverse activities that had continuously crowded our church space. Our church is rather large, having been constructed at the turn of the twentieth century as a magnificent Loew's theater seating 2,000. With our renovations over a period of 30 years, the building was serving us well, but not enough for 2,000 parishioners and some 50 assorted groups and auxiliaries with the building open every day of the week. Our multipurpose center was to address most of this current space need. We had barely occupied the building in late 1998 when this awesome question of considering the building for charter school operation became the center of our concern.

For some, the opportunity to be a part of a new educational venture overrode the initial use concept; however, many others were disappointed that the space would not be available as originally desired. Another quantum leap was called for: somehow, to proceed with the school project, we had to devise a plan for realistically sharing space. We ultimately came up with a formula for 85% of the space to be used exclusively by the school, and our main gathering room, "The Hall of the Ancestors," would serve as school program space during the weekday and for church program activities during the evenings and weekends. This extended to the commercial kitchen facilities, a very important service area for a well-run school. Our development corporation is housed in the community center building, and four of those spaces were set aside as exclusive use for our purposes (corporate office, conference room, resource and technological services, and a small retail shop for our teen job skills program).

"We had barely occupied the building ... when this awesome question of considering the building for charter school operation became the center of our concern."

What made this work at all? The building was brand spanking new and not yet filled with furniture. We were thus able to plan furnishings that were fashioned to fit the shared space concept. In 1999, close friends who owned a recently closed school in upstate New York consulted with our pastor and offered to donate all the furniture the school would need. They had a far larger elementary and middle school than the one we intended, and this act of generosity was greatly appreciated, especially because of the lack of time in our schedule. The selected furniture was scheduled for delivery in early August.

During the summer months, our church calendar is also in recess, and this provided more time for incisive planning on space needs. The pressure was on to be both economical and visionary. After all, the promise of a new day with charter schools raised the bar for everyone. The school management plan projected occupancy of 248 K–2 students. The physical plant provided (on paper) 10 classrooms.

"The project *was the queen bee!* We were all workers, highly dedicated and experienced, but workers serving the queen bee.... Lawyers, architects, insurance brokers, realtors, all were in the beehive mix."

Space and more space. Every time a space problem was accommodated, we had to face additional requests. This one physical aspect tapped our expertise and resources extensively. The coming event of this charter school started to grab a lot of press print. We knew that we would undergo a lot of scrutiny from those who had the responsibility to inspect everything as well as those who sought to satisfy their curiosity. We had to satisfy New York City's fire, building, health, and environmental protection departments to ensure our compliance for school safety. Never mind that it was a new building; it was not built as a school space, and that meant recertification.

OUR BEEHIVE ENVIRONMENT

The project *was the queen bee!* We were all workers, highly skilled, dedicated and experienced, but workers serving the queen bee. This was no place for amateurs. Lawyers, architects, insurance brokers, realtors, all were in the beehive mix. Implementation by any newly formed community group would have been an extremely tough job of complying with such time frames without access to similar resources. Those of us in our planning group were using every professional contact and the muscle of our respective organizations and companies to get this done. We had people power, money, plant resources, technology, political clout, business acumen, and a constant watchful eye on the refinement of the curriculum and those who would be selected to be school leaders.

"Although the EMO cast a long shadow and brought many talented people on board, the Canaan operation had to sustain its normal everyday commitments in addition to our emerging profile as a landlord."

Cost factors also loomed. Although the EMO cast a long shadow and brought many talented people on board, the Canaan operation had to sustain its normal everyday commitments in addition to our emerging profile as a landlord. We weren't quite there yet, so there was no income to underwrite the participation during this formation. Our senior administrative staff very quietly and admirably rose to the occasion. Errands, photocopies, telephone calls, research, and tasks of every sort were attended to as the days got longer and longer.

Our pastor is renowned for his activist history and highly respected organizational skills, and our congregation is progressive in support of community developments, yet we remain traditional in the manner of how churches work and prosper. No matter how busy the beehive, this charter school proposal would have to follow approved steps and be submitted for congregational approval by July 1999.

Right in the middle of this passage of time, our planning group considered yet another important issue: What would be the name of this groundbreaking, first-in-New-York charter school?

During the long struggle against apartheid in South Africa, Dr. Walker had protested the unjust imprisonment of Nelson Mandela and his associates. Our church became the unofficial host to many of the African National Congress activists and special envoys to the United Nations. After Nelson Mandela was elected president of South Africa, his first stop in the United States was an all-day visit to Canaan Baptist Church in October 1994. Another hero of the struggle against apartheid, right at the side of Nelson Mandela and in prison with him at Robben Island, was Walter Sisulu. Mrs. Albertina Sisulu had spent time with us during the prison days, and their daughter was serving as a UN representative. Dr. Walker reached out to the Sisulu family, explaining the importance of giving this new charter a shining example to follow, and they consented to allow the use of his name.

This gave the charter school application another heightened dimension: the school was named for a living international hero, a man whose strength and purpose were known to everyday folks in our community. There's a lesson here: no matter the complexities, it matters not what they call you, it's what you answer to that counts! Sisulu! Liberation! Justice! Walter Sisulu Day has been established as an important recognition day in our school.

THE PROFESSIONAL TEAM PARTICIPATION

The EMO team of advisors, consultants, and educational practitioners did a very good job of preparing the charter application. In light of its precedent-setting overtones, the glaring spotlight was on every nuance of their submission to the SUNY trustees. Steve Klinsky's earnest devotion to this charter school was clear, and those in charge of the approval process must have known how important this was to him. The vice chancellor of SUNY and trustees seemed pleased to be at the school when they visited the site. Many of these persons were known to us through the general press, and we were pleased to meet them. They took time to discuss the entire charter application with the Planning Committee members during their full-day visit.

The lawyers, architects, insurance brokers, and realtors involved in the process all faced isolated tasks as well as coordinated tasks, and each had superior talent, but there was also another discovery: like the Canaan committee, these pros had never put together a school-based project either!

We were especially sensitive to time constraints, so their findings, reports, and verbal comments all had to be streamlined by the Planning Committee to activate only those recommendations and requirements that absolutely had to be completed before September. On our side of the table, Canaan had always fostered and used the services of African American professionals. This certainly gave us an opportunity to recommend those individuals and companies for myriad services required by the EMO for the immediate start-up and the future. Too often businesses of the community are not considered seriously for participation when such projects come into our neighborhood.

OUR NEW LEXICON

There is no teaching, without learning. In this project, we had to learn a lot. We had to learn new words, with obvious and sublime definitions. One word was *lottery*—not a game at all. The public charter school at the very outset was anticipated to be oversubscribed. That would mean our children would be subjected to selection by lottery. How would it work? Would the families believe in its fairness? What alternatives would be presented to those who were disappointed?

Another word we learned was *capitation*: getting paid by the state educational system based on the census of the school and related attendance. All of the nightmares of the existing public bureaucracy hovered over us. Some school districts in the state received as much as $30,000 per student and others received as little as 25% of that amount. The New York City rate projected for public charter schools was to be approximately $6,600 per student. Would the management company provide all of the extras from the very first day while waiting for public funds to flow?

Prompted almost daily by press stories speculating on privatization, charter confusion, teachers' union fears, and a host of other questions, the phones began to ring off the hook. The management company filled this need by hiring temporary personnel for the sole purpose of being available for community concerns, and we provided office space. Even before applications were ready and lottery dates were announced, we could feel the growing excitement of surrounding residents. Summer had approached and many people did not have access to regular school admission offices or any way to receive accurate information. This public information office on our premises proved to be a valuable asset to the community, especially as the EMO promoted distribution of flyers throughout the borough.

Our three-person Canaan team had agreed on division of labor. Minnie Goka's strength was curriculum design, knowledge of Board of Education policy and practices, and teacher training, development, and certification. She settled into the difficult position of analyzing and if necessary challenging the intended curriculum of *Direct Instruction* and *Core Knowledge*. The EMO's curriculum consultants had daily contact with her. Without her expertise, parents and other interested persons may not have received correct information when making inquiries.

Dr. Walker took the responsibility to coordinate and sometimes precipitate valuable commentary affecting us politically and socially. He was also continuously available for press inquiries, and he persuaded our local councilman to join our board of trustees. In addition, because he was the chief executive officer of the church, the entire official presentation rested with him.

The "business" of Canaan's role in the charter school implementation came to me. This covered all areas of compliance, personnel, systems, and coordination of the outside professional team with Steve Klinsky's EMO executives. This school preparation had to coexist with our ongoing economic development programs sponsored by our development corporation. We were operating a full-time catering service, a retail training program, and a professional gift-wrap service for the teens. Our development included the acquisition of school uniforms from a major U.S. manufacturer and post-construction purchase of interior furnishings for spaces *not* used by the school, as well as various subcontract construction details.

Faster and faster the time seemed to run out as the task lists became longer. Once we had committed ourselves to see it through, we also had to adopt a reasonable attitude when others asked, "How's it going?" Did we dare confess that we were on the edge of exhaustion? Actually, for our collective ages, we were in pretty good physical shape, so the exhaustion came really from the anxiety we faced. Our anxiety was apprehension in dealing not with *things*, but with people. From this point onward, our daily attention would be first and foremost the people to be included in the charter school scenario. Well, you can't cross a chasm in two steps, so we just took the leap and began the process.

"The selection method—the lottery—had to be as Caesar's wife: 'above reproach.' Too many families had been aggrieved in the past with unfilled promises, and their suspicions of such a selection method had to be removed."

CHASMS AND KINKS

Pastor Walker made a cogent presentation to our corporate church meeting in July, which essentially provided the green light for our use of the building for the Sisulu Children's Academy. However, the academic team had yet to be assembled, and what was supposed to be a liberating aspect of charter school operation—namely, freedom from the traditional bureaucracy—now loomed as a major task. A well-drafted charter application could glibly project using "qualified classroom teachers." The reality was somewhat different. Tenured, qualified, and certified teachers were not in abundance. State law required that 70% of teachers had to be certified. Running parallel to this scarcity was the well-publicized search by the Board of Education for the same "qualified" teachers.

It also became clear that the selection method—the lottery—had to be as Caesar's wife: "above reproach." Too many families had been aggrieved in the past with unfilled promises, and their suspicions of such a selection method had to be removed. Here we were in August, and the numbers had to fit: total number of children for the legal square footage available; total satisfied parents whose children (K–2) were chosen in the lottery; total teachers and aides hired by end of August to be in place by opening day. Another element was the rising interest in this new venture because of repeated press coverage in the *New York Times* and other newspapers.

One younger member of our team was Marshall Mitchell, a dynamic gentleman who had been a *pathfinder*. He had a background as a congressional legislative assistant and had created a public policy entity several years prior that emphasized research and marketing on parental concerns of school choice. New York state had lagged behind the charter school movement (it was the 34th state accepting charter schools), and his work with other viable charter school state markets had brought him to New York state, advocating this legislation. The management team had solicited his help in locating a suitable school space. Now he pressed for an aggressive campaign throughout the community and surrounding zip codes. He recruited and worked the field with a team of young adults to distribute 50,000 flyers, and he advertised for students and school workers through churches, community organizations, and at subway stations. His focus was sound: *Children First!* As long as every major problem was turned to this focus, we could move along with credibility.

THE DOLLARS

School was not yet open, so where were the start-up dollars coming from? The EMO had to meet the advance expenses head on, with no excuses. They had opted to be in the forefront and needed to finance all school costs: early academic hires, curriculum consultants, educational supplies, space preparation, site administrative and maintenance staff.

With the advent of for-profit EMO's, debates had arisen over the source of advances to the newly formed school for all kinds of expenditures. Strangely enough, this seemed to be more publicly argued than any substantive doubts within our team. The public was tantalized by some adversaries as to the motives and accountability of a for-profit management company receiving and applying state educational funds in charter school operations. Our private concern was that the management company was retained by and responsible to the trustees of the nonprofit Sisulu Children's Academy. We knew even at this early stage that the ongoing reviews of the state would be directed toward the stabilization of this relationship.

Although we had not yet executed a lease with Sisulu, we felt confident our planning process assured us our building would be used properly.

Even in this matter, we were caught up in the fast pace of current events. In 1999, our Harlem community was experiencing the reality of a major revitalization by private developers and empowerment zone forces. Our concerns for a multiple-year lease with the school had to include future expectations of increased property value—which, indeed, was increasing each day! In the best interest of supporting a new charter school, we had offered the building to the school at the exact monthly rate of our mortgage obligation for the first year. In addition to working with the school team, we had to work with our own real estate analysts to acquire valuable information for our fiscal reports to the Canaan congregation.

WHOSE SCHOOL IS IT, ANYWAY?

One reporter erred badly by saying in a front-page article that "the school is helping to rejuvenate the church." Pastor Walker quickly wrote a letter to the editors, objecting to poor and careless reporting. After 35 years of intensive community development and as the primary catalyst for quality housing created in our Milbank-Frawley section of Harlem, we were *not* being rejuvenated by the school. This highlighted for us a new resolve to be vigilant and *responsive* as to what kind of public reporting was in place.

"To most community observers, every visible indication of the school's operation was associated with Canaan church. . . . We knew we were creating a brand-new model of parallel concerns involving both *church and state*!"

Untangling an identity can be very difficult. To most community observers, every visible indication of the school's operation was associated with Canaan church: the pastor's support in Albany, the contiguous building location (on the immediate southeast side of the church building), similarity of street addresses (West 116th vs. West 115th Street), and press items as well as parishioners and friends referring to it as "Canaan's school." Historically, most neighborhoods have been quite comfortable with the existence of a school on church property and with the school belonging to the church and using the church's name, albeit these were *always* religious schools. More than one parishioner or neighbor felt the church could intervene with either student placement or new hires. *Isn't this the church's school?* The church persuasion is to be sensitive to all people when a problem is presented. Applying objectivity to this identity dilemma was a skill we had not considered. We were committed, and we knew we were creating a brand-new model of parallel concerns involving both *church and state*!

We devised straightforward orientation for administrative church staff so they would have valuable, reliable referral tactics. All new school staff were thoroughly indoctrinated into keeping separate physical traffic patterns. All telephone and mail services were strictly segregated, right down to the mail carriers who had been quite accustomed to dropping off at our church reception office any mail that even remotely appeared to belong to the church. This public relations feat carried us through the mild turmoil that brought us to opening day— September 8, 1999.

SCHOOL DAYS, SCHOOL DAYS

Open at 6:30 a.m.! School security desk in service by 7 a.m.! Food delivery by 7:15! School administrators and teaching staff on site by 7:15! Arrival of students and breakfast served by 7:30! School bus arrivals! Classes at 8 a.m.! As students streamed through the doors with their parents, grandparents, older siblings, or other caregivers, we looked upon this day with great pride. The children wore navy-blue bottoms and tops with white shirts and navy ties. They were beautiful from the very first day.

Another reality shot home: whether in a traditional public school or charter public school, every child deserved a good start every day. They needed to be safe, fed, and encouraged to like school and prosper there. The new principal had her work cut out for her to maintain the exuberance and expectations of this first day throughout the school year.

A HANDSHAKE WITH NATIONAL MEDIA

Sisulu Children's Academy opened in September 1999 and we wound up right in the middle of a campaign platform issue in October. The frontrunner in the 2000 presidential election, Republican Governor George W. Bush of Texas, championed charter schools, and before we knew it the largest mass press event we had ever seen occurred in our midst. More than 200 members of the press descended on us, preceded by the Secret Service, members of the New York City Police Department Intelligence Division, Texas Rangers, and a host of other security and campaign personnel. The new little Sisulu students were very excited as they were interviewed at the school during their "up close and personal" visit with New York Governor George Pataki and Governor Bush.

This unusual event disrupted school most of the day and was reported in the major media. Once again we were reminded that we had *no days to spare for publicity and photo ops.* It was encouraging that all of the team—trustees, administrators, and management company—felt the same. Each day had to be a stepping-stone. Although the school day was extended, parents were already pressing for news of a weekday after-school program. This issue alone would be a constant source of discussion for the remainder of the year.

ORDINARY EXCELLENCE

With our unique curriculum of direct instruction and core knowledge, each ordinary day was expected to be a challenge well met. We were a public school, and the school population reflected the realities that prevailed elsewhere. There were children with special remedial needs and those already working above grade. There were experienced teachers and some in their very first year of classroom reality. This charter school with 248 children would seek to have extensive involvement of parents and bring enlightenment to the public.

We settled down to building the trustee board and an improved agenda for the next school year. This compressed time execution from April through September had taught us we were not going to survive just because we had done one good new thing on a very fast track. The model we had achieved for bringing academicians and community and business interests together was proving fruitful. And so, our work began toward proving this educational venture would succeed. We knew we had best remember our rallying call: "Children first!"

9

A DISTRICT SCHOOL

Libia S. Gil, Lowell Billings, Ana Tilton, Rick Werlin, and
Dennis Doyle, Feaster-Edison Charter School

BACKGROUND, BY LIBIA S. GIL

Dr. *Libia S. Gil was appointed to the superintendency of the Chula Vista Elementary School District in August 1993. During her tenure, the district has experienced continuous growth and is currently serving more than 24,000 students in 39 schools. Gil has fostered the successful implementation of numerous school change models including five charter schools and partnerships with Edison Schools Inc., School Futures Research Foundation, Accelerated Schools, Comer, Standards-Based Instruction, and the Ball Foundation. In 1998, the community passed a $95 million school bond with a 76% voters' approval to support modernization of learning environments. Gil began her teaching career in the Los Angeles Unified School District and has taught in various programs, including English as a Second Language and Gifted and Talented programs. During her teaching experiences, she and her colleagues created a successful K–12 alternative school and numerous alternative classroom programs.*

Chris Whittle was one of the keynote presenters at California's statewide Superintendents' Symposium in January 1996. This was the pivotal event that provided the exposure to the Edison Project, which grabbed my immediate attention and desire to learn more. Within a week, I was corresponding with Chris Whittle to exchange information about our school district and the Edison Project goals and timelines.

The following month I contacted all principals to determine if their schools had any interest in exploring a potential partnership with the Edison Project. To our surprise, 11 out of the 33 principals responded affirmatively. Additional Edison program materials and project overviews were distributed to all interested principals.

In May 1996, Bill Kirby, former Texas State Education commissioner representing Edison, met with a group of interested principals. Due to conflicting schedules, actual participants in this session represented six schools. There was high receptivity and enthusiasm for the Edison program design, with the emphasis on restructuring instructional time, reorganizing school governance, and providing a comprehensive curriculum in each content area supported by intensive staff development. With the addition of technology as a teaching-learning tool, the focus on improving student achievement was most appealing. The enthusiasm dampened when the topic of reconstituting staff, including the principal, was presented. Although most principals readily welcomed the opportunity to select staff members, they found it difficult to apply the process to themselves.

In the next several months, discussion continued among principals and with executive Edison staff members. In August 1996, we formally contacted the teachers' union and the classified employee organization to inform them about a board presentation by Chris Whittle, who provided an overview of the Edison Project that highlighted the conceptual framework for supporting student achievement. All of our board members were intrigued with the Edison model and responded positively to our continued exploration.

In September 1996, several planning sessions between executive administrators from both organizations occurred. Questions on potential school site options, financial parameters, development of support, and overall timetable were addressed. It was quickly determined that a schoolwide Title I qualified school would be most desirable to create the necessary economies of scale in addition to the need for improving student performance. Seven schoolwide Title I schools were identified as potential partnership options. Subsequently, nine principals of Title I schools were contacted to determine interest level. In this round, two principals expressed a definite interest. Edison staff visited the interested school sites and met with each principal to discuss the Edison concept and implications for implementation.

"Ironically, parent and student feedback rated the school and teachers positively, in contrast to teachers' rating parents and students poorly."

To support a successful Edison project implementation in California, Chris Whittle created the three-legged partnership model to include philanthropic entities for start-up capital. Numerous regional donors were contacted, and initial expanded facilities and technology investments were supported by major donations to the project.

School Selection

By October, the Feaster principal remained the only one with serious interest in exploring the Edison project. Simultaneously, Feaster was considering school change vehicles to address the dismal pattern of student achievement, unruly student behavior, poor attendance, negative school climate, and one of the worst school reputations in the region. All common school data, including customer satisfaction survey results, indicated a low-performing school with low staff morale and low expectations for students. Ironically, parent and student feedback rated the school and teachers positively, in contrast to teachers' rating parents and students poorly. The discrepancy in attitudes demanded strong interventions to raise the level of expectations for student learning in a community that had accepted school failure as the norm.

Dialogue participants expanded and continued at multiple levels of the organization, including Feaster school staff, parents, district administration, and Edison staff members. In November 1966, a representative team composed of the Feaster principal, teacher, parent, two school board members, and I visited an established Edison Project school in Colorado Springs. The teachers' union president decided to join us at the last minute. The observations and interactions with students, parents, and teachers reinforced our interest and created greater excitement to pursue a potential Edison partnership. The Feaster school representatives returned to their school community with renewed energy and spirit.

The positive energy and hope for a new future at Feaster school was quickly challenged by the teachers' union, whose leadership attempted to sabotage the interest. It was not unusual to have a parent meeting disrupted with charges that all staff would be fired and other unfounded allegations to derail support for the Edison Project.

Feaster Edison Charter

In January 1997, a team of representative teachers and principal, Dr. Catherine Rodriguez, toured one of the original Edison Schools in Wichita, Kansas. They wanted to observe firsthand the program implementation process and impact on students, parents, and staff. The outcome of this visit solidified the team interest and commitment to pursue the Edison model. They were all impressed and convinced that the program design provided a high potential to maximize student learning.

"Despite the regular ongoing discussions with the local teachers' union leaders ... [they] continued to bombard individual staff members with misinformation and intimidation tactics."

Despite the regular ongoing discussions with the local teachers' union leaders and daily responses to inquiries regarding a possible conversion to a charter, the union leaders continued to bombard individual staff members with misinformation and intimidation tactics. Tenured teachers were understandably nervous to hear that they would lose many rights, including seniority and tenure status in the school district. They were also concerned that they could be terminated at any time in a charter school without due process and would have no right to return to the school district. Although charter legislation already provides job protection for teachers who do not wish to teach at a charter school, we responded immediately with board action to reinforce that "any Feaster teacher who does not want to be part of the program will be guaranteed a teaching position in the district."

This action contradicted all the misconceptions of teacher status perpetuated by the local union; however, it served to intensify their local, state, and national propaganda distribution to staff and community to raise public opposition. The issue now focused on the lack of inclusion in the process and anti-privatization sentiments. Fortunately, all segments of the community had been included in a proactive communication plan: I had personally met with elected officials, including the mayor, members of the CV Chamber of Commerce board, Council of PTAs, District Parent Advisory Committee members, other community leaders, and the press corps.

On March 4, 1997, the Chula Vista Elementary School Board unanimously approved the Feaster staff charter school petition supported by over two-thirds of the teaching staff despite teacher union allegations of improprieties with the voting process. On March 13, 1997, a representative team of a parent, a teacher, Edison staff, district staff, and I went to Sacramento to witness the California State Board of Education approve the Feaster-Edison Charter School petition. Prior to that meeting, I had contacted and lobbied every state board member for their support on the petition. It was now official: the first Edison charter school partnership in the state. We felt the joyous culmination of many months of effort to create a new school model for our students, as well as a new beginning with renewed staff and community enthusiasm and dedication to increase student achievement.

PUBLIC/PRIVATE PARTNERSHIP:
A BUSINESS PERSPECTIVE, BY LOWELL BILLINGS

Dr. Lowell Billings has spent 26 years in public education as a K–6 teacher, principal of West View School, and director of research and technology in the South Bay Union School District. In 1991, he was appointed assistant superintendent for instructional services and is currently the assistant superintendent for business services for the Chula Vista Elementary School District. He serves as chief financial officer, chief planner for school construction/renovation, and director of district operational support services.

Feaster Elementary School had a long and well-documented history of providing substandard educational programs. By any measure, its success with students was well below Chula Vista Elementary School District and state standards. Consistently, Feaster was the poorest-performing district school. When Feaster became a charter school, a number of staff left, which provided flexibility to reinvent expectations and standards for instruction. Simultaneously, class size reduction was implemented, which brought one new staff member for every two teachers in grades K–3. At the same time, over $3 million in modernization renovation and repair was completed. Additionally, four acres of adjacent property were acquired to augment what was one of the smallest school sites in the district. The resulting partnership with Edison brought over $800,000 of capital funds to provide classrooms for the rapidly growing student population in this sector of the district.

"When Feaster became a charter school, a number of staff left, which provided flexibility to reinvent expectations and standards for instruction."

These circumstances proved beneficial for start-up of the project partnership. California per-pupil funding was marginal for the program-rich Edison. The large size of the school was countered through creation of school-within-a-school houses, which reduced the size of the school to more manageable components.

Creation of a fiscally independent public/private for-profit venture was daunting. Support for this model, although unanimously supported by the local Governing Board, was not routinely embraced by various state agencies. The State Teachers' Retirement System, the Public Employees' Retirement System, the San Diego County Joint Powers Authority Insurance/Liability consortium, and the San Diego County Office of Education all questioned the fit with our public education charge. Chula Vista Elementary School District's standard reply was that public education constitutes a multimillion-dollar for-profit business opportunity.

Textbooks, insurance, construction contracts, software, computer hardware, furniture, and equipment have long provided for-profit opportunities. The Edison Project merely requested equal business opportunity, only this time for direct services in a teaching and learning delivery model.

Formation of a public/private for-profit partnership threatened the existence of established institutions, roles, functions, and areas of real or perceived jurisdiction. Nowhere was this clearer than with the teachers' association. Elements of the charter such as merit pay, differentiated teacher job descriptions, extended school day/year, and charter precedence over union contracts, coupled with the voluntary flight of some senior teachers, were some of the impacts and effects that the union viewed as negative and threatening. It's interesting to note that the classified union, through an interest-based approach, found the charter and the public/private for-profit partnership to be a new and unique opportunity for students in the school. Under this arrangement, issues were openly discussed and resolved.

"Formation of a public/private for-profit partnership threatened the existence of established institutions, roles, functions, and areas of real or perceived jurisdiction."

Edison staff worked very hard to involve both classified and certificated bargaining units while developing charter language. This effort was undertaken to create buy-in and support. The teachers' union efforts to disrupt the process and waylay the charter were ultimately unsuccessful.

Due to the complexity of the Edison partnership design, there was a need for a solid fiscal independence model with clear operational structure that defined district and charter roles and responsibilities. Great efforts were made to develop this foundation document, which later served as a template for numerous other charters within and outside the district. This afforded the district opportunity to reflect on its service and support model as cost centers were defined and quantified. Value added became a key definition for support.

REFORM EFFORTS, BY ANA TILTON

Ana Tilton is a senior vice president of the School Division for Edison Schools Inc., the largest educational management company in the United States. She oversees all school operations for the Western Division of the company, encompassing approximately 65 schools in eight states, with an enrollment of approximately 40,000 students. Prior to joining Edison in 1999, she had a long career as a California public school administrator; she served as superintendent of the Soquel School District, assistant superintendent for the Chula Vista School District, and principal in the Carlsbad Unified School District.

I love a simple story with a profound message. One of my favorite children's books is *The Little Engine That Could*. You know the one: "I think I can, I think I can, I think I can." As a teacher, I thrilled at the chorus reading and discussion that followed from all ages regarding the little engine that saved the day for all the children on the other side of the mountain. As you may guess, I am also the eternal optimist when it comes to providing a world-class education for *all* children.

In 1995 and 1996, as a cabinet member in the Chula Vista Elementary School District, I coached a school in crisis. Feaster Elementary School students continually scored at the bottom on all indicators of success: attendance, norm-referenced testing, district criterion-referenced assessment, community involvement, and mobility. Teacher morale was low, students did not display pride in work or self, excuses were made for low performance, and schoolwide decisions were not made based on student needs but on adult wants.

It was clear to district leadership that this was a "Little Engine That Could" in need of a shove to start the journey in reaching *Our Shared Vision*. One of the sentences in the district's vision statement reads: "The entire educational community accepts the challenge of change and is motivated to acquire skills and values for a rapidly changing world." Both the superintendent and the entire school board embraced change and sought out partnerships in creating a challenging educational experience for all children. Through an inclusive effort, Feaster joined other schools in examining different reform efforts.

Edison School design is highly ambitious, encouraging fundamental change in school structure. They offer a longer school day, longer school year, rich and challenging curriculum for all students, extensive professional development for teachers and administrators, technology for an information age, and careful assessment that provides accountability. In partnership with the district reform efforts, Edison Schools offered a new vision of the future.

In August 1997, Feaster Edison Charter School opened its doors to students and families. This was only the beginning of a five-year journey to dramatic reform on behalf of children. This Little Engine not only had a heavy load to take up the hill, but also had people blocking the tracks. Despite the obstacles, Feaster Edison Charter School is on the other side of the hill and delivering on its promise to children. In the fifth year of design implementation, it has demonstrated steady and significant growth in student achievement evidenced by multiple measures.

This story of success is not over. The staff and community are looking for new mountains to climb and are not satisfied with the great gains. They want to continue their reform efforts and increase the gains for all children. I am proud to say I was part of this story. I have since left the district to become a superintendent and now work for Edison Schools overseeing the operations of 30 Edison School partnerships across the nation.

FEAR OR FACT, BY RICK WERLIN

Rick Werlin received his bachelor's degree in elementary education from the State University of New York and master's in educational administration from Texas Southern University in Houston. He has served as a special education, bilingual, and general education elementary teacher. His instructional leadership experiences include elementary assistant principal and principal, middle school principal, and alternative high school principal. He has worked in human resources in three major districts in Texas and has served as the assistant superintendent for human resources services and support for Chula Vista for the past five years.

"Watch out, you're going to lose all your benefits." "There go all your teacher rights out the door." These were all too familiar comments made to teachers at Feaster-Edison Charter School when they were trying to make a decision on collective bargaining per the Migden Bill (AB 631), which required all California charter schools to make a decision by March 31, 2000, as to whether they were going to declare themselves or the school district the "employer for collective bargaining purposes." The latter would automatically allow for the sole representative, Chula Vista Educators, part of the California Teachers Association and NEA, to represent them and have a closed shop.

Teachers at Feaster-Edison voted not to declare their charter school as the "employer for collective bargaining purposes," therefore disassociating themselves from the teachers' union. The union not only lost approximately $800 annual dues from almost 80 teachers but faced the shocking reality that all five of our district charter schools had elected the same path.

Rather than choosing the path of fear and deception, district representatives provided factual information so that teachers would be well-informed prior to their election of their options. This district approach is directly related to our core belief that it is our responsibility to empower our staff with the tools and knowledge to better provide students options for success.

THEN AND NOW, BY DENNIS DOYLE

Since 1997, Dennis M. Doyle has served as an assistant superintendent in the Chula Vista Elementary School District, the largest K–6 district in California. Prior to accepting his current position, he was director of educational partnerships for Lightspan, Inc., a multimedia educational technology company. Previously, he worked as an administrator for eight years in the San Diego Unified School District.

Francisco Escobedo, Feaster-Edison principal, showcased the data to the Chula Vista Elementary School District Board of Education in June 2003. Feaster-Edison Charter School was making the school's annual presentation to the board, a requirement assumed by all charter schools. Prior to the Edison conversion, Francisco explained, Feaster's enrollment consisted of 781 students. Six years later the school had grown to 1,137 pupils. Students who routinely left their neighborhood school for spaces in other district schools had all come home. There was space at the local school, programs were exciting and appealing, and all neighborhood students could be accommodated.

The student population, Francisco noted, had become more Hispanic over that period of time, growing from 72% to 80% Latino. The percentage of Feaster-Edison students who were Limited-English Proficient/English Language Learners climbed just slightly, from 50% to 54%. The population is poorer than it was before Feaster became an Edison School; the percentage of students qualifying for free or reduced-price lunch grew from 74% to 100%. Of particular interest was the change in mobility rates. Edison data show declines sharply from 58% in 1996–97 to 19% in 2002–03. With additional facilities, Feaster-Edison was becoming a more stable learning environment over time. Attendance showed demonstrable improvement as well, with reductions in absenteeism every year in succession.

"Data [on mobility rates] show declines sharply from 58% . . . to 19% [four years later]."

By every measure, academic achievement was up. More students were reading at grade level (6% in 1997, 72% in 2003). The number of bilingual students who began English reading on an annual basis had grown steadily as well.

What Francisco did not know was that new standardized test scores had just been released and the spring reading scores had risen dramatically from the baseline year. Indeed, graduating sixth-graders saw their cohort Normal Curve Equivalent (NCE) scores grow from 30.0 as second-graders in 1997–98 to 42.0 NCE in 2002–03, a 12.0 NCE change. Math scores, too, had risen to new heights. The same graduating sixth-graders showed cohort gains from 30.0 NCE in 1997–98 in second grade to 48.3 NCE last year, an 18.3 NCE improvement. Language scores grew for the cohort from 27.0 NCE as 1997–98's second-graders to 49.8 NCE last year (22.8 NCE change). Spelling improved from 31.0 NCE to 43.7 NCE (an 12.5 NCE net gain) for the cohort over five years. (See table 9.1.) More students than every before were meeting district

Table 9.1.   Sixth-Grade Cohort NCEs

2nd Grade	3rd Grade	4th Grade	5th Grade	6th Grade	Final NCE Score
Reading					
30.0	34.1	37.7	40.1	42.0	12.0
Math					
30.0	32.8	37.3	45.8	48.3	18.3
Language					
27.0	35.4	39.8	45.1	49.8	22.8
Spelling					
31.0	34.9	33.3	41.6	43.7	12.5

standards, as measured by a set of conjunctive multiple measures. Just 37.76% of students met district reading/language arts and math standards in 1997–98, rising to 44.23% last year.

Student, staff, and parent ratings of the school as measured by the prestigious Harris Interactive Survey have soared. For example, before Edison, 68% of parents graded the school an "A" or "B" for atmosphere. In the last rating, 82% graded Feaster-Edison an "A" or "B." In the recent student-led Quarterly Learning conferences, 98% of parents attended.

"There were parents with tears in their eyes, grateful for the transformation."

Earlier in the month, Francisco met with parent members of the Feaster-Edison Charter School community. Over 159 parents attended. There were parents with tears in their eyes, grateful for the transformation Edison had provided. It was a very emotional meeting. The principal reported that the idea of an Edison Middle School Academy was brought up. Parents, Francisco stated emphatically, love the Edison model.

For students, there have been other major changes. For example, once staff discovered through data analysis that 20 students accounted for 73% of disciplinary referrals, it took just five months' implementation of a Resiliency Mentoring Program (each student was adopted by one staff member) to reduce referrals for those 20 students to just 28%.

SYSTEMIC CHANGE, BY LIBIA S. GIL

We have supported and encouraged charter schools in our district based on some of the following assumptions:

- Belief in providing options and alternative pathways to improve student learning. We are committed to high expectations, common standards, and accountability goals for student achievement, but we do not subscribe to a single model or program to meet the unique needs of all children.
- Belief that increased flexibility at the school level provides increased opportunities for ownership and responsibility for student learning outcomes. This is a natural extension of a highly decentralized approach to our district operations.
- Belief that charter schools provide a strong vehicle with the potential to not only transform student learning at their particular site but also to impact the entire educational system.

"'Why have you given up on public schools?' Our best response is 'Quite the contrary: we are strengthening our public schools because we will not give up on our children!'"

What impact has Feaster-Edison Charter School made on the district? Debunking the myths that for-profit privatization is inherently evil and that we had betrayed the public education system was the first attitudinal challenge we had to address districtwide with skeptics and resisters to change. The most common questions are:

"Why for profit? Why allow them to make money off our children?" We can point to the myriad of equipment, services, textbooks, other materials, facilities, technology, etc., that the public school system currently purchases from private vendors who are profit making.

"Why have you given up on public schools?" Our best response is "Quite the contrary: we are strengthening our public schools because we will not give up on our children!"

"What can they do that we can't do ourselves?" Our response is: We can write our own curriculum, train our teachers, extend the school year, and do our own research, but how long would it take to accomplish what Edison has already completed with their investment of time and resources in research and development?

Other general impacts include:

- The process for creating a charter proposal is a model for building a unity of purpose with staff and community engagement.
- We challenged the status-quo thinking and stimulated new practices to open minds to other possibilities for service delivery models. A major attitudinal shift occurs from "can't do" to "can do" that permeates all levels of the system. From a traditional public school principal's perspective: "The charter school movement has opened doors for traditional public schools. Many of the innovations used by the charter schools are applicable within the confines of a traditional bureaucracy. Processes include program planning, peer coaching, differentiated staffing, extended day programs, etc." Charter schools have modeled possibilities for other school change efforts.
- One of the most significant impacts is raising the expectation and demand for responsive customer-service orientation from the central office. For example, when the first charter school contracted with a private landscaper, our district landscaping crew was stunned and dismayed. They quickly learned what value-added service and customer satisfaction meant. You can be assured that they started immediately removing all grass cuttings instead of piling them where children can trip on them and avoided mowing outside a classroom during instructional time, and they certainly improved their response time to staff requests at every school.
- Establishing accountability has raised expectations for all schools and refocused the entire system on outcomes and results.
- Efficiency concerns and cost-effective practices caused the analysis of cost centers for services and goods.
- The expectations for performance outcomes were raised and aligned with appropriate compensation based on a merit system rather than longevity.

- Ultimately, the greatest impact area was collective bargaining. The fact that all charter schools staffs voted to disassociate themselves from the local teachers' union sent a clear message that teachers value flexibility and do not want to be constrained by a collective bargaining agreement that demands uniformity. Some of the practices in charter schools, such as a differentiated pay structure, teacher peer evaluations, home visits, and calendar and schedule changes, would be difficult if not impossible to implement under current collective bargaining agreement and philosophical differences.

There is no question that charter schools, and in particular Feaster-Edison, have made an impact on the traditional public schools in the Chula Vista Elementary School District. The question for us is how do we determine the significance of impact on student learning?

10

BUILDING ON THE DREAM

Jim Blew, Watts Learning Center

Jim Blew helped found the Watts Learning Center charter elementary school in 1997 and continues to serve on the school's board. He has worked since 2000 with the American Education Reform Council and its companion advocacy organization, the American Education Reform Foundation. AERC provides information about school options, and AERF seeks to expand school options for parents in low-income urban areas. The organizations are based in Milwaukee, where more than 12,000 students attend charter schools and nearly 15,000 low-income children attend private schools at taxpayer expense. Before joining AERC, Blew worked at political and marketing communications firms in New York and California. His experience includes several issue campaigns and high-profile corporate crises. He attended LAUSD public schools, received a BA from Occidental College, and earned an MBA from Yale University.

The Watts Learning Center charter school quietly yet successfully serves about 200 elementary students in a neighborhood that ranks among the state's most economically disadvantaged. Reflecting a correlation that sometimes seems inescapable, the area also has some of the state's worst-performing schools. Of the 49 traditional elementary schools that are in zip codes adjacent to the Watts Learning Center, 45 ranked in the lowest decile on the California 2001 Academic Performance Index (API); the other four were in the lowest quintile. In contrast, the Watts Learning Center's API just missed placing it among the top half of California schools. The five-year-old school has not yet achieved its goal of becoming a world-class academic institution, but it has taken the initial steps. The recently published API rankings for 2003 show even higher achievement for the Watts Learning Center, which was given a 7 out of 10. The neighboring traditional schools continue to receive 1 or 2 out of 10.

When people hear of the Watts Learning Center's success, they often suspect that its students must come from unusually privileged homes. The suspicions are wrong. Nearly all of our students qualify for the federal free and reduced-price lunch program. All are minority, mainly African American. An overwhelming majority live with a single parent, who typically did not complete high school.

This book is about the challenges facing urban charter schools, and the temptation is to list and define the many trials and obstacles confronted by the Watts Learning Center. This chapter instead focuses on why the Watts Learning Center works well in spite of the challenges. Along the way, it naturally mentions the obstacles, inequities, and injustices that all urban charter schools confront, especially in California and Los Angeles. Four themes emerge as the core reasons the Watts Learning Center succeeds where other urban schools fail:

- Shared and strong vision of purpose
- Great teachers with good support
- Empowered parents
- Careful stewardship of resources

SINGLE VISION

When the Watts Learning Center (WLC) officially opened in the fall of 1997, it had three students and three teachers. Within a couple of weeks, about 60 kindergartners were enrolled, and the school had moved to a second location. By 2001, the school had moved to its third location, had grown to about 200 students and 10 teachers, and was serving grades K–4. The school now serves grades K–5 and 210 children. We have requested permission in our renewal petition to grow to grades K–8 and 400 students.

Our nomadic existence and growing student body are not the only changes. Already the school has had to sever its relationships with one principal, a couple of teachers, and the management company that helped the school get started. More changes and challenges are expected. In 2002, for example, when the school petitioned for a renewal of its charter from the Los Angeles Unified School District (LAUSD), the initial response was lukewarm and we were told that our draft petitions did not demonstrate a "sound educational program," as required by law. The school was finally granted a five-year extension of its charter—six months after our original charter had expired. During the gap, we continued to operate as if we had a charter, while we wrestled with various factions within the LAUSD bureaucracy. In the end, intervention by board members forced the staff to let our charter come before the board for a vote.

At the Watts Learning Center, very little remains constant, with one exception: our vision.

THE VISIONARY

Perhaps as many as 20 people have been essential to the birth and development of the Watts Learning Center. Most of those have been teachers; a few have been board members; one is a philanthropist. Yet, were it not for one single inspiring individual, the Watts Learning Center would not be. She brought together a committed, competent team to plan the school, and she gave us her vision. It is a vision that has outlived her. In a bitter twist, she died before LAUSD granted our petition in 1997 to open the school.

Nira Hardon Long was an attorney, a business consultant, and a person who knew how to enjoy life. She knew how to be a friend, and she knew how to bring her friends and acquaintances together on behalf of a good cause. Nira was destined to promote progressive causes. Her first name was derived from one of America's greatest progressive experiments, the National Recovery Act of 1933. No one could be surprised that she took an active role in the civil rights movement, the women's movement, and the cause of international development. It should not have surprised anyone that her chief passion in her final years was helping low-income children get a good education.

"Perhaps as many as 20 people have been essential to the birth and development of the [school]. . . . Yet, were it not for one single inspiring individual, . . . [it] would not be."

Nira was a product and proponent of Los Angeles public schools. She recognized, reluctantly and sadly, that the system was failing low-income children, especially blacks and Hispanics. She pointed out that only a small percentage of blacks were learning to read proficiently (just 12% of fourth-graders, according to the 2000 National Assessment of Education Progress) and a large percentage of black teenagers were not graduating from high school (a shocking 44% nationwide in 2000, according to a study by the Black Alliance for Educational Options). She resolved to do something constructive about it—even if constructive meant controversial.

When confronted with the educational chasm between African Americans and non-Hispanic whites, Nira realized she had to decide between two explanations. The first, which might be labeled "blame the victims," holds that black families are culpable for their low achievement. Either because of genetic predisposition or a dysfunctional subculture, under-achievement among black children is thought to be inevitable. Few say it so bluntly. Fewer still would admit that this explanation is their intellectual framework. The alternate view is that something is wrong with the system—that somehow it has not evolved to serve the needs of African Americans and Hispanics, especially those with limited means. This view holds that a different system could produce better results, and that the existing system will continue to produce generally good results for the affluent and generally atrocious ones for the poor. If one accepts that the problem is systemic, then it is easier to conclude that the solution needs to be systemic as well.

Charter schools offer systemic change and a way to close the achievement gap. The reasons go beyond the notion that charter schools are, at least in theory, welcome to try new and different approaches—sometimes radical, sometimes slight, always based on the goal of improving achievement. The school districts, again in theory, could adopt and replicate successful experiments. More important, successful charter schools could inspire systemic change because their existence provides a modicum of competition. By giving parents the power to leave, charters provide an incentive for traditional schools to improve.

In middle- and upper-income neighborhoods, competition and the ability to choose a good school are essentially taken for granted. If a family is unhappy with the local public school, it either moves to a new neighborhood or sends children to private school. As a consequence, public schools either learn to perform or students leave (along with their funding).

In disadvantaged, urban communities such as south L.A., this competitive dynamic does not exist. Children are trapped. Schools are overcrowded. There are few incentives to perform better, except perhaps the moral imperative that is weakened by low expectations and the "blame the victims" syndrome. When charter schools reach critical mass in urban areas, they provide strong competitive pressure to improve. Even in overcrowded L.A. schools, no one in power willingly gives up a student or the associated funding.

"Nira learned that the city's elite recognized the school system's ineptitude but had little political will to change it. In fact, many were benefiting from the current system and were committed to protecting it."

As Nira crystallized her views on charter schools and education reform, she conducted an extensive research project on behalf of the School Futures Research Foundation. She helped conduct dozens of interviews with African American and other leaders in Los Angeles, as well as several focus groups comprising low-income parents. Her research culminated in a report entitled "Handwriting on the Wall." For Bible-literate Nira, the title was no accident. She knew well what happened to King Belshazzar after Daniel had interpreted the handwriting on the king's palace wall.

From leaders she interviewed, Nira learned that the city's elite recognized the school system's ineptitude but had little political will to change it. In fact, many were benefiting from the current system and were committed to protecting it. From the parents she learned that, in spite of the lip service, schools sent most parents unmistakable signals that they should not "interfere" with their children's education. From everyone, she heard frustration and hopelessness.

At that point, lesser folk might have walked away, depressed and defeated by the consequences of inaction. Nira decided to persevere. As she articulated her motivation, the country simply could not afford to lose another generation of poor children to prisons and dependency. She decided to open a charter school.

THE TEAM

By the time I heard in 1996 about Nira's dream to start a charter school, she had already recruited a handful of distinguished friends to help her. Many would eventually become the board of the Watts Learning Center Foundation. Gene Fisher, a chemical engineer, had a long career in government service, including with the California Air Resources Board. Dr. Owen Knox, a nationally recognized expert on effectively teaching low-income and African American children, had been an assistant superintendent with LAUSD. Gloria Nabrit was CEO of the Kedren Community Health Center, one of L.A. County's largest providers of mental health services and operators of Head Start centers. Sandra Porter (later Fisher) had been an LAUSD elementary school principal. Later Nira supplemented this working group with Eugene Ruffin, the president and CEO of the School Futures Research Foundation, Mary Idella Coleman, the director of the Urban League's Head Start program, Sylvester Hinton, a local public school activist, and me.

For almost a year, our group planned and discussed a vision and mission for the school. Without much debate, we decided quickly to focus solely on low-income children. Local Head Start programs would provide an ample supply of children ready to excel, although research indicated that Head Start alumni in public schools were failing as badly as other low-income peers by the third grade.

Determining how to work successfully with low-income children took more discussion, which the board continues to this day. Dr. Knox provided the key insight: children of poverty have often learned special coping and life skills that could be effectively leveraged for academic performance. Most of these skills are ignored and, indeed, viewed with disdain. They are usually stifled in traditional classrooms. WLC would mold our instructional methods to take advantage of such skills.

The working group agreed to set the highest possible standards for our students, long before a presidential campaign speechwriter pointed out the "soft bigotry of low expectations." The logic was simple. It's far more inspiring to train for the Olympics than a pickup game. If we set our goals low, our students would certainly achieve them.

The working group also wanted to create a self-reinforcing community that embraced all stakeholders. We imagined that an effective school could inspire a neighborhood renaissance in a way that government housing or subsidized commercial zones simply could never do. It enumerated the different stakeholders and outlined each one's responsibilities. The team decided to build the school's student body over time. Rather than hatch whole, we decided to start with kindergartners and add a grade each subsequent year. Such an approach allowed us to ramp up more effectively, even as we educated some children without compensation and the district received money for students it no longer served (due to state funding rules).

Finally, the working group wanted to create a school that was driven exclusively by concern for our students and their achievement. To the extent possible, the nascent board encouraged adults to put their own agendas aside for the sake of the children. Eventually, the concepts were captured in the following statement:

> The Watts Learning Center will be a world-class, child-centered elementary school with strong ties to families and the community. WLC will produce

high academic achievers who are self-confident, ethical, and motivated to be lifelong learners. The Watts Learning Center will build on the success of Head Start and other pre-school programs by creating a culture of learning in which all stakeholders—students, parents or guardians, faculty, and staff—have clearly defined roles and expectations. WLC students will acquire:

- Reading, writing, math, and critical thinking skills that meet or exceed those expected of students at the world's top elementary schools.
- A base of core knowledge common to well-educated Americans.
- Emotional maturity, including empathy and the willingness to accept responsibility for personal actions.
- A clear understanding of responsibilities and rights concerning their schoolmates, staff and faculty, family members, community, country, and world.

As the primary educators and advocates of their children, parents or guardians will participate actively in the school. They will obtain the skills necessary for motivating their children to become responsible students and lifelong learners.

The WLC faculty team will be role models for lifelong learning and professionalism. Because the faculty team will be held accountable for assuring that WLC students achieve high standards, it will be deeply involved in developing the WLC academic program.

The WLC operations staff will set new standards for efficient and effective management, freeing more resources for the education of our students.

VISION AND ACTION

Nira died just days before we submitted our final petition to LAUSD. Her leadership lingers with us, but she has not been here physically to reiterate, reinforce, and spread the vision. That task has fallen largely to Gene and Sandra Fisher. Gene, who serves as the president of the WLC board, is an intelligent, charismatic, and good-humored advocate to the community. Sandra, equally bright and good-natured, also has significant experience as an educator and school administrator. With significant prodding from her fellow board members, Sandra came out of retirement to serve as the school's interim principal and director. The board recruited John Allen to be principal beginning in fall of 2003, and Sandra continues to serve part-time as executive director.

Gene and Sandra devote scores of volunteer hours to the school each month. Most people who know the Watts Learning Center today do not associate it with Nira Long. They do associate it with Gene and Sandra Fisher. And of all the things that Gene and Sandra do, nothing is more important than guarding and reiterating the vision inspired by their friend Nira.

"[Our board] has been repeatedly grateful that we spent so much time up front articulating our vision and mission. . . . It has not shielded us from heartache, but . . . has allowed us to act decisively."

As the Watts Learning Center has grown and faced small and large crises, the board has been repeatedly grateful that we spent so much time up front articulating our vision and mission. Time and again, we return to those fundamentals. It has not shielded us from heartache, but the shared vision has allowed us to act decisively when confronted with challenges. One of the biggest heartaches involved WLC's relationship with School Futures Research Foundation (SFRF). Based in San Diego, SFRF was organized in 1995 as a nonprofit educational management organization (EMO). It had plans to open as many as 50 charter schools in five years. WLC appeared to be just the sort of charter school that was worthy of SFRF's investment.

While WLC was going through the petitioning process, SFRF was a constant, comforting support. It provided our working team with needed technical assistance, particularly in the area of school finance. At a time before planning grants, it picked up the expenses related to developing our petition. It even provided a $250,000 line of credit that LAUSD demanded before it would allow our charter school to open. By the time the school opened, SFRF had invested a lot in WLC, and WLC owed SFRF much. We were united in our goal of opening a quality school for low-income children. No one doubted the marriage would endure.

For all of our careful planning together, WLC and SFRF failed to communicate clearly what role each would play after receiving the charter. WLC's board expected that its role would be limited to governance and that SFRF would pick up management. SFRF at first seemed to expect the board to manage the school, but it later observed (correctly) that the WLC directors had begun micromanaging.

The warning signs were there but were easily overlooked. For example, at one meeting before the charter was approved, the board was shocked to learn that SFRF did not plan to help the board locate a permanent facility. The board was forced into micromanagement, literally cruising block after block, looking for empty buildings that might accommodate our school. After we received our charter and were added to SFRF's portfolio of schools, SFRF management became even more preoccupied by their efforts to start other schools. Additional items ended up being delegated to the board, including the areas of recruiting and training teachers, ensuring we had a strong parent organization, developing personnel policies, and hiring and firing staff.

Before long, the board was intimately involved with operating the school. When SFRF asked to increase its management fees, the board demurred, essentially questioning SFRF's added value. SFRF departed soon after. WLC students and parents never knew the difference.

The key lesson here is not about governance versus management. Indeed, our board remains very skeptical about playing a management role, and we have intentionally begun to distance ourselves from our flawed but necessary early days. Rather, the lesson is about vision. The easiest thing to do would have been to accommodate SFRF's minimal but expensive role. Remember, we owed them a lot; they were absolutely critical to getting the school started. SFRF's flaunting of the Watts Learning Center as their creation was harmless enough and close to true. We also felt good that our association gave them credibility needed to get other good schools started. It took a while for us to start questioning whether our relationship with SFRF aligned with our vision and mission. Did SFRF's involvement get us closer to becoming a world-class school? Did SFRF reflect good stewardship, focusing dollars where they make the most difference? Sadly, in both cases, the answer was no.

It is popular in education reform literature to credit any successful urban school to the work of heroic, larger-than-life leaders. It's a seductive theme, and one that is promoted, perhaps subconsciously, by some of those successful school leaders. Such a theme is ultimately restrictive and defeatist, for it implies that only a breed of super-human leaders can reverse the yawning achievement gap and fix failing urban schools. The Watts Learning Center offers a refreshing contrast to that restrictive hypothesis. WLC can attribute its success to one common vision, not an extraordinary school leader or board. Certainly, the school's nominal leader is a wonderful and talented individual, and the school's board includes several outstanding people. But that ignores a critical fact: people of equal quality are also involved in the failing schools surrounding WLC. We perform better not because we are better, but because we have better focus—a clear idea of what we want to achieve and how we plan to get there.

We hope that Watts Learning Center prompts others to ask why equally dedicated and competent people are not making progress within the traditional public schools. One part of the answer is that everyone involved with WLC is encouraged to envision a world-class school and accept nothing less. Another part is our teachers.

GREAT TEACHERS WITH GOOD SUPPORT

As part of his State of the State address in 2000, Governor Gray Davis acknowledged the dedication and teaching skill of Marques Allen. Young, male, and African American, Marques learned his trade at WLC and has served on the school's faculty since our opening day. For our school, it was a moment of pride. For me, it was also a moment of irony. Our school's view of teachers—their qualifications, training needs, and significance—stands in sharp contrast to traditional views embraced by most Californians and the politicians that represent them.

It should be obvious that the Watts Learning Center has well-qualified teachers. The achievement of our students, who would otherwise be labeled "at risk," is as much evidence as most people would need. Yet, according to the measures that our public school establishment uses to judge the qualifications of teachers, our faculty comes up wanting. Most of our teachers come to us without full credentials, sometimes without having suffered a single course in pedagogy.

Because of misguided amendments to California's original charter school law, Watts Learning Center teachers must have the same certification and credentialing as teachers in the traditional system. We do abide by the law, but we find it an unproductive annoyance. From direct experience, we have learned that a teaching credential has little to do with a teacher's true qualifications. The main reason so many good teachers have credentials is that they were forced to get them. Such people would have been good teachers even if they had never jumped through the credentialing hoops. Conversely, far too many people with impressive credentials are weak teachers, even though they are good, smart people. What we look for in teachers can be summed up in one word borrowed from the church: "calling."

Visitors to the Watts Learning Center are often struck by the ethnic and gender composition of our staff. In a field that remains dominated by whites and females, especially at the elementary level, our faculty is almost all minorities, and women only barely outnumber men. We don't know if this helps our students achieve or not. We do know that our teachers, especially the men, become powerful role models. Perhaps that alone is enough to inspire better achievement.

> **"From direct experience, we have learned that a teaching credential has little to do with a teacher's true qualifications. . . . What we look for in teachers can be summed up in one word borrowed from the church: 'calling.'"**

Visitors also ask questions revealing an underlying assumption that our teachers must work harder and longer than teachers at traditional schools. Sometimes such questions are wrapped in crafty references to our teachers not being represented by the local United Teachers of Los Angeles, so we are allowed to make them work harder. Our teachers may work harder than other good teachers, but I doubt it. Don't misunderstand. Our teachers are very committed and work very, very hard. They put in long hours, often followed by independent coursework at local colleges and universities. They have little time for anything other than their students and their chosen careers. Yet I know teachers in failing public schools who are working just as hard. Indeed, given their environments, it seems they work harder, and certainly more heroically. Good teachers everywhere work very hard.

So if it's not credentialing and it's not more effort, what accounts for our faculty's superior results? The answer is complex, but the reasons include the people we attract and how we treat them. WLC works hard at making sure their hard work matters. We hire potentially talented teachers, and then we empower them to teach. We seek individuals who have a passion for children and lifelong learning. We seek people who have been gifted with the raw communication skills and strong substantive backgrounds. We seek people who see our students' achievement as a personal mission.

We are not opposed to experience; in fact, we would welcome it. But we are simply not in a position to lure veteran teachers away from LAUSD, which pays its most senior teachers close to $75,000 for 10 months' work and offers one of the state's richest benefit packages. Because we receive from the state a fraction of what LAUSD receives per student, salaries like that would mean serious cuts in other parts of our program. We pay our teachers as well as we can, always wishing we could pay them more. Teacher salaries take the highest priority in our budget. We have pegged them to LAUSD's salary scale—meaning that our starting teachers make about $38,000 per year. We decided to pay the higher-than-average LAUSD salaries mostly to communicate that we value our teachers. A residual benefit is that comparable salaries defend against LAUSD raiding our faculty.

Beyond salary, we work to provide an environment that lets our faculty know that we consider them central to our success. Because our teachers are held accountable for student performance, they are involved in all decisions affecting their ability to improve achievement, including curriculum selection and parental empowerment. Our board has yet to deny a teacher proposal or recommendation, save one or two that have been tabled until resources to support them can be raised. Meanwhile, the state teachers' union, the California Teacher Association, announced in 2002 that its highest legislative priority is to incorporate such powers into its collective bargaining negotiations. Their attempts to muscle through such legislation were opposed by every major editorial board in the state, as well as erstwhile ally Governor Gray Davis. Eventually, the legislation was withdrawn for want of votes. For all its political power in the state, CTA was unable to convince decision-makers to relinquish such powers. At the Watts Learning Center, we cede those powers willingly because we know our teachers only have the best interests of students in mind.

"Because we value our teachers, and because our teachers recognize there is always more to learn, coaching and peer interaction are central. . . . It is . . . our desire to empower good teachers to teach. . . . We also empower ineffective teachers to leave."

Because we value our teachers, and because our teachers recognize there is always more to learn, coaching and peer interaction are central to the culture at Watts Learning Center. The school's director spends much of her time in the classroom and in private meetings, helping our teachers hone their skills. This past year, the board hired an experienced educator specifically to be an on-site coach and supplement the director. It is all part of our desire to empower good teachers to teach. One of the reasons the board chose John Allen to be the principal was his commitment to coaching our faculty, especially in the area of mathematics, an area where we need to achieve the same excellence we have in reading instruction.

We also empower ineffective teachers to leave. My personal philosophy is that there are three types of teachers: those who are strong and can get better, those who are weak but can get better soon, and those who are weak and will not get better in time to avoid harming students. We tend to treat all new faculty as though they fit in the second category. In a couple of cases, it becomes clear over time that the person will never be a good teacher, and we badly misjudged their potential when we hired them. The easiest thing to do in such situations is nothing. Terminating a teacher means finding a replacement, never an easy task and close to impossible mid-term. There is never a guarantee that the replacement will be better, and there is a chance he or she will be worse. Termination also means hurting someone's feelings—someone we have come to like and respect. Terminations occur, however, because of our vision of a world-class school.

PARENTS

When the NAACP announced a $100 million advertising campaign to encourage more "involvement" from parents in schools—a campaign that would be financed largely by their longtime political ally and financial supporter, the National Education Association—I cringed. First, the press release came dangerously close to blaming the victims of failed schools, a sad and ironic position for one of the country's leading civil rights groups. Second, involvement is a weak, ambiguous word. One school's involvement is another's interference. In the inner cities of America, the system has too often taught teachers that many, and perhaps all, urban parents are incompetent and the ultimate reason for a child's inability to learn. The parents, in turn, have learned that in spite of the rhetoric, they are not really welcome at school, much less in the classroom.

At the Watts Learning Center, we focus on parent empowerment, not involvement. We teach WLC parents that they are critical partners in their children's education—irrespective of their own level of education. Parents are not only welcome on campus, they are expected to show up regularly. We reinforce the empowerment theme through dozens of formal and informal communications throughout the year—often delivered to parents by other parents. One of the most controversial is the contract we ask all parents to sign before the child attends the Watts Learning Center. (This practice is explicitly prohibited in many states.) In this unenforceable document, parents acknowledge that they will be expected to make sure their child is read to each night, attend a few parent meetings each year, and volunteer at least 30 hours per year. Like many contracts, its main purpose is to spell out expectations clearly. It helps reinforce the school's culture, and many parents far exceed the minimum requirements.

The empowerment messages extend to school management. The Parent Organization is not some rubber stamp or impotent shell. The Parent Organization's president, who is a member of our board of directors, regularly reports on parent activities and organizes the parents to make policy recommendations. The board deliberately requests input and recommendations on vexing areas. There are several examples of parent recommendations becoming the school's policy, including our uniform policy, our response to tardiness and excessive absences, and our parent volunteer policies.

Parent empowerment generates positive results in several areas, including student achievement, and other public schools would be stunned by the amount of money these low-income parents raise on behalf of the school. They raise the funds independently and decide themselves where to invest the funds. Recently, they purchased and installed five computers in our classrooms. Each of those computers is highly valued and will make a big difference in the classroom. At the suggestion of the parents, the board also purchased five computers, making sure that each of our classrooms received a new one.

STEWARDSHIP

We have not invested much in technology up to now. It is not even a high fund-raising priority of ours, although it is certainly on our comprehensive wish list. Given our commitment to stewardship, I predict that our investments in technology will continue to lag behind personnel and other areas that we believe yield higher returns for student achievement. If it comes down to a choice between a new teacher and new software, the teacher wins easily. If it is between another, faster Internet connection and teacher-support personnel, again the staff wins. And if it is a choice between a new high-speed local area network and welcoming, comfortable facilities, the facilities win. We resist the temptation to be state-of-the-art when low-tech investments will mean more for improving student achievement.

In the context of a school, stewardship should mean making sure that every dollar goes toward ensuring student achievement. The government, ultimately the taxpayer, has entrusted charter schools with using the resources granted them wisely and prudently. Each expenditure should be scrutinized with the questions "How will this affect student achievement?" and "How might we get the same outcome with less money?"

"We have not invested much in technology up to now. . . . We resist the temptation to be state-of-the-art when low-tech investments will mean more for improving student achievement."

The Watts Learning Center practices good stewardship partly because it is consistent with our vision and, in our view, the right and moral thing to do. Anything else would violate the public trust. But, in practice, there are other powerful motivations. One is that we have less money than traditional schools, so we are under more pressure to make every dollar count. Not that we are the least funded of inner-city schools. The Watts Learning Center receives almost $6,000 per student, an allotment that must cover everything from teacher salaries and benefits to facilities to special education programs and hot lunches. When compared to nearby Catholic parochial schools, we are flush; they get by on about $3,500 per student, with only about $2,500 coming from tuition. The consistently positive performance of urban Catholic schools is all the more remarkable given their budgets.

As a rule, though, we do not compare WLC spending against urban parochial schools. The better comparison is with the Los Angeles Unified School District, the leviathan that imposes its mind-numbing regulations and ultimately its cost structure on our 200-student school. With a budget of about $8.8 billion and 740,000 students, LAUSD receives more than $11,000 for each enrolled student, or roughly twice what WLC receives. This per-student amount does not include the hundreds of millions of dollars of bond funds that allow LAUSD to build, or try to build, its schools and other facilities. WLC receives no funds for facilities, although we hope that will change in the next couple of years. Given our performance and desperate need for facilities, we hoped we would be given a portion of the funds earmarked by voters for charter schools in 2002; however, the funds for the L.A. area went instead to a successful, unionized charter school.

Legislators, frustrated by the lack of student achievement in urban schools and concerned about potential financial malfeasance, have continuously placed more and more regulatory burdens on schools and districts. Cumbersome regulations, for all their good intentions, lead to higher costs. Charter schools in California are not protected from this pattern. If one of our state's 300 or so charter schools misbehaves, all of us can rely on a new set of restrictive policies and regulations the following year. As at least one education lobbyist has pointed out, adding more regulations is what most lawmakers believe they are paid to do. In their world, the idea of removing regulations seems radically irresponsible.

The upward pressure on salaries also seems justified. In nationwide comparisons of teacher salaries, California ranks in the top ten. Putting aside how these higher than average salaries clash with claims of lower than average spending, any teacher representative and most California school board members and legislators can articulate why teacher salaries in the state are not sufficient. They argue that California must attract upward of 200,000 new teachers into the profession over the next six to 10 years to accommodate a growing student body, replace retiring teachers, and implement smaller class sizes. Degreed professionals have lots of competing employment options. If we are to meet the demand for teachers, we simply must raise salaries. Their argument misses many economic and social nuances, and it blows past some details that mitigate the alleged crisis, but the general premise is solid. To attract good teachers, the salaries, especially starting salaries, have to rise. And when teacher salaries increase, you can bet on concomitant salary increases for everyone else in the system, especially administrators.

The problem is not that LAUSD receives $11,000+ per child; it's that WLC receives half that amount and must cut into our general allotment to pay for facilities in one of the most expensive real estate markets in the state. The comparison hints at the second reason beyond our values that causes us to practice good stewardship: if we did not, we would not survive.

Every traditional school within miles of WLC can have the lowest possible achievement, and the system keeps them open. If we falter, we would be closed. Every traditional school around us receives special funds to accommodate their poor performance; if they fail to improve achievement, the system keeps them open. Again, if we did that, we would be closed. WLC does not chaff at this double standard. We truly embrace it. It's the sort of accountability that makes charter schools work. One wonders what similar accountability would mean for the traditional public schools.

CONCLUSION

The birth and growth of the Watts Learning Center parallels my own journey from vaguely concerned citizen to radical school reformer. I am forever grateful to a friend like Nira Long for nudging me into the journey. Today, I wish that more vaguely concerned citizens would take time to work at and for urban charter schools, for every reformer longs for comrades. If others did take the time, I believe they, too, would come to see our urban education system as fundamentally flawed. They would delve beyond those glib sound bites of superintendents and union officials to dialogue sincerely with the teachers, parents, and students who grapple with the broken system every day. They would see that without systemic change—that is, trading in the current system for a new one with different incentives and power relationships—society will continue to see 50% plus dropout rates at urban schools, too often unemployable graduates, and rising crime and violence.

Like me, they would begin to challenge and question the apologists for the broken system. When they hear pleas to stifle charter schools because they "drain" money from the traditional public system, they would begin to ask, shouldn't we care more about *whether* a child gets educated than *where* he or she gets educated, and more about who helps to pay, not which school receives the money? Like me, they might even begin to wonder if it would be so terrible if low-income children were empowered through taxpayer-financed scholarships to attend private schools or religious schools.

Perhaps the greatest obstacle to confronting and closing the education achievement gap between whites and minorities is that the public school system actually works fairly well in predominantly white, middle- and upper-income neighborhoods. Many educators (and politicians) see this and wistfully recommend that low-income black and Hispanic families act, in effect, more like middle-class families. It sounds like pretty good advice, especially when wrapped in terms like parent involvement, because the recalcitrant system seems incapable of educating anyone other than middle- and upper-class children. But such advice is unrealistic. It fails to recognize the enormous pressures faced by low-income parents, and it ignores the extensive and subtle training that has empowered middle- and upper-income families to assist with, and advocate for, their children's educations.

It is provocative and dangerous to point out the underlying racism and classism in our public education system. As a society, we are shy about confronting such things. But I submit there is a deep reason that most apologists for urban school performance begin their presentations with a litany of statistics about how different urban children are from the country's white, middle-class norm. There is a reason society allows so many black and Hispanic children to languish and ultimately fail in public schools. We expect nothing more.

"If we really want to change the performance of an urban school, we will give black and Hispanic parents the same power that most white parents take for granted: . . . to choose what you think is best for your own child, . . . to change a school or a classroom if you aren't satisfied."

Is it too mind-bending for people to imagine that the urban system, not the families, should be what changes? California, like most states, has seen repeated "reforms" fail to make a difference with urban children. Even wildly popular (and expensive) reforms such as smaller class size have not closed the gap and may have actually aggravated the problem. Still, our educators and politicians continue to insist on "reforms" that do not spur the system to act differently. The huge bureaucracy continues to operate as if the whole world is one white suburb.

Conservative economists view this problem as one of market incentives. Not until a school is threatened with losing the money associated with a child, they argue, will the school system have an incentive to change. Perhaps because my training is stronger in politics than economics, I believe they overstate their case. The more fundamental problem is one of political power, for ultimately, schools and school districts are political organizations that respond to potent constituencies. If we really want to change the performance of an urban school, we will give black and Hispanic parents the same power that most white parents take for granted: the power to choose what you think is best for your own child, the power to change a school or a classroom if you aren't satisfied.

Up until now, urban charter schools such as WLC and others in this book are less a challenge to the existing public schools than they are a defiance of societal expectations. They are proving there are ways to engage low-income parents productively in public schools. They are showing that all low-income minority children (and I do mean all) can learn and succeed in life. If urban charter schools are allowed to continue growing and reach critical mass, their impact will extend beyond serving as important examples. They have the potential of empowering low-income parents, transforming public education for the better, and providing equal opportunities to the next generation of urban children.

⏸ THE PHOENIX

John von Rohr, Rocky Mount Charter School

Rocky Mount Charter School is the largest charter school in North Carolina, with nearly 1,000 students enrolled for the 2002–03 school year. The school has withstood many trials and tribulations, including the complete destruction of its facilities by Hurricane Floyd, and has made impressive academic improvement each year. Dr. John von Rohr, superintendent of the Rocky Mount Charter School, is a 21-year career army officer. He was an instructor at the U.S. Military Academy at West Point, during which time he earned a doctorate in educational administration and supervision from Fordham University. His military background concentrated on the areas of military police and military intelligence, and he was provost marshal (chief of police) at a military installation and chief of operations for the U.S. Army Criminal Investigation Division Command in Europe.

The history of the Rocky Mount Charter School encompasses both tragedy and triumph. The idea to create the school was fermented in the minds of past presidents of the Rocky Mount area Chamber of Commerce, most notably Robert R. Mauldin, past chief executive officer of Centura Bank, one of the largest financial institutions in the state of North Carolina. In late 1995, this group of successful business people met to discuss the possibility of starting their own charter school in

Rocky Mount. With knowledge of the success of the public "charter-like" School of Math and Science and School of the Arts in Wake County, and a limited knowledge about the charter school movement in other states, the groundwork was laid for the school's future. To them, the most attractive aspect of the charter school movement was the premise that charter schools would have "freedom" from the normal bureaucratic controls placed on regular public schools. After numerous meetings, it was decided to wait until the North Carolina legislature enacted its own charter school legislation before proceeding further.

"Being astute business people, the core group quickly concluded that they did not possess enough educational expertise to operate the school by themselves."

In March 1997, this same core group met again for more serious discussions. At that time they decided to apply for a school charter under the state's new charter school laws. The school would begin as K–5 and would add one grade each year, ending up with a K–12 school by the 2004–05 school year. Their goal: provide a better education to the children of the Rocky Mount area, which includes both Nash and Edgecombe Counties. Another change at this time was the election of a school board with a diversity that more accurately reflected the demographics of the local population (50% African American, 50% white).

Being astute business people, the core group quickly concluded that they did not possess enough educational expertise to operate the school by themselves. They researched several educational management companies and finally formed a joint partnership with one, which included site management, curriculum, construction financing, faculty hiring, etc. After finding no other suitable building, it was jointly decided to gut and totally renovate an empty J. C. Penney retail facility at the Tarrytown Mall in Rocky Mount. The mall itself had been built during the 1960s. The initial build-out consisted of approximately 60,000 square feet of classroom space, and it was a first-class facility, at least inside, in every way. There were, however, no playground areas and the outside of the building was, by virtue of its mall location, quite "austere." The management company and the school board mutually agreed to start school in August of that same year, which resulted in an abundance of logistical problems (this is an understatement).

"In regard to school leadership, the school went through a very turbulent period for the first two years."

The charter school opened for the first time in August 1997 with 563 students, although not at the Tarrytown Mall, but in several locations in the Rocky Mount area, including six different churches and additional classroom space at North Carolina Wesleyan College. This transient situation lasted until October of that same year, at which time the students moved into their permanent home at the Tarrytown Mall facility. There was never any shortage of textbooks or other classroom materials while the school was at this location.

In regard to school leadership, the school went through a very turbulent period for the first two years. The initial school director lasted just two months, finding the job of starting a new school and having the dual role of school and business leader to be overwhelming. The second school director lasted six months, leaving because unable to succeed in the multiple roles required of this position. For some time after that, other members of the administrative staff (curriculum director, business manager, and behavioral specialist) ran the school on a daily basis. Eventually, school director number three reported, serving in an interim status as a "troubleshooter" from the management company's corporate headquarters. The school board was, by necessity, more heavily involved in the day-to-day operation of the school as a result of not having a permanent educational leader in place.

The school's educational philosophy was directed by the management company and focused on Direct Instruction programs for reading, language arts, and math. The ultimate goal of these programs was for students to reach the mastery level of learning. The success of these programs depended heavily on small ability groups to ensure that children were constantly being challenged and reaching mastery level. This required the hiring of a plethora of teaching assistants, who actually taught these small groups in conjunction with regular classroom teachers. The number of staff members needed to properly conduct these programs put a drain on the school budget.

A strict Code of Conduct was enforced, along with the wearing of uniforms. A longer school day and longer school year were in place. A major premise of the program was that children were not routinely given enough positive feedback when they successfully accomplished a task; therefore, praise became a watchword for all teachers to incorporate into their daily teaching regimens. A very structured character education program also played a significant part in the educational process at the school, with the goal of producing model citizens. Each of these programs was research-based and was seen as most applicable to the needs of our students, which consisted of a largely urban population. By virtue of the impact these programs had on our students, they later served as some of the many justifications parents gave for enrolling their children in the Rocky Mount Charter School. From the beginning, a big emphasis was placed on parent involvement with the school. To reinforce this, the parent, student, and school director signed a pledge to support school policies on both academic and behavioral issues.

"The 'flight' of the previously locally employed teachers definitely contributed to feelings of animosity between the charter school and [the school district]."

Initial efforts at teacher recruitment were somewhat of an ordeal, as was expected. Recruiting ads were placed locally and nationally, and by the beginning of the school year all necessary staff was on hand. Several of these teachers came from the local Nash-Rocky Mount school system, while others were recruited from as far away as New York state. The "flight" of the previously locally employed teachers definitely contributed to feelings of animosity between the charter school and Nash-Rocky Mount Schools, the local education authority (LEA). Although some noncertified teachers were employed (allowable by the State of North Carolina under charter school regulations), the majority of the staff was certified.

Before the school opened its doors in 1997, local resistance popped up in the form of a lawsuit filed by Nash-Rocky Mount Schools, the LEA. The superintendent for Nash-Rocky Mount Schools argued that a for-profit management company should not be taking away local school funding for the operation of a charter school. The lawsuit was dropped before the school year started, but this is an example of the "bad blood" in evidence during the early years of the charter school's operation.

The school board faced many challenges during the early years of the school's existence, most notably in the area of financing the school's construction. As charter schools in North Carolina receive absolutely no federal, state, or local money for school construction, members of the school board had to guarantee loans that were backed up by their personal assets. These were bold people indeed, particularly when many millions of dollars would be needed to construct a school large enough to hold over 500 children. The Self-Help Credit Union in Durham was one of the only financial institutions in the state willing to take a chance on financing our charter school. The school board was also able to gain the support of several major businesses in the community, who committed themselves to making financial investments in the form of ongoing funding to the charter school. The management company also assumed risk in this new venture, which was a definite plus in getting the school built.

"A perception in the community was that the charter school would raid all of the white schools in the area....At the same time, there was a concern among the charter school founders that the public school system would use the charter school as a 'dumping ground.'"

One definite lesson learned early on, according to Robert R. Mauldin of the core group, is that it would have been more advisable to wait another year to open the school. It takes a significant amount of time to get a school off on the right foot. He has further remarked that if he had it to do over again, there would be much more planning and less building at the onset of the granting of the charter. The school board, however, did take the great leap, and it succeeded because they were simply not going to let the school fail, no matter what the cost.

One perception in the community was that the charter school would raid all of the white schools in the area and create some sort of elite, white "public prep school" by means of a "brain drain" of students at the expense of the Nash-Rocky Mount school system. At the same time, there was a concern among the charter school founders that the public school system would use the charter school as a "dumping ground" for their low academic achievers, behavior problems, and exceptional children that no one else wanted in their classrooms. None of these perceptions came to pass. The charter school's first class consisted of about 65% African American students and students functioning at varied levels of academic achievement. The percentage of exceptional children enrolled in the charter school matched other public school settings. It was determined, however, that in regard to academic levels, the students tended to be at two extremes: those way ahead of their peers and those significantly (several grade levels in some instances) behind. It was impossible to determine whether or not the enrollment of the low-performing students was a result of a purposeful "dumping" by the local public school system or simply a result of so many parents wanting to enroll their children in a school where they could experience academic success. What was known was that the charter school board was giving parents a feeling of ownership in the school through their required participation in their child's education.

From its very first day of operation, the Rocky Mount Charter School was the largest in North Carolina. Dr. Grova Bridgers, director of the Office of Charter Schools in North Carolina, called the Rocky Mount Charter School "North Carolina's Flagship Charter School." That designation remains today as everyone at the school does their very best on a day-to-day basis to live up to that reputation.

In March 1999, the author of this chapter assumed duties as the school's fourth educational leader, the school by this time having an enrollment of 750 students. The management firm had found me through a headhunter firm in Maine. As a result of my prior administrative and teaching experience, I felt I was more than prepared for any challenges that this position might offer. I certainly would not have considered myself naïve in regard to financial affairs, having done considerable budget-related work while in the service. I quickly ascertained, through immediate personal experience, that the business side of leading a charter school was just as important, if not more important, than being a good educational leader.

"The business side of leading a charter school was just as important, if not more important, than being a good educational leader."

One problem encountered by Rocky Mount Charter School was the "disconnect" between the curriculum our management company provided and its alignment with North Carolina's "Standard Course of Study," the curriculum upon which state accountability testing is based. Wearing two hats, being responsible to both the management company and the school board, I did my best to identify this issue without harming the relationship with either. Curriculum alignment would prove to be a very thorny issue in the school's future due to state-mandated accountability.

It was obvious that our students were learning under the Direct Instruction curriculum in place, and our kindergarten children were very often reading at the second-grade level by the end of their first year. State testing, however, did not necessarily identify this growth, due to the misalignment with their testing goals, with the result that the school received a "No Recognition" designation at the end of the 1998–99 school year (the same as the year before). This label is above "Low Performing" but below "Meets Expected Growth," falling into the twilight zone of nondescriptive academic achievement.

Another issue came up shortly after my arrival at the school. Were we going to go along with the state's waiver for percentage of certified teachers (75% for elementary, 50% for secondary)? My decision was that we would not, that in the future we would hire only certified staff, and furthermore, if those already on the faculty did not already have their degrees and certification, they could keep their teaching job only

as long as they were actively working toward a bachelor's degree and a
teaching credential.

"Our kindergarten children were very often reading at the second-grade level by the end of their first year. State testing, however, did not necessarily identify this growth, due to the misalignment with their testing goals."

The entire summer of 1999 was spent preparing for the 1999–2000
school year and the 800-plus students we expected to enroll. When we
opened school in mid-July (remember, our school year is longer), 820
students were on hand, the maximum we could logistically support.
While school was in progress, construction was already underway to
build out classrooms for eighth-graders for the next school year. A new
gym was to be completed no later than early October, just a short time
away. A new, state-of-the-art playground was built adjacent to the school
building at a cost of $35,000, shared equally by the school and its very ac-
tive Parent Advisory Council. It was used for a few short weeks in September 1999 before disaster struck, which brings us to the "And Then
There Was None" chapter in the school's rather tumultuous history.

"By early morning ... the [school] was submerged under more than five feet of raging water. . . . . The truly beautiful, almost-new school facility was lost forever."

During the first week of September 1999, Hurricane Dennis had inundated eastern North Carolina with extremely heavy rainfall. That water had no place to go but into local rivers and their tributaries, which
were quickly filled to the top of their banks. At this point there was no
serious problem for either the Rocky Mount Charter School or the local

community at large. Just two weeks later, shortly before midnight on September 15, 1999, Hurricane Floyd, with its accompanying 100 mph winds, suddenly veered inland into eastern North Carolina, bringing with it a deluge of rainfall in proportions unpredicted in even the 500-year floodplain. By early morning on September 16, the Rocky Mount Charter School was submerged under more than five feet of raging water. Almost as fast as the water had risen, it receded, but the damage was done. The truly beautiful, almost-new school facility was lost forever.

A few days later it was possible to go into the school with some degree of safety. From the outside entrance of the school, it was quite easy to see where the water line had been, 5 feet 3 inches above the ground level. Classroom furniture was overturned onto the floor, desks were covered in a brown slimy substance, and the entire library was now just a pile of smelly paper products rather than a source for learning. The interior of the building, where the administrative offices were housed, was pitch black; all electricity was gone as a result of the water damage to electrical outlets. At first it was believed that at least some adjustable student desks might be salvaged (the only items thought to be redeemable out of the entire school facility), but this proved to be a false assumption due to the presence of e-coli, streptococcus, and staphylococcus contamination and the inability of anyone to ensure that any amount of washing could properly disinfect them to such a degree that children would not have been harmed. In other words, all school and personal property, including items that some teachers had accumulated for 15 plus years, was lost.

"Within three days, classroom space had been secured at three churches in the . . . area."

How can you realistically account for what was lost, both professionally and personally, as a result of such a disaster? We never could, and eventually we stopped trying, deciding instead to move on, for our sake and for the children. It was a horrible, totally disheartening experience to see what six hours of Hurricane Floyd could do to a $5 million investment dedicated to the improvement of student learning. The only living thing that survived the floodwaters in the school, along with three water moccasins we found, was a newt (an amphibian) kept in a teacher's classroom as a class pet. The newt had been in a fish tank with a glass top on it, and the floodwaters never seeped in. The newt still lives today, the school's only living "survivor" of Hurricane Floyd.

On Sunday, September 19, 1999, just three days after the destruction of the school, a strategic planning session was held at my residence (spared by the flood) with members of the school board and administrative staff. At that time it was decided to begin calling local churches in an effort to locate classroom space so that our school could survive. Not one person at that meeting would even remotely consider closing the school or giving up on it; this is how much every single person involved was dedicated to seeing to the school's continued existence.

Within three days, classroom space had been secured at three churches in the Rocky Mount area: First Presbyterian, First Baptist, and Englewood Assembly of God. Grade 2 and Middle School were to be taught at First Presbyterian, grades 3–5 at First Baptist, and K–1 at Englewood Assembly of God. We owe our very survival as an educational institution to these churches, which opened up their hearts and doors to us. By their actions, they eloquently demonstrated that they are truly examples of the southern hospitality that still exists in the "Bible Belt" section of our great country.

On October 2, 1999, two weeks after the flood destroyed the school, 95 percent of the students showed up for classes at the churches. Some parents had to drive from one of the two churches downtown to the third site seven miles away to pick up their children. In addition, complicating matters even more, approximately 35 of our students and their families had lost their homes and possessions as a result of Hurricane Floyd, as did four of our staff members. There was a tremendous amount of psychological trauma experienced by every man, woman, and child who lived in Rocky Mount. It was obvious that we had a very strong commitment from our parents and teachers toward the continued existence of the Rocky Mount Charter School. Remarkably, all of our students continued to apply themselves toward learning under some very stressful conditions, which included having no textbooks for almost five months.

What was used to teach the children? The school begged, borrowed, and did everything else short of some illegal act to obtain teaching materials. Donations came in from all over the United States, as the school's plight was well publicized. Without this help, the school could not have survived. "Scrounging" efforts resulted in approximately $200,000 worth of school furniture being placed into a Federal Emergency Management Agency (FEMA) sponsored school site on the west edge of town. The local public school system donated a large quantity of school furniture from a school that had closed. The relationship between their school system and ours had, without a doubt, significantly improved. The logistical support given to us by Nash-Rocky Mount Schools reminded us that "what once was, does not have to be again."

"Our teachers worked together like a family in time of crisis and as a result came out of all of this much stronger, both personally and professionally."

Teachers had to be very creative to teach under these circumstances, and they did a truly wonderful job, for in June 2000 the school received the "Meets Expected Growth" designation from the State Board of Education for its academic achievement during the 1999–2000 school year. This is a particularly admirable accomplishment under "normal" circumstances, but under these extremely adverse conditions it is, without question, a testament to our teacher's dedication and unparalleled professionalism. Not one teacher complained during the entire six months we were in the churches (October 2, 1999, to April 10, 2000). Our teachers worked together like a family in time of crisis and, as a result, came out of all of this much stronger, both personally and professionally. Whatever obstacle was placed in their way, it was efficiently overcome by the team effort.

After six months in the churches, our students moved into the FEMA-sponsored site, in actuality a mobile home park. The school facility was composed of 53 classrooms, situated in a double-wide configuration. Although certainly not an ideal place in which to educate children, it was a step up from our cramped existence in the churches'

Sunday School rooms. It was amazing to watch our students get right back into the learning mode, never missing a beat from one school location to another.

As time progressed, we decided not to renegotiate our contract with our local transportation source for buses and to instead run a joint operation with another transportation company, with the end result that in three years we would take over the running of the transportation system ourselves. To say that a tremendous amount of planning was involved in this move would be an understatement.

Also at this time, questions began to arise about the continued relationship between the management company and the school board. In March 2000, the school board and management company parted amicably, by mutual agreement. From this point on, administrators at the school were responsible for the daily operation of the school. Long-range planning and goal setting were also constantly on their agenda. As the school director position would now assume overall responsibility for the "big picture" issues, a role once taken by the management company, the title was changed to superintendent. Two new principal positions were created, one for elementary, one for middle school. These principals would handle routine day-to-day activities, to include disciplinary actions when required. Each principal had, at a minimum, a master's degree.

> ## "No matter how 'creative' a charter school ... might wish to be, the state's big stick of accountability is always lurking there in the background."

Disciplinary problems were usually few due to the school's continuing strict enforcement of its Code of Conduct. With high expectations not only for academic achievement and behavior, children routinely followed the established rules for behavior, with some minor but unavoidable exceptions. We often remark, "What gets us upset would make a regular public school administrator laugh." Discipline is always administered in a firm but friendly way. When children know exactly what is expected of them, they tend to be much more compliant.

In the period since the charter school became locally operated, we have learned a wide variety of lessons. We continue to tweak our curriculum to ensure that it is aligned with state standards, for no matter how "creative" a charter school in North Carolina might wish to be, the state's big stick of accountability is always lurking there in the background. We have learned how to follow the state's Standard Course of Study and still be creative in the classroom by using supplemental material and giving teachers the ability to use common sense.

How are we different from other public schools? We definitely emphasize higher expectations, both in academics and behavior, our belief being that children will rise to our highest level of expectations, both academically and behaviorally. Our parents are also much more involved in our school than in most other public school settings, to the point that they are overwhelmingly supportive of the standards we've established. How else could we remain the largest charter school in North Carolina, still growing, after being forcefully evicted from our home?

How do the students feel about the school? They've increasingly accepted the fact that their primary "mission" is to come to school prepared to do some serious learning. They also know that school is a place where they are not just a number and that their teachers take a personal interest in them. Believing that a small school setting is best, we purposely separated our elementary, middle, and high school students from each other by placing them in separate buildings on the same campus. Therefore, although a single LEA, the Rocky Mount Charter School consists of the Rocky Mount Elementary, Middle, and High Schools.

"'We don't have to behave like you; we don't go to the Rocky Mount Charter School.' . . . The entire school staff took that comment as a compliment of the highest order."

The intent of the school board is to provide an extremely rigorous curriculum to students to prepare them for entry into college. For this reason, math in particular is required in every single semester in grades 6–8.

Although we obviously place a strong emphasis on the achievement of academic excellence, we do have student dances, sports programs (we won the state charter school middle school basketball championships on two occasions), and clubs. We continue to look forward to offering an extremely rigorous and challenging academic program, while at the same time supporting the institutionalized indoctrination of appropriate socialization skills. We have a school guidance counselor on staff to keep the focus on achievement and to deal with any personal problems our students might have. We firmly believe that there is a connection between academic excellence and proper citizenship skills. While our students are out in the community, their behavior reflects what they have learned in our classroom settings. From all the feedback we have received thus far, it appears we are doing our job. For example, our girls' basketball team had pointed out to them by female athletes from another school, "We don't have to behave like you; we don't go to the Rocky Mount Charter School." The entire school staff took that comment as a compliment of the highest order.

In regard to new school financing and construction issues, after initially being turned down for grants to replace the lost school facility and its contents, FEMA eventually had a change of heart. The school received grant funds for both projects.

In late 2000, school staff and school board members began making plans for the new school facility. Members of the school board and administration reviewed several building systems and builders in an attempt to identify the most efficient and cost-effective way to erect a new school facility. A trip to Tennessee was included in this effort at choosing the best possible builder for our new school. At this same time, other interested parties were searching for an actual physical site on which to build the school.

North Carolina Wesleyan College had a 25-acre section of land at the sound end of their property that was not being used, so an offer was made to purchase it. Their reply was that they would lease the land to us. Our school board did not find this an attractive alternative and the search continued. Shortly thereafter, property became available just west of the college, about a block and a half away from the previously mentioned plot. This 34-acre tract of land was purchased by the school.

Contrary to our earlier efforts to secure financing, which were at times problematic, this time numerous financial institutions offered to fund the building of the new charter school. This trust in us was based to a great degree on our demonstrated ability to operate within a set budget after our separation from our management company. After FEMA grant money was finally received, groundbreaking ceremonies were held on October 21, 2000, with actual construction beginning within 30 days thereafter.

Final construction on the elementary and middle school buildings at a cost of $8 million was completed in time for students to begin school in August 2001. The new school facility consisted of a V-wing configuration, with an elementary wing, grades K–5, in the left wing, an administrative building and library in the middle, and grades 6–9 in the right wing. Total classroom space was in the 72,000 square foot range. A new 15,000 square foot gymnasium/multipurpose facility was completed in December 2001, and final build-out of the school (the high school wing) was completed in July 2002, with an additional 14,000 square feet of classroom space. This final construction expenditure of $2 million brought the total construction cost for the campus to $10 million dollars.

Since the school has opened at its new location, it has become a "learning laboratory" and source for professional development for the staff at our school and our college neighbors across the street. The school frequently serves as a base for student teaching and other professional experiences, including routine student observations and case studies. Curriculum in the high school encompasses some very innovative ideas, including honors courses in archaeology, meteorology, art history, Shakespearean studies, and medieval history. In regard to extracurricular activities, to date our charter school is the only one in North Carolina to be admitted into a regular public high school athletic conference, where we compete in a wide variety of varsity sports. Once again, the goal is simple: provide a private-school quality experience, tuition free.

Because of our easily identifiable emphasis on college preparatory teaching, in July 2003 our school board officially changed the school's name to the Rocky Mount Preparatory School to more easily identify the school's educational mission in our community. For the 2002–03 school year, we were honored by the State of North Carolina with its

"School of Progress—High Growth" designation, a reflection of the school's highest level of academic achievement to date. The intention of the entire staff and school board alike is to continue to make measurable and tangible gains in achievement each year the school is in existence.

So goes the story of the Rocky Mount Charter School, once proud, then destroyed, temporarily impoverished, and finally rising from the floodwaters of Hurricane Floyd into a model charter school for the entire United States of America.

12

PLANTING LIFE PRACTICES

Richard Lodish with Joanna Lennon and Cathleen Micheaels,
East Bay Conservation Corps Charter School

Tell me, what is it you plan to do
with your one wild and precious life?
(Mary Oliver, *The Summer Day*)

Richard Lodish *has spent over 35 years in the education profession, be-*
ginning in Cleveland as an elementary school teacher in urban public
schools. He spent over 20 years as an administrator at the highly re-
spected Sidwell Friends School in Washington, D.C., before being asked
by the East Bay Conservation Corps to serve on a national advisory team
convened to design a new charter school. This led to his taking a one-year
sabbatical from Sidwell Friends to become the founding head of the ele-
mentary level of the EBCC Charter School. Published widely on educa-
tional matters, including articles in the Washington Post *and* New York
Times, *he holds a doctorate from the Harvard Graduate School of Edu-*
cation. He received a National Distinguished Principal Award from the
U.S. Department of Education and helped to establish a bilingual, inter-
cultural school in Beijing, China. He is the author of A Child in the Principal's Office: Laughing and Learning in the Schoolhouse.

Joanna Lennon is the founder and CEO of the nonprofit East Bay
Conservation Corps (EBCC) in Oakland, California, dedicated to pio-
neering programs promoting the civic engagement of children and

*youth within the context of improving public education and strength-
ening the larger community. She was the founding board president for
the National Association of Service and Conservation Corps (NASCC)
in Washington, D.C., that provided the platform for the creation of 170
local corps nationally. She also helped to draft and pass Assembly Bill
2020 (the "Bottle Bill") and the National Community Service Act,
which Congress passed with strong bipartisan support and President
George H. W. Bush signed in 1990. Since 1998, she has served on the
Kellogg Foundation's Learning in Deed Initiative Steering Committee,
which was convened to address how service learning can be dissemi-
nated nationally as a strategy for promoting civic engagement in public
education. She has a BA in social and political philosophy, an MS in
forestry and resource management, and a California Secondary Teaching Credential from the University of California at Berkeley, and she
was the recipient of UC Berkeley's Peter E. Haas Public Service Award
for 2001, an award given annually to a Berkeley graduate who has
made a significant public contribution to the betterment of the community and society.*

*Cathleen Micheaels is a consultant with the East Bay Conservation
Corps and the EBCC's Institute for Citizenship Education and Teacher
Preparation, where she served as director from 2001 to 2003, overseeing
curriculum development, research, teacher preservice and professional
development, and dissemination and public policy projects, including
supporting the opening and ongoing implementation of the elementary
level of the EBCC Charter School as a demonstration site. She also facilitated agency partnerships with universities and organizations and
the development of institute publications. From 1998 to 2000, as the
EBCC Charter School curriculum manager, she facilitated a team comprising staff and national leaders in the fields of citizenship and civic
participation, service learning, and education reform, public and private
education, research and evaluation, and ethics and theology convened to
develop the framework of the elementary level of the EBCC Charter
School. Prior to 2000, she managed Project YES (Youth Engaged in Service), the EBCC's school-based service-learning program.*

The idea of rediscovering the civic purpose of public education became a reality for the East Bay Conservation Corps (EBCC) before we
opened the doors of the elementary level of the EBCC Charter School

in September 2001. The EBCC was started in 1983 as a summer demonstration program in a condemned school in the East Bay area. The idea was to engage a diverse cross section of young people to meet real needs in their communities while helping them to complete their high school education. During the past two decades, the EBCC has grown to be a $10 million nonprofit organization with over 300 staff and members serving thousands of children annually through four primary programs. Those programs are:

- The EBCC Charter School, which includes both the corpsmember program division serving 17- to 24-year-old students and the elementary-level division currently serving students in grades K–6.
- Project YES (Youth Engaged in Service), a school-based service learning program in partnership with the Oakland Unified School District, which provides training and technical assistance to teachers and educators locally and nationally.
- AmeriCorps, one of the largest national service programs in the country, which engages volunteer members to help elementary schools in the Oakland Unified School District meet the literacy and health education needs of students in early primary grades.
- The Institute for Citizenship Education and Teacher Preparation, which provides an infrastructure for fostering civic engagement among public school students through the development and dissemination of curriculum with a holistic approach to teacher preparation involving the EBCC Charter School demonstration site and the integration of academics and service-learning strategies.

Since our inception, we have been at the forefront of education reform through the development, implementation, and dissemination of model youth development, service learning, and national service programs engaged in innovative community partnerships. We have translated our mission into practice locally and nationally in order to achieve the larger goals of building alliances, informing policy, and promoting the most effective and powerful practices in the urban conservation corps, national service, service learning, and charter school arenas.

Today, many education reforms are focused on academic standards, with particular emphasis on preparing students for high achievement in literacy, math, and science. Concerned business leaders and politicians engaged in school reform emphasize student performance and assessment in an effort to prepare students to assume productive roles in the workplace. What is not addressed is how such reform initiatives will prepare students for their lifelong roles as citizens. Through service learning, the practice of linking academic learning with service that meets real community needs, the EBCC partners school and community resources to prepare students for their full and thoughtful participation in our diverse democracy. This approach to education reform and community development is founded on the belief that young people are our most valuable resource and that it is the urgent responsibility of all our schools and communities to engage young people in creating a safe and civil society.

"Today, many education reforms are focused on academic standards, with particular emphasis on preparing students for high achievement. . . . What is not addressed is how such . . . initiatives will prepare students for their lifelong roles as citizens."

The story that follows, told by our first head of the elementary school, Rich Lodish, is a snapshot of how all of our experience, along with the tremendous efforts of many, many committed staff, volunteers, partners, and funders, opened the doors of the elementary level of the EBCC Charter School.

THREE YEARS AND 140,000 MILES

My journey to the EBCC Charter School encompassed three years and 140,000 miles. It began when I received a call from EBCC's founder and chief executive officer, Joanna Lennon, asking me, really convincing me, to serve on a national advisory team that was being convened to design a new charter school in Oakland, California. For the previous 25 years, my career had been rooted at Sidwell Friends School, a 125-year-old Quaker institution, first as the lower school principal and then as the associate head. As a Quaker school built upon the foundation of service, Sidwell Friends School has a mission and values similar to those of the East Bay Conservation Corps, so my participation in helping to plan for the opening of a school committed to service learning, spiritual development, and creative expression was not only professionally purposeful but personally compelling.

While I believe deeply in the mission of Sidwell and hold a deep affection for the students and families who are part of the school's community, I missed the challenges and complexities of urban education, which launched my career in education. Prior to my many years at Sidwell, I taught elementary school and so-called "behavior problem students" in the Cleveland public schools. My four years in graduate school had concentrated on urban education, and most of my volunteer and board work has centered on helping children in Washington's inner-city schools.

From nearly 2,000 miles away in Washington, D.C., I agreed (with gracious support from Sidwell) to fly out to California once a month to participate in the EBCC Charter School Curriculum Development Team, which received national funding to plan the elementary level of the EBCC Charter School as a model for schools across the country. This team, convened to think through the framework for the school, included a remarkable and eclectic collection of minds—professionals and leaders in the fields of service learning and education reform, public and private education, citizenship and civic participation, research and evaluation, and ethics and theology.

A REMARKABLE VISION

The elementary level of the EBCC Charter School was created as part of a natural evolution of the education programs and services already offered by the East Bay Conservation Corps. Since 1983, the EBCC has provided leadership in serving low-income urban youth and in developing active learning strategies that imbue young people with a sense of their role in the community. The EBCC Charter School emerged out of the organization's 20-year history in pioneering programs which promote the civic engagement of children and youth within the context of improving public education and strengthening the larger community.

The EBCC Charter School includes two divisions: the corpsmember program division, which opened in September 1996 and is focused on meeting the immediate educational and employment needs of students between the ages of 17 to 24 years, and the elementary level division, which opened in September 2001 to serve K–4 students, expanding to include grade 5 in September 2002 and grade 6 in September 2003 (middle and high school grades will be added in subsequent years).

For nearly two decades, the EBCC has been dedicated to promoting youth development through environmental stewardship and community service and furthering education and social change. The foundational beliefs that shaped the EBCC as a youth and community development organization were also the foundation for the guiding principles that shaped the elementary level of the EBCC Charter School. As the mission of the school is stated: "The EBCC Charter School was created out of the belief that public schools must prepare children for the challenges, opportunities, and responsibilities of life in a democratic, pluralistic society. Through service learning, the curriculum and culture of the school integrates service, spiritual development, and creative expression across a full range of academic subjects."

"Our team had the luxury of time to think and reflect. . . . Most important, we had the support of a well-organized and well-respected organization with a long and proud history."

Two years before the school opened, the EBCC Charter School Curriculum Development Team completed a comprehensive document, *The East Bay Conservation Corps (EBCC) Charter School Framework*, which articulated the educational philosophy of the EBCC Charter School and demonstrated how service learning provided us with the methodology to carry out our guiding principles. This part of the journey—planning and envisioning an ideal charter school based on core beliefs of the EBCC, while complex and time consuming, proceeded rather smoothly. Our team had the luxury of time to think and reflect, and most important, we had the support of a well-organized and well-respected organization with a long and proud history in California and across the country for its commitment to youth and service learning.

The closer we came to opening a real school with real kids, the more I felt compelled to continue to be an integral part of this creation. Joanna Lennon, the founder, dreamer, and doer behind the school, sensed my need. After many discussions with Joanna and the head of Sidwell Friends, its board, and my family, I decided to commit the next year to serving as the founding head of the elementary level of the EBCC Charter School. Fortunately, I received a generous sabbatical from Sidwell Friends to do so.

UNCHARTED TERRITORY: OPEN TO CHALLENGES, OPPORTUNITIES TO GROW

Just as our team created the time and opportunity to plan and reflect, our newly hired faculty participated in a three-week Summer Teacher Training Institute where we planned curriculum, discussed ways to integrate service projects, and heard from experts on topics ranging from spiritual development of children to math and reading programs. Yet, even with this time to reflect and plan for our new school, the reality of 120 children from all across the East Bay area, from all kinds of family situations, promised to be filled with the unexpected. You can only plan so much for the unknown—the energy, the angst, the tears, the laughs, the anger, the joy, the perceptions, the misperceptions, and yes, the love that goes into starting a new school. Often during our three years of planning, I would say to the team that our real challenge would occur the first September that the school opened when the inevitable, multiple collisions and unexpected detours began.

This part of the journey as the school's first principal was, for me, like a scene from the popular movie *Back to the Future*. From my early career teaching in the late 1960s in inner-city Cleveland to leading a charter school in urban Oakland in 2001, I found that, sadly, very little had changed. The poverty and the predominantly single-parent families with access to few personal or institutional resources were still dominant. Parents harbored tremendous love for their children, coupled with the hope that life for the next generation would not be filled with the same hardships they had endured. So many parents would do anything for their children even though often overwhelmed by the exigencies that life presented them. All this was hauntingly familiar to me; in fact, it was almost identical to my experiences 35 years earlier while teaching in Cleveland.

Personally, I have found that life in the Oakland/Berkeley area has also been like a return to the 1960s—it's a ponytail world with psychedelic painted VW buses parked on nearly every street and coffeehouses on every corner. This change of venue has proved healthy, if a bit disconcerting. (In my first stab at the faculty handbook, I included snow days, unaware of the need for earthquake drills.) This new journey has posed many professional questions as well: what traits, talents, knowledge, and so-called expertise from my 35 years as an administrator and teacher would be transferable to a new setting with fresh and different challenges?

A FAMILY AFFAIR

As I write this, we are in our fourth month of school. Also, as I write this, two students have rushed into my office proudly boasting that they have honored their signed commitments to "not hit and try to help each other until 3:30." I pat both of them on the back and they give me a big hug and we all shake hands over the background music of the next-door kindergarten class singing an insect song: "head, thorax, abdomen, and wings" to the tune of "head, shoulders, knees, and toes." With 12-hour days as the norm, I have very little time to reflect on what is going on, let alone to write about it. I have rarely felt so exhausted or so valued. My spirits are high, my body fatigued. I wonder where people in true service professions find time to reflect or write. Our journey is in overdrive and it is hard to downshift.

Luckily for our school (and for me), we have recruited an exceptional teaching staff (from the over 200 resumés we received to fill our nine positions) to join us on our charter school journey. We hired six K–4 teachers, a full-time music teacher, a full-time support teacher, and a part-time art teacher. They are teachers who not only share our vision for the school but also are equally passionate about teaching, learning, and creating classrooms full of joyful learners and independent thinkers.

Our second-grade teacher, in her first weekly newsletter to her students' parents, wrote: "It is very exciting to be challenged in such a purposeful way. I am grateful to have such a profoundly meaningful job. Together, all who are involved in the vision of our school are embarking on a voyage to push the limitations put on public education and open doors for our children and our communities. I am happy to be a part of this transformation."

"Because of the help from our 'parent organization,' I have been free to spend most of my time where I belong—helping students, teachers, and parents."

I was also fortunate that our newly opened K–4 school was one division of a much larger service organization—the East Bay Conservation Corps. Many responsibilities were lifted from my shoulders and handled effectively and efficiently by the EBCC. The Development, Accounting, and Human Resources Departments all contributed expertise in planning and opening the school by taking care of everything from revenue projections to fund raising and employee benefits. Because of the help from our "parent organization," I have been free to spend most of my time where I belong—helping students, teachers, and parents.

To complete our journey, we needed students, of course. We recruited students who represented the ethnic, religious, and socioeconomic diversity of the San Francisco Bay area, with the majority of the students drawn from Oakland and neighboring East Bay area communities. We met with prospective parents in libraries, recreation centers, church basements, kitchens, and dining rooms around the city. All of our prospective parents participated in a two-hour mandatory meeting describing our school's mission and purpose. In my talks with parents, however, it became clear to me that many parents ultimately chose our school to avoid a former school in which their child had a negative experience, rather than from a clear desire to participate in our school's vision.

The site we ultimately found was the site of a former charter school that disbanded in the middle of their third year (sadly, an experience paralleled by a number of other charters across the country). The school building—which was constructed in the early 1900s and served as a Catholic parish school, most recently to a predominantly African American Catholic community—was an unbelievable mess. It appeared that everything but the students and teachers had been left behind; the building was filled with desks, chairs, tables, student papers, sweaters, lunches, and even a working copying machine. Because of the EBCC's history in the community and St. Columba's desire to maintain a neighborhood school, we were welcomed with open arms. Father Jayson, the much-loved priest who was instrumental in helping us to secure the site, continues to visit us often and more than once has remarked that we have accomplished a miracle in bringing the school back to life.

> **"It became clear to me that many parents ultimately chose our school to avoid a former school in which their child had a negative experience, rather than from a clear desire to participate in our school's vision."**

To prepare the school for its opening, we relied heavily upon EBCC corpsmembers (17- to 24-year-olds completing their high school education through the corpsmember program division of the EBCC Charter School). They helped us to get the school building and grounds into shape. The staff and corpsmembers picked up trash and debris and planted trees to beautify the school grounds. We were involved in extensive renovation of the school site, including lead and asbestos abatement, mold removal, tiling, carpeting, and painting. Construction crews put up walls to create additional classrooms on the upper level of the school building, demolished old rooms in the lower level to create a larger downstairs space, and installed handicapped-accessible bathrooms in the upper and lower levels of the school. Nearly all of the renovation work was donated or contributed at cost by vendors and partners of Webcor, the construction firm that also designated the EBCC as the "Christmas in April" project (now "Rebuilding Together") in 2002. Parents and faculty came on Saturdays to paint, plant, build, chat, and eat. A sense of shared ownership and involvement began, and what seemed initially impossible—actually renovating the site by September when the students would start the first day of school—occurred with the tremendous assistance of staff and volunteers and the unrelenting drive of our leader, Joanna Lennon.

"Our task during the first month was to develop a school culture . . . routines and rituals that have brought our school community closer together."

FINDING OUR PARTS AND WORKING TOGETHER

On September 5, 2001, the first day of school, the real journey was launched with 115 students enrolled in two kindergarten classes, one first-grade class, one second-grade class, one second/third-grade class, and one-fourth grade class. Our task during the first month was to develop a school culture—a balance of structure, discipline, and caring—that would help carry us forward. We established the procedures and ground rules to guide us in the hallways, the playground, and the classrooms—routines and rituals that have brought our school community closer together.

Every Monday morning, all our students and teachers sit in silence in a large circle in our music room. Out of the quiet, children and adults are invited to share their reflections and thoughts with the entire school. On Fridays, all students participate in an assembly where our school song is sung. There is also time set aside in which students and teachers can honor or praise one another. During our first "honoring," a second-grader stood up in front of everyone and proudly said, "I want to thank all the people who volunteered their time to clean and build our great school."

Yet, every new endeavor has growing pains. As I anticipated from the beginning, discipline and class management presented a large challenge and needed to be tightened. Our second-grade teacher included this note to her parents in her second weekly newsletter: "One of the areas where I have been most challenged thus far is in classroom behavior. I realized a little too late that this class needs a little more structure than I had originally thought. Now I am backtracking just a little bit and pulling the reins more tightly. Structured procedures and high expectations are necessary in maintaining a classroom environment that fosters both interactive and independent learning. I ask that parents support me in this by discussing with your children the importance of listening, following directions, and working toward collective goals in the classroom."

At our first parent Back-to-School Night (which 80% of our parents attended), I stressed the need to balance firmness, structure, and clear disciplinary policies with lots of gentleness, love, and academic challenge. I told our parents that this balance would help us create a cooperative school environment. However, I also emphasized that in order to have a school free of violence, we needed to take our discipline policies one step further. We had to maintain a school environment that was safe, secure, and provided an opportunity for all students to learn. We had to honor our mission and guiding principles.

"'You will respect each other, you will listen to your classmates and your teachers. You will not hit or fight in *our* school. We need to be a comfortable and safe place where everyone can learn the best they can.'"

On the second Monday of school, after our initial period of silence, I stood in front of our 115 students and sounded a lot like Sidney Poitier in *To Sir With Love*. I told the students in no uncertain terms: "You will respect each other, you will listen to your classmates and your teachers. You will not hit or fight in *our* school. We need to be a comfortable and safe place where everyone can learn the best they can." I forcefully stated that "any hitting or physical violence would result in suspension for the rest of the day." I explained that our school would not tolerate any student disrupting a class to the point where it took teacher attention away from other students.

During the first month of school, we established a "Reflection/Work Room." If a child is acting in a way that significantly or repeatedly disrupts other students, is disrespectful, or hinders the learning process, the student is sent to the Reflection/Work Room, where they complete class work and a written commitment to return to class ready to participate in the learning process. We hoped that this room would not only provide necessary time for students to reflect on their behavior and its impact on others but also allow our teachers to focus on their planned classroom activities without disruption.

One month after the opening of school, five AmeriCorps members—national service volunteers participating in the EBCC's AmeriCorps program—were assigned to our school. They could not have come at a better time, as many of the teachers, even with class sizes of 20, needed assistance with their students. The AmeriCorps members (including an older sibling of one of our students and a parent hoping to attend college) have been supporting student learning through partnering in the classroom and small-group tutoring as well as assisting with our After School Care Program, which nearly a third of our students attend.

We were also fortunate to have a thoughtful, hardworking parent, who grew up across the street from our school, volunteer to lead our Parent Association. I continue to be amazed and gratified by the support and generosity of our parents—especially in a new school in existence for only three months. Our parents established a parent listserv, organized family picnic and work days, initiated and contributed to a fund to provide assistance to families for the purchase of EBCC Charter School uniform shirts, donated classroom supplies, supported classroom teachers, organized free parenting classes, improved the school grounds, and hosted fun events (a harvest carnival/Halloween Parade and a winter holiday bazaar) that have forged our community and enriched our children's experience.

During the first month of school, I felt like an EMT, rushing from one crisis to the next—taking care of everything from instructing kindergartners about bathroom protocol to mediating violent outbursts during recess to helping children move past name calling and teasing—only occasionally stopping to catch my breath.

BEING RESPECTFUL OF THE DIFFERENCES WE SHARE

After the first three months of school (it seems like three years), we have begun to establish a school culture based on our mission. Discipline infractions are decreasing, cooperation and respect are increasing, treasured school rituals have been established, and service learning is being implemented. As a third-grade parent wrote to me just before our winter break: "I am extremely impressed with the way the school has evolved in such a short duration of time. My daughter is absolutely thriving. . . . When I pick her up after school she is bubbling over with information about her day. At night, she is excited and diligent about her homework. Her reading has improved immensely in just these four months and she is writing stories and poems that aren't even assigned! At home, she paints pictures and sings songs that are peaceful and kind. . . . [All this] has infused a simple sense of spirituality in her that she carries throughout her daily life."

Our students are involved in a number of community projects, including learning about nutrition and hunger through serving lunches at a neighborhood soup kitchen, learning about the overall importance of providing service in our community through working with senior citizens at our neighborhood recreation center and tending a neighborhood garden, and learning about conservation and recycling through participation in Project YES (Youth Engaged in Service), the EBCC's school-based service-learning program. There is a different kind of energy igniting our students. Just this week, our kindergartners are working with a fourth-grade reading buddy to research 10 new vocabulary words for use in a story they will share with the class and their parents. Down the hall, third-graders are reading poems that celebrate older people and writing poems of tribute to residents at the local Center for Elders Independence, where they read aloud every week. All of our classes have taken on a service project to improve the school. Projects include recycling, playground and grounds beatification, and lunchroom, hallway, and bathroom cleanup.

In her November letter to parents, one of our teachers wrote: "By now, students have a good sense of classroom expectations and their importance in creating a positive environment. I am pleased to say that I am already seeing steady progress in all your children. In both quality of work and attitude, your children have much of which they should be proud. . . . On Monday, we will concretely delve into our service-learning purpose. We will begin to look at the community surrounding our school and assess ways in which we can improve it. Our goal is to give service to our neighborhood and then learn from our service through reflection. I know our class is ready for the challenge!"

"Talking about lofty goals and putting them into practice are two vastly different activities. Because we are a public school and because many parents chose our school to avoid problems encountered in previous schools, we have our fair share of students with significant behavioral and academic problems."

Yet, for every three steps our school moves forward, some issue or incident brings us one step backward. We have developed clear "Life Practices" about how to participate in the life of our school, which are boldly posted in our school's entryway and in all our classrooms:

- Be honest to yourself and others.
- Be a thoughtful listener.
- Speak from your heart.
- Be respectful of the differences we share.
- Be open to challenges and opportunities to grow.
- Be alive with purpose and practice thanks.
- Find your part and work together.

However, talking about lofty goals and putting them into practice are two vastly different activities. Because we are a public school, and because many parents chose our school to avoid problems encountered in previous schools, we have our fair share of students with significant behavioral and academic problems. These students (and their teachers) need extra help and professional guidance. The reality is that these students crave individual attention and often disrupt the class, which takes away critical teacher time from the rest of the students. Because of budget considerations, we were unable to hire a counselor/learning specialist to work with the students who require specialized attention. The Oakland Unified School District has provided some basic assistance: a speech therapist, an occupational therapist, and a resource teacher each visit a few times a week, but only serve five students who came to the school with an IEP (Individualized Education Plan). We have at least a dozen more students who are in significant need of counseling and remedial help. Volunteers from programs such as the University of California, Berkeley Psychology Clinic have helped a number of our students, but much more sustained intervention and one-to-one help is needed to make a real difference in these children's lives.

The largest difference between charter and private schools is not in the quality of teachers (there are good and poor teachers in each), or the schools' unique missions (both are mission driven), or class size, or even educational materials, or teaching methods. The real difference between these types of schools is in the student peer group. Private schools can select students; charter schools cannot. We have only lost three families from our school (other than those who moved) since we opened. All were middle class and their primary reason for going to another school was their lack of comfort with a few "disruptive" students from "difficult" families.

Just as we try to help children respect differences, we need to help their parents appreciate and understand families from different backgrounds. In order to maintain a truly diverse school such as the EBCC Charter School, we need to provide the time for parents to get to know one another and the opportunity for these parents to share their perceptions honestly and openly with one another. We need to understand that the more comfortable parents become in our school community, the easier it will be for them to share their feelings with other parents, and to reach common ground. Perhaps we are making progress. Recently, a parent posted this note on our parent listserv: "I really feel our community coming together and developing a lot of heart."

On the first day of school and almost every day since, our dean of students and I have greeted each student in the morning car pool in front of the 50-year-old, 14-foot fence that surrounds our school. On the first day of school (and every day since), Samuel (not his real name) drops off his son Isaiah (not his real name) and reminds him (with a wink to me), "No spitting, no hitting, no punching, no kicking, and don't kiss the girls." Perhaps not words to live by, but it would help!

The qualities needed for successful teaching in our school are more difficult to categorize. Assuredness, confidence, discipline, order, comfort, and the ability to engage students are needed to teach in our school. Persistence, patience, careful listening, calmness, gentleness, firmness, and passion also help. Like all school administrators, I struggle with how much to intervene in classes, when to step back, when to tighten the reins, when to loosen them, and when to give teachers a shot in the arm without letting them feel the needle. Many parents are beginning to appreciate the quality of our teachers. A letter sent to me during the third month of school expresses a growing sentiment: "Your school exceeds any new parent's expectations and my daughter's teacher seems to go above and beyond not only to teach but also to understand each and every child. For that, I am extremely thankful."

ALIVE WITH PURPOSE: SPEAKING FROM THE HEART, PRACTICING THANKS

"The ultimate test of the value of what is learned," wrote John Dewey some 80 years ago, "is its use and application in carrying on and improving the common life of all." As the EBCC Charter School journey continues, putting our mission of service learning and a solid, yet creative academic program into concrete practice will be the ultimate test of our success. But how we adults—teachers, administrators, and parents—treat each other, how we make decisions, how we deal with disagreements and tensions, how we hold ourselves accountable, how we treat others above and below us on the economic ladder, how we treat people different from us, and most important, how we provide service to our own communities will determine what that success feels and looks like.

During the first three months of school, I have cried privately. I cried when Michael (not his real name), a struggling fourth-grader, whose dad is in prison and whose mom is struggling to make ends meet, came into my office, gave me a hug, and asked, "Mr. Principal, will you teach me to read?" I cried when a single father rushed into my office, grabbed his child in a panic, and announced that his ex-wife, just out of jail, had demanded that she receive custody of the son he had been raising on his own for three years. (After repeated calls and meetings, we were able to help mediate the conflict in the best interests of his son.)

Just this past week, one of our parents was involved in a car accident and was unable to pick up her son from school. As I drove Malcolm (not his real name) to meet his grandpa at the BART station, I asked, "What are you learning in kindergarten?" Malcolm hesitantly responded, "Letters and numbers." I probed his five-year-old mind a little deeper and asked, "What do you think is the main thing our school is trying to teach you?" I cried privately as Malcolm responded, "To help and respect each other."

"I cried when Michael . . . , whose dad is in prison and whose mom is struggling to make ends meet, came into my office, gave me a hug, and asked, 'Mr. Principal, will you teach me to read?'"

At this point in our school journey, the road to success may still be under construction, but right now success is beginning to feel pretty darn good. "I sleep well at night," a parent recently wrote me, "knowing my child is receiving a balanced education and that she is happy and loved at her school." This parent is not the only one who is finally able to get some well-needed shuteye.

13

OWNING WOBEGON

Doug Thomas, Minnesota New Country School

Doug Thomas is director of the Gates-EdVisions Project and president of EdVisions, Inc., the nonprofit corporation hosting the effort funded by the Bill and Melinda Gates Foundation to replicate the learning model of the New Country School and the teacher-owner model of Ed-Visions Cooperative. Thomas was the University of Minnesota's Center for School Change outreach coordinator for southern Minnesota for 10 years, working to create new kinds of public schools in rural communities. He served four terms on the Le Sueur-Henderson Board of Education and six years on the board of the South Central Minnesota Service Cooperative. He has five years of teaching experience in rural towns and for 10 years was a small-business owner. His special areas of interest are rural community development, secondary education reform, and leadership for educational change.

It's now been over 10 years since the first planners met to discuss the creation of what was to become one of the most unusual and celebrated charter schools in America. The New Country School planning process began in the halls and basement of the 1900 portion of the old Henderson High School, located approximately 60 miles southwest of Minneapolis, farm country along the Minnesota River Valley. A couple of teachers, myself, and a few local business people first met in the teachers' work room to sketch out a plan for a new kind of computer-infused high school. That first meeting was invaded by the local superintendent, who sternly warned the group, "You had better not be talking about a charter school." He subsequently banned the group from meeting on school grounds.

"The … superintendent … warned … 'You had better not be talking about a charter school.' He subsequently banned the group from meeting on school grounds."

So it was in bars and coffee shops for the next 18 months that this group of entrepreneurs and school reformers pursued their dream. I was the convener of sorts. I was two years into a position at the Center for School Change at the Humphrey Institute for Public Affairs at the University of Minnesota and knew a little about the landmark charter law Minnesota had passed the year before. I also had access to the best minds and activists around the school reform work of the early 1990s: Joe Nathan, Ted Kolderie, Wayne Jennings, Ted Sizer, and others. My job was to help create new kinds of public schools, schools-within-schools, magnet schools, and charter schools if possible. Thus, it was not so accidental that I came to be involved in the making of a school.

What was more accidental was the place where that school began. Most people find it highly unlikely that such a school would be found in the heart of rural Minnesota, where the kids are all "above average." I had been on the local school board for about five years in 1992 and was committed to making high school more interesting and friendly. My own experience as a teacher, relatively short at four years, was one of boredom and frustration. My own small high school education, in Henderson, was one of tremendous personalization and nonstop activity, total immersion in sports, drama, music, community service, and academics (when we could fit them in). I knew school could be more than regimentation, rules, and elitism. The local school had consolidated with the bigger neighbor, taking local kids out of their community and giving them less opportunity to participate in the kinds of activities that develop true active citizenship and leadership. What tipped the scales for me was a survey done in the local high school in which 70 percent of the students indicated their school "was not a good place to be." How could we stand for that many students being unsatisfied? It had to affect the entire culture of the school and community.

"My own experience as a teacher ... was one of boredom and frustration. ... What tipped the scales for me was ... 70 percent of the students indicated their school 'was not a good place to be.'"

So I began to recruit and we began to meet. I recruited teachers, ex-teachers, board members, former board members, mentor teachers from Minnesota State University–Mankato, and business people who were both entrepreneurs and reformers. We even got a few students to join us. We met every couple of weeks for a year before we let our plans be known. Our premise was to take the typical high school and look at each major design feature and decide whether that piece made sense in terms of what it did for the students. At the end of the year, we had nothing left that looked like a traditional high school: no classes, no grades, no bells, no principal, a weeklong break every six weeks, personal work stations and a computer for every student, public presentation of student work, and a building that would look more like a busy office. And it would be small, no more than 150 students.

When the news of the new school came out, some were shocked and insulted, others inquisitive and interested. The school board was not impressed and turned down the request for sponsorship 6–0 (I had to abstain). We were disheartened but immediately turned our attention to a neighboring district, which subsequently refused to take a vote for not wanting to appear anti-reform. Little consolation for us. But Le Sueur-Henderson's new superintendent, Dr. Harold Larson, came back to us and asked if we would like to participate in a districtwide, strategic planning process to take place in the summer of 1993. We agreed, and the resulting plan called for a new kind of high school model. Later that fall, the board unanimously voted to sponsor the Minnesota New Country School.

At that point, the real planning began. We had less than a year to recruit students and teachers, find a place to locate, and develop a program that no one in the country had yet to try. We had only our good intentions and advice from folks like Joe Nathan and Wayne Jennings, who
had started the St. Paul Open School 20 years before. We began meeting weekly, and with no start-up funds and only our good name and in-
tuition, we created a school from scratch.

We had one big political hurdle to overcome yet. Three months after
our sponsorship, we were ready to take the contract back to the board.
In many ways this was more crucial than sponsorship because it committed the district to three years of experimenting with an autonomous,
new, and different kind of public school arrangement. We were asking
the district, in Ted Kolderie's words, "To trust someone other than the
typical district and its employees to provide the service of public education." It was a very intense couple of weeks. The opposition and the
press wanted all the answers now. They wanted to know where we
would locate, how students would be bused, and how many students
from the district would attend. We didn't have many of the answers. The
board took testimony for six and one-half hours, mostly from current
high school teachers opposing the reform ideas and the need for such a
school. We got a few experts to come in and support our ideas but
mostly relied on our ability to convince people of our sincerity and the
growing need to change high schools.

"'This is not your money. This is not our money. This money belongs to parents and their children, and if 60 or 70 of them choose to spend it differently, I can't stand in their way.'"

The stars must have been aligned the following week when the board
voted 5–1 to approve the contract. The key point in the process was when
the board chair, Virginia Miller, spoke eloquently about the reality of
school choice coming to a small Minnesota school district. She looked at
the crowd that had gathered, many of them opposing teachers, and said,
"This is not your money. This is not our money. This money belongs to

parents and their children and if 60 or 70 of them choose to spend it differently, I can't stand in their way." The superintendent nodded in agreement and the contract vote was approved. Years later, I still think about
that moment and how important that statement has become and how
charged the question of public school choice remains. It seems never
about doing the right thing but about money. We wouldn't create big
boxes with 2,000 students if it wasn't about the money.

"Ted Kolderie . . . asked if we'd be interested in creating a school that had no employees. . . . The idea was for a teacher professional practice, legally organized as a cooperative, . . . [that would] own the instructional service at the school."

The rest is history. Well, not exactly. Charter schools are always evolv-
ing. They never take a break from change or controversy. We set about
preparing for our opening in fall 1994. We found a couple of empty
storefronts in downtown Le Sueur and remodeled up to the opening
day. Parents and potential students helped out immensely those first few
months prior to and after opening. I still can't believe they were so pa-
tient and trusting that first year. The program was totally unknown and
untried. The buildings were less than adequate, and some of the first
students were troubled, having come from a variety of school districts
(this seemed to be their latest stop). The original teachers (Ron Newell,
Nancy Miller, Kim Borwege, and John Brosnan), two who came from
the traditional school, one a local techie, and one a MSU mentor with
25 years of experience, were motivated but unsure. I think what saved
us that first year was that the planners were there almost daily, trying to
help the teachers pragmatically and with the big picture. We kept re-
minding them at our weekly meetings that they were doing groundbreaking work and others would be looking at their success or failure.
Admittedly, we put pressure on them they probably didn't need.

Shortly after our initial contract approval, we put another twist on this
story. Ted Kolderie approached us with a question and an idea. He

asked if we'd be interested in creating a school that had no employees. As you can imagine, we were puzzled but very intrigued. I'd always been interested in alternative business practices. The idea was for a teacher professional practice, legally organized as a cooperative, to own the instructional service at the school. In other words, a cooperative made up of teachers and others would contract for the learning program at the school. The staff would receive a lump-sum amount of money (for compensation, staff development, etc.) and then decide among themselves how it would be spent, thus eliminating the board from the tedious work of negotiating every person's worth and pay. The group was not all that excited about the idea, especially since Minnesota charters were governed by a teacher majority board already. After several hours of discussing and selling the idea, I was able to convince everyone it was worth a try. If we didn't make history with our unique school design, we were certainly going to with the teacher ownership and professionalism model.

I and others were especially excited about EdVisions Cooperative because the group decided to allow for "at large" membership. This allowed those of us who had been part of the planning team to remain involved at the learning program level. The initial group included about 14 members, including Dr. Larson, the superintendent. Essentially, we directed the program those first years of the school. Today, EdVisions Cooperative has grown to include nine schools, 125 teachers, a dozen at-large members, a small group of consulting members, and a nonprofit arm that has set about creating more New Country–like schools. A recently published book about the professional practice idea, *Teachers As Owners*, is available through Scarecrow Press.

The New Country School itself has evolved. Although still holding true to its original premise, it has developed a bit more structured, but very respected, project-based learning model. The school still has no courses or bells and no formal principal. Still run by the teachers, it is now located on Main Street in Henderson in a new facility that was designed to mirror the unique learning program. There are the high-tech personal work stations for each student, lots of room for project work, a science lab and media resource center, and a stage area for public presentation of student work, plays, and community events. The building project in 1998 was a unique partnership between a local development group, the City of Henderson, the U.S. Department of Agriculture Rural Development, and a local bank. The New Country School has become an economic development success story. It attracts over 500 visitors from around the world each year, and the cooperative has created several jobs for this small community of 1,000 residents.

The school has had a measure of success beyond the novelty and publicity, as well. Standardized and other measures are positive, and student and parent satisfaction is always tremendous. The combination of technology and self-directed learning is very popular and works with all ability levels. The staff at New Country has spent considerable time over the years improving the learning process and fine-tuning the project system, weaving in the state performance standards, making sure the basic skills are attained, and preparing young people for the world of work and postsecondary school. About 70 percent of New Country's graduates go on to further schooling. Nearly all the students attend some college while in high school through Minnesota's postsecondary enrollment program.

"Some still think the school is either for 'tech-heads' or at-risk students."

Reaction to the school has been mixed over the years. I think generally the public has accepted the idea that we need a variety of schools to serve students' needs. Many still don't understand or appreciate the differences in our school. They see on the surface that the school doesn't have its own sports teams (they have a pairing arrangement with the district). Some still think the school is either for "tech-heads" or at-risk students. The building is getting more and more community use, so that tends to break down the barriers to a certain extent.

After eight years, there are no original board members left on the district board, and Superintendent Larson has retired. The former high school principal is now the superintendent and is generally supportive. The various board members have been helpful over the years, especially when the different academic program is explained and they get firsthand knowledge of how it works well for students. They appreciate, too, the teacher cooperative model, especially when they see how many of their own issues are tied to collective bargaining and union vs. management politics. Those difficulties are virtually nonexistent in the cooperative model or are internal to the cooperative group.

Some of the original planners are still present but working in different capacities. Ron Newell is the learning programs director for the Gates-EdVisions Project of EdVisions, Inc., the nonprofit arm of the cooperative. He recently authored a book about project-based learning, *A Passion for Learning* (Scarecrow Press). The Gates-EdVisions Project is a multimillion-dollar replication project funded by the Bill and Melinda Gates Foundation. I am now the president of EdVisions, Inc. (nonprofit), and director of the Gates-EdVisions Project, after spending 10 years with the Center for School Change. Nancy Miller returned to the local high school to retire and take advantage of a lucrative severance package. Kim Borwege spent seven years with New Country until accepting a position in the district where she lived. John Brosnan returned to the private technology company he had been employed by before teaching at New Country. Two of the original planners, Dee Thomas and Dean Lind, are now teacher/advisors at the school. Dee Thomas is a member of the Minnesota State Board of Teaching and president of the Minnesota Association of Charter Schools. Dean Lind and Ron Newell are active members of the board of directors of EdVisions Cooperative. Together, we all keep the fire burning.

"If a group of naïve country [educators] in a typical school district can do this, anybody can."

The Gates-EdVisions Project is charged with creating 15 new schools like New Country School and 10 new teacher-owner models like EdVisions Cooperative. We now have a small staff, located in downtown Henderson, and have nine new schools up and running in Minnesota and Wisconsin and are working on a national scale-up effort. It is truly a dream come true for many of us who started the New Country School. Our mission was to create a great, small, innovative school and to change the world of high school education. We often joke about being "farm kids with attitude" and trying to "save the world." The truth is that the charter venture is hard, sometimes scary work. If you don't have a passion to make things better for kids and adults, you tend to run out of energy or lose interest in the fight. As Joe Nathan reminded me so often at the Center for School Change, "This is a marathon, not a sprint."

My personal reflection is quite positive. I've heard all the clichés about small groups doing great things. Now I've seen it happen and know it can happen over and over again across this country. If a group of naïve country kids in a typical school district can do this, anybody can. The heart and soul of public education is the entrepreneurial spirit that comes from parents, educators, and students joining together to create something wonderful. I can't help but think this is the beginning of the reindependence of public education, this infusion of spirit that has often been zapped by the bureaucracy.

Leadership is all about ideas and people. It's the infusion of ideas into people's hearts and minds and helping them do something extraordinary. I'm certain there will be a new culture created around charter schools, one with a new freedom and motivation to say "we can" when dreaming about what might happen for kids. We often say this is "missionary work," converting one soul at a time. For me, the past 10 years have been just that, working with one person or a small group to help them realize the possibilities of acting on their dreams.

⑭

NO CATS

Vickie Kimmel Forby with Paul Seibert,
Tomorrows Builders YouthBuild Charter School

Vickie Kimmel Forby earned a master's degree in architecture from the
University of Illinois at Urbana-Champaign while participating in the
East St. Louis Action Research Project from 1990 to 1994. She has been
the executive director of the Emerson Park Development Corporation
since 1996 and worked as a volunteer for them from 1990 until 1996.
EPDC has operated one of the best YouthBuild Programs in the country
for the past five years, opened the Tomorrows Builders YouthBuild
Charter High School in September 2002, and has partnered to bring the
second largest park and ride station on the MetroLink line to the Emerson Park Neighborhood. EPDC has also partnered to bring the largest
private, multi-family, mixed-income development to the city in over 30
years. EPDC is a testament to the fact that partnership and resource
sharing are the key to redeveloping neighborhoods while breaking the
barriers for minorities into the trades.

    With more than 30 years of experience in business, education, and the
business of education, Paul H. Seibert is a nationally recognized figure
in education reform and has made charter public schooling his specialty.
As the director of Charter Consultants, he works with individuals and
groups, including parents, teachers, for-profit and nonprofit corporations, public and private schools, and state universities in their quest to

reform education. He supported the passage of Illinois's charter public school law and later assisted in the development of Missouri's charter school legislation. His proposal for the Fort Bowman Academy Charter School was accepted in 1998 by Cahokia District 187 and the Illinois State Board of Education to create the first Charter Public School in Southern Illinois. Charter Consultants' proposal for the Tomorrows Builders Charter School, a construction trades charter school based on the YouthBuild model, was approved by East St. Louis District 189 in May 2002 and opened with Illinois State Board of Education approval on September 16, 2002.

It took almost three years to get approval to open our charter school. Illinois charter school proposals must be presented to the local board of education, in this case the board of East St. Louis District 189. The first vote was a unanimous denial; a year later, it was a six-to-one denial. We appealed both local denials to the Illinois State Board of Education but were denied there on technicalities. Illinois is not a charter-friendly state. But something happened in local politics that gained us unanimous approval on our third attempt. Now the Tomorrows Builders YouthBuild Charter School serves about 60 of the district's most troubled high school dropouts in a building trades program.

"The 2000 Census data for track 5041 [in East St. Louis] show 430 housing units, with 103 of them vacant."

The story really begins when the Emerson Park Development Corporation was formed. The EPDC is a community development corporation organized in 1985, incorporated in 1989, and recognized as a not-for-profit 501(c)3 organization in 1995. Organized to enhance the quality of life for residents of the Emerson Park Neighborhood of the City of East St. Louis, EPDC focuses on community development, housing and economic development, code enforcement, infrastructure improvement, public safety, education, and job training.

The demographics of the neighborhood we serve reflect blight, deterioration, high levels of poverty, and low education levels. The 2000 Census data for track 5041 show 430 housing units, with 103 of them vacant. Of 894 residents, most are African American and low income. Average median income is $20,089, 41% below the poverty level. Nearly half of the families in the area are single female-headed households with children, 70% of households receiving some form of government transfer payment as their primary source of income. Unemployment is 8.6%—5.4% above county average.

As the second of our five-year plans evolved, it became clear that the need for vocational educational opportunities in the neighborhood was tremendous and unfulfilled. While the residents are aware that the neighborhood is filled with undereducated and unemployed individuals, the acknowledgment that East St. Louis School District 189 has the highest dropout rate in the state at 52% made it clear to the residents that we would have to narrow our efforts to serve a limited population. The research for opportunities to provide vocational skills and education launched a search of potential funders for these activities.

The search yielded a wide variety of possibilities and natural partners for this project. Therefore, in 1997, EPDC began applying to the U.S. Department of Housing and Urban Development to acquire a Youth-Build Grant. YouthBuild funding allows organizations a five-faceted program to provide the opportunity for at-risk young people age 16–24 to achieve their high school diploma or GED, gain construction trades training, and gain counseling, leadership development, and job acquisition, placement, and retention skills. Natural partners to the YouthBuild programs across the country are the construction trade unions, the Department of Education, the Department of Justice, and the Department of Health and Human Services at both the federal and state levels. In 1999, EPDC was awarded YouthBuild funding and in February 2000 decided to partner with Charter Consultants to develop a charter school to make this opportunity of education and construction trades training more sustainable.

Charter Consultants is the educational consulting division of the Governor French Academy of Belleville, Illinois, the premier private school in our area. They had already started and supervised the operations of two downstate Illinois charter schools. Due to their qualifications and 20-year track record in both private and charter school operations, they were selected to assist EPDC in developing the Tomorrows Builders YouthBuild Charter School. The amount of learning that had to go into this endeavor surpassed anything we had ever attempted. Paul Seibert, director of Charter Consultants, inundated us with information both technical and inspirational, and the learning process began. Once our board of directors was comfortable with the knowledge, the application process began. This endeavor would take three trying years!

"Board members questioned a charter school's ability to do a better job than their own, a laughable criticism, as District 189 had been listed as one of the three worst academically performing districts in the state."

We continued to operate the Tomorrows Builders YouthBuild Program as we partnered to develop our charter school proposal. The proposal met much opposition from the school district in the first year. Board members questioned a charter school's ability to do a better job than their own, a laughable criticism, as District 189 had been listed as one of the three worst academically performing districts in the state, with their errant finances under the control of a state-appointed oversight panel. Opposition to charter schools was one of the few things the district administration and the local teachers' union could agree on. At least four charter school proposals had been before the district board since the inception of Illinois charter schools—all summarily denied.

We were an uninvited guest in the district boardroom. Ignoring the lessons of kindergarten, District 189 was not inclined to share and did not play well with others. Though we targeted to serve only those whom the district had failed or expelled, we were not welcome. Thus, our 1,500-page proposal was unanimously denied.

We appealed to the Illinois State Board of Education at a time when Illinois law only allowed the state board to remand errors back to the local board to be corrected. The local board had committed several errors in its lack of an approval process. The judgment from the state board forced the local board to reenact its public hearing and its vote. Their being forced to repeat the process gained us only more animosity and another unanimous denial. However, we promised to return next year, and so we did.

With proposal number two, we thought we really had it. We made all the corrections suggested by the state board staff. We incorporated all the new information garnered by Charter Consultants in their ongoing work with Illinois charters. The local superintendent contacted us with an offer of partnering with the district to ensure passage. But you already know that we didn't get approval of our second proposal.

The superintendent's offer seemed to be the clincher. He suggested that the district really wanted this high school alternative. But what it also really wanted was a middle school program to reach those same students with an earlier intervention. If only we would expand our target from grades 9–12 to include grades 6–8. Why not? We, too, believe in early intervention. We, too, thought we could be successful with this other troubled group. We spent the next four months working with the school administration, board members, and local politicos to develop "the right stuff" for local approval. At every step, we got the message to go forward. The day of the vote, the straw poll said we had at least six of seven votes assured. We had thousands of support petitions. We had some 60 local high school dropouts marching peacefully in the streets, meeting with the board president on his doorstep with television crews, and filling the board room with one plea: give us this school and we will come back. The state superintendent of schools happened to be in East St. Louis and commented to the press that it was pretty incredible to see a group of high school dropouts fighting for their own school.

"I don't suppose we will ever know what happened in that [school board] executive session that sank our ship. But sink it did."

The agenda for the board meeting put the vote on the charter school after a closed session recess. The six members present retired to closed quarters. When they returned an hour later, they were joined by the seventh member, who had just arrived. The superintendent's recommendation to the board was to deny the charter school. We received only one affirming vote, that of the late-arriving board member who, like ourselves, was shocked that the other six votes had turned against us. I don't suppose we will ever know what happened in that executive session that sank our ship. But sink it did.

Shocked and infuriated, we again appealed to the Illinois State Board of Education. This time, the state legislature had added teeth to the appeals process. The state board could now overturn a local decision and grant a charter directly. Off to Springfield again. Again we incorporated every hint dropped by the state board staff and by our consultants. But when one writes a proposal as a partnership with a local board and the partner pulls out, such a proposal is doomed. As expected, the state board denied the proposal for lack of such items as a special education provider. No surprise, since the law and the district had required that the proposal specify the district as the special education provider. With the local denial, we had none. But if we have learned nothing else (and we have learned much else) doing what we have done over the last 18 years, we have learned to take adversities like this, regroup, and hit again. So began Tomorrows Builders YouthBuild Charter School proposal number three!

This time we would again do it our way. It was clear that the local board did not want a middle school program. That was apparently the superintendent's idea. We would return to our original grades 9–12 formula and again incorporate our current YouthBuild GED program for 18 to 24-year-olds into a high school diploma program for 16- to 21-year-olds. We would target high school dropouts and students previously expelled. We would ask the district to send us their most troubled students. We have been successful with the 18–24 age group, and we would be successful with the 16–21 group.

The proposal had expanded to fill three, 5-inch binders. We had again incorporated every new refinement learned through Charter Consultants' experiences. The country had just passed the No Child Left Behind Act, and the pressure was on for greater local results. The proposal was submitted to the local superintendent. Meetings began immediately with the board president, the board lawyer, the local politicos, Emerson Park Development Corporation, and Charter Consultants staff. First we were asked for concessions that were not legal. We declined. Then we were asked for concessions that were not feasible. We declined. Then we were asked for concessions that were practical. We agreed. The proposal was amended. The contract was revised. The proposal was approved unanimously on May 22, 2002.

In Illinois, local approval is imperative for the granting of a public school charter. Denial will get you before the State Board of Education, but the state board has not approved an appeal since the law was first initiated. Local approval means the state board will approve your charter, but not without intense review that brings monumental requests for additional information and adjustments. The next several months were consumed with this next step of gaining final state approval. Questions were answered. Documents were submitted and amended. Contracts were renegotiated. Special board meetings were held, including a special local board meeting to make final approval of the final corrections minutes before the state's deadline. We all waited pensively for final state confirmation.

Final state approval came by fax at 4:35 p.m. on Thursday, September 12, 2002. Under Illinois law, a charter school must open between August 15 and September 15. September 15 fell on a Sunday this year. Fortunately, the state board allowed us to open our school on Monday, the 16th. We started calling students immediately and set up the chairs over the weekend. Monday morning, about 60 students arrived.

"All are minorities; the local district reports that 98.8% of district students are black."

At this writing, Tomorrows Builders YouthBuild Charter School has just completed four months of classes. We currently have about 40 students, as some of the first 60 dropped out again. Some were too old for the high school and went into our GED program. Two were expelled for slashing another student with a razor. Even the 40 most serious students are mostly problematic. Their reading levels are often third grade. Most have children of their own. All are low income. All are minorities; the local district reports that 98.8% of district students are black.

Tomorrows Builders Charter School will open its doors to new students again on February 17, 2003, as it begins its second semester of its 12-month school year. We will again take a small number of new students and do our best to turn bad habits into good choices. We will continue to stress reading, writing, and math along with construction trades skills. Our students will engage in building and rehabbing local homes for low-income families. Our charter school and our YouthBuild Program will work together to overcome all the missing parts for our students, even for those students who appear committed to thwarting our endeavors to provide them with a good education and job-skills training.

"We will not be deterred in our educational efforts, either, for we know that inside each and every one of these young people is a commitment to succeed."

Having succeeded against all odds to open this school, we will not be deterred in our educational efforts, either, for we know that inside each and every one of these young people is a commitment to succeed. We will not reach them all, as their commitment may not align with our own. But like our previous YouthBuild graduates, those for whom we are a match will find themselves graduated and enrolled in college or admitted to a union apprenticeship program, and yes, even accepting a $26 per hour job offer from a local contractor.

Post Script: When I first came to East St. Louis as a University of Illinois graduate student, I made a note in my class journal: "There are no cats." I first met the founders of what was to be the Emerson Park Development Corporation in the most destitute public housing area I have ever seen. It was a cold day. They were standing around an old oil drum, burning trash to keep warm. Most buildings were damaged beyond repair. Half were vacant and burned out. Lots were overgrown and strewn with trash. Street lights didn't work. Manhole covers were missing. But the people were so real, so full of hope and vision. They spoke to us college students about how the neighborhood used to be and how they hoped it would be again. They had hope. I wondered how they could. There were no cats. There were only a few mangy dogs with bones showing. The neighborhood was so poor that there wasn't even food for the rats, and the dogs had eaten whatever cats hadn't starved.

The people that I have come to know in East St. Louis are rich beyond my dreams; many have acquired survival skills that surpass anything I have ever seen. But their spirit and hopes are *alive* and the residents that dare to dream in the Emerson Park Neighborhood plan to stay right here to be part of the revitalization. They have proven not only that they have dreams and ambitions, but that they can fulfill them. We have gotten the street lights back on and the manhole covers replaced; about 40 old homes have been refurbished or rebuilt; 174 new multi-family, mixed-income units have been constructed, and about 328 derelict buildings have been demolished since my first visit there. We have another 110 new mixed-income homes to complete in the next two years, along with the first 12 of 150 single-family homes, with a community center, some wonderful parks, and a light-rail transit stop. And we have a charter public high school.

"They have proven not only that they have dreams and ambitions, but that they can fulfill them."

The power of hope, prayer, and commitment combined is really the answer when people ask me, "Why East St. Louis?" I respond simply, "I could sure be making more money somewhere else and could sure have more comfortable surroundings elsewhere. But nowhere could I find more fulfillment than being part of bringing to life the dreams of the neighborhood residents of Emerson Park." This story is dedicated to those residents, most of whom are quite old now—to them and the community's children they have committed to serve. Through their joint efforts, Emerson Park Neighborhood is again becoming the diamond that was lost from the jewel setting that used to be East St. Louis. Together, we will revitalize one of the most destitute cities in the United States. And I know we will succeed. For now there are cats in Emerson Park. Thank you who have believed enough in me for us to accomplish all that we have together: Ceola, Richard, Peggy, Cathy, Kathy, Henry, Jean, Pinkie, Herbie, Rev. and Marie, Marinella, Geraldine, Miss Sarah, Mr. Hall, Louis and Marie, Carrie and Anna. Thank you to those I have not named, thank you for all of you who have made me feel at home with you! Thanks to all of the young people who have fought for another chance to fulfill their dreams! And thank you Jake, Zack, Percy, Mom, Dad, Emmy, and Grandma Minnie for all of the love, support, and guidance you have provided me!

⑮

DARKNESS BEFORE DAWN: THE ARTS-BASED ELEMENTARY SCHOOL

Hal Johnson, BB&T

Hal Johnson became involved with the Sawtooth Center for Visual Art in 1994. The Arts-Based Elementary School (ABES) concept grew out of the strategic planning process conducted with the Sawtooth Center board. The Sawtooth Center served as an incubator for the school until it became a separate organization in 1999. Since 2001, Johnson has been an executive vice president of BB&T, one of the nation's 12 largest bank holding companies. His tenure with the company began in 1985 when Southern National Corporation hired him as a marketing research assistant. Two years later, he was promoted to the position of marketing director for the corporation. His creativity in this role produced the slogan "You can tell we want your business." This tag line embodied the spirit of SNC's corporate values and continues to be used in current marketing promotions. In 1989, he developed a strategic planning department. Working with the bank's executive management and the corporation's board of directors, he helped shape the future of Southern National through his work with the corporation's strategic plans and acquisition strategy. He has been involved in 98 acquisitions, including 29 banks and thrifts, 52 insurance agencies, and 17 nonbank companies. He has seen the company grow in asset size from $20 billion to over $90 billion.

The Arts-Based Elementary School (ABES) is located in Winston-Salem, North Carolina, a city of about 285,000 in a region (the Piedmont Triad Region of North Carolina) of about 1.2 million. Winston-Salem has a national reputation as being a community steeped in the arts. That reputation is built on a heritage of strong funding for the arts by RJ Reynolds, Hanes, and Wachovia. In fact, Winston-Salem bills itself as the "City of the Arts."

THE SEED

ABES began as a seed concept in 1996. At the time, I was a board member and the strategic planning chair for the Sawtooth Center for Visual Art in Winston-Salem. The Sawtooth Center is a Visual Art School that provides training for a range of interests from the hobbyist to the professional. The school's mission is to train artists, not to provide a formal education or grant degrees.

We were conducting a strategy session for the organization, trying to set the course for the organization's next five years in the face of declining funding for the arts, increasing demands for our services, and the desire to expand our reach in the community. The planning session was facilitated by Arthur Andersen and had representatives from the board and staff of the Sawtooth organization, the Winston-Salem Arts Council (a major source of funds for the organization), and the community at large. The session suggested many themes for the Sawtooth Center to develop, one of which was the idea of becoming a degree-granting institution.

"Jim and I became energized about combining . . . arts-based reforms in education with the idea of expanding . . . to become a degree-granting organization."

During the period when the brainstorming session was held, legislation permitting charter schools in North Carolina was at the conceptual stage. Much discussion followed about expanding Sawtooth's scope to become a degree-granting institution. As a board, we also explored many of the other options developed during the session for expanding the reach of Sawtooth.

During the time we were working on implementing programs that were developed at the planning session, Jim Sanders, the executive director of the Sawtooth Center, started to pursue a doctorate in educational curriculum and instruction. Jim and I became energized about combining the research he was undertaking in arts-based reforms in education with the idea of expanding Sawtooth's reach to become a degree-granting organization.

"Early on in the process of forming the school, we made philosophical decisions that would prove critical in the years to come."

We followed the progress of charter legislation in the North Carolina General Assembly and educated the Sawtooth board on what was happening with the charter school movement. We encouraged the board to consider setting up a sister organization to run the school. The Sawtooth board reviewed the North Carolina charter school legislation when it was enacted, and additional debate on Sawtooth becoming the sponsor for a charter school ensued. We considered structures in which a common holding company would be created and the Sawtooth Center for Visual Art and the Arts-Based Elementary School would be sister organizations under its common umbrella. Ultimately the Sawtooth board agreed to allow Jim to use some of his time as an employee of Sawtooth to write the charter and submit it for approval. However, the Sawtooth board did not want to be the sponsoring organization for ABES.

EARLY ORGANIZATION

Jim and I formed an organizing committee and began work. Early on in the process of forming the school, we made philosophical decisions that would prove critical in the years to come. Just how critical these choices would be we could not have ever conceived at this early stage.

We spelled out the basic philosophy for the school. Jim was the primary architect of the vision as we began to develop our concepts:

- The school would serve K–5 and the curriculum would be delivered using the arts (music, dance, visual art, theater).
- The school would strive for a racial balance that reflected the larger community (67% white, 26% African American, 7% Hispanic).
- The school would be located in a racially neutral site in downtown Winston-Salem within easy reach of the city's arts organizations.
- The school's campus would extend to include the entire city.
- Students would learn how to navigate an urban landscape.
- Each child would develop and build upon an educational portfolio as they progressed through their educational experience from kindergarten through fifth grade.
- The school would become a partner with the city's arts organizations and would also seek out other partnerships that could strengthen its curriculum.

SECURING THE CHARTER

There are two ways to submit a charter application in North Carolina. One can submit it either to the local education authority (LEA), that is, the local public school board, or one can submit it directly to the North Carolina Department of Public Instruction. Most charter schools bypass the LEA in favor of applying directly to the state. There are three reasons for this pattern: (1) if the LEA turns down your charter application, you cannot appeal to the state; (2) most charter schools maintain adversarial relationships with their LEA; and (3) if you submit through your LEA and they approve it, the application still needs to be approved by the state, thus adding another level of approval.

The ABES board did not believe it served our interests to be at odds with our LEA, and thus we submitted our charter application to the Winston-Salem Forsyth County School Board. This decision was also consistent with our mission of seeking local partnerships that could strengthen our school. The LEA unanimously endorsed our charter application and sent it on to the state for consideration. The local Chamber of Commerce also endorsed our application to the LEA and to the state. One of the lessons we would come to learn is that you can never have too many friends and allies.

Our charter was granted in early 2000 and we had permission to open our school in the fall of 2000. Our plans, however, called for a year of ground work, with the school scheduled to open for the 2001–02 school year. Our next challenge was to find a suitable building for the school.

"One of the lessons we would come to learn is that you can never have too many friends and allies."

FINDING PHILANTHROPY DIFFICULT

My leadership role with ABES was about to begin in earnest. Jim asked if I would serve as chairman of the board of the new organization that was to be formed to take the concept of an arts-based charter school forward. We started with all the usual perfunctory tasks, forming a corporation, writing bylaws, recruiting board members, and so forth.

We put together a task list of all the critical functions to be accomplished in order to open the school. We recruited a very strong board that provided the organization with expertise in many different disciplines, as well as a team of people who were willing to roll up their sleeves and work hard together. Our initial board consisted of individuals such as Peter Perret, the conductor of the Winston-Salem symphony and creator of the Bolton Project, a proven arts-based reform based on the positive impact of music on developing the brain. Other founding members came from such organizations as Wake Forest University, Volvo Trucks, BB&T Corporation (a major bank), the United Way of Forsyth County, the Wake Forest University School of Medicine, Womble Carlyle Sandridge & Rice (a major law firm), American Express, the Winston-Salem Housing Authority, and the community at large. Thus, we had a strong cross section of academics, business professionals, and supportive community volunteers.

We began to work on many things concurrently, meeting as a board every two weeks and feeling as if we were all holding a second job. We began to hold student recruitment meetings at the downtown public library during the winter of 2000–01. We had a good response from parents interested in putting their children in the school when it opened. We also embarked on what would turn out to be our most difficult task, finding a building to house the school.

"We learned that our city building code for a downtown school was much more restrictive than state requirements. . . . Collectively, these standards removed almost every site from consideration."

In keeping with our founding principles, we wanted to secure a building in downtown Winston-Salem within easy reach of the arts venues and on ground that would be considered racially and socioeconomically neutral. We recruited a real estate professional to our board (the head of facilities for a major corporation) and retained a local commercial real estate broker to review space options.

As we toured available buildings, it became apparent that the task of finding space that was both suitable and desirable was not going to be easy. We learned that our city building code for a downtown school was much more restrictive than state requirements. The code requires 100 square feet per child, a 5,000 square foot playground on site, and the kindergarten and first-grade classrooms on ground level, with two exits per classroom. Collectively, these standards removed almost every site from consideration.

We began to focus in on the Lowey building, in the heart of the central business district, which seemed to satisfy all the required code issues. We hired an architect to lay out the floor space and determined the building would work. We then began to negotiate a lease with the building owners. During the negotiations, which were proceeding as planned, we had the architect complete construction drawings and put the project out to bid with three contractors. The bids came in at about the cost expected, and we selected a contractor to do the work.

"We had 120 families ready to send their children to the school. Delivering the news that we would not be able to open in the fall was one of the hardest things we had to do."

We finalized the negotiations on the building lease, including an upfit allowance sufficient to do the majority of the renovation work that would be needed. Our attorney worked through the final details, and the lease was ready to sign when, at the last minute, the building owners (an out-of-state group) pulled out of the transaction. It was now late spring of 2001. At this point, it was going to be almost impossible to find a new location and get it ready to open a school in by fall. The board worked feverishly to try to identify another building. We found one possible location but decided that the building's current use and its designation as a historic landmark would preclude making the necessary changes within the time remaining to get the project done.

"Many alliances were formed during this ongoing trial by fire that would play a major role in the ultimate success of the school."

We had 120 families ready to send their children to the school. Delivering the news that we would not be able to open in the fall was one of the hardest things we had to do. However, we felt that we had an obligation to the families to let them know in enough time that they were not shut out of all their other education alternatives. We continued to maintain a dialogue with our families by e-mail and with face-to-face meetings over the course of the next year as we started over on the building search. It would have been easy to throw in the towel and blame our failure on an unfortunate real estate transaction, but to quote NASA: "failure was not an option."

THE SEARCH CONTINUES

Many alliances were formed during this ongoing trial by fire that would play a major role in the ultimate success of the school. The two individuals who were responsible for creating our unique curriculum were the heads of two major art organizations in Winston-Salem. Jim Sanders was the executive director of the Sawtooth Center for Visual Art and Peter Perret was the conductor for the Winston-Salem Symphony. Both of these individuals had long records of providing services to the public school system in the county through their respective organizations.

In the spring of 2002, the Winston-Salem Forsyth County School (WSFCS) system was awarded a federal grant to create an arts-based magnet school in the district. A staff member responsible for the magnet program at the WSFCS system contacted Peter Perret to determine if the ABES board would be interested in supplying the curriculum for the magnet school. This eventually led to meetings with the senior staff at the WSFCS system, including the superintendent, Dr. Don Martin. A proposal was developed that called for the magnet school to become a district-run charter school to be managed by the ABES board, which would have a dotted-line relationship with the WSFCS board instead of being entirely independent, as with most charter schools. The ABES board had to decide if it should join forces with the WSFCS system to run one of its schools under this arrangement.

"We had to decide between making a major financial commitment . . . or accepting somewhat less autonomy in a relationship with a strong partner who would be a major asset to . . . our program."

We had identified a building (a facility we called the sewing building) that would be an excellent home for our school, and the board was divided between developing our own building or joining forces with the WSFCS system. We had to decide between making a major financial commitment in the face of an unsuccessful attempt at opening the previous year or accepting somewhat less autonomy in a relationship with a strong partner who would be a major asset to building our program.

We knew that the task of converting the designated public school location to a charter school would not be easy. The school was in an impoverished part of town and adjacent to a large public housing neighborhood and a major highway. We held meetings at the school to determine the interest of our constituents as well as the residents of the neighborhoods surrounding the school that would be impacted by the change from a community "zone" school to districtwide magnet.

Our board voted to pursue this opportunity with WSFCS. We decided that our program could reach more children and that we would be removed from the administrative burdens of running a school under this arrangement. We were also confident in the strength of our curriculum and decided that if it proved itself in this setting, it would become an indisputable model to apply to a broader universe of schools and students.

Little did we know, we were blazing new trails that were not anticipated under the current charter law. To do what we wanted to do would require an affirmative vote of the majority of the current families at the school that was to become a district-run charter, a similar majority vote by the school's teachers, and a change in the state's charter law to allow the district to establish another LEA under its umbrella. The board, in collaboration with the staff of the WSFCS system, now found itself lobbying in Raleigh, the state capital, for a change to the law and politicking with the community being served by the school to support a change of the school to a district-run charter.

The boards of both the ABES organization and the WSFCS system worked hard to make this proposal work. The delegation of elected officials from our county was supportive of trying to change the legislation to allow our proposal to work. We met with the staff of the state's Department of Public Instruction and Division of Charter Schools to work out the details of what would be required to make this proposal work. As with most things dealing with politics and bureaucratic organizations, there were those who did not support a change to the status quo, but we generally found people to be very supportive of our concept to blaze new ground.

The people involved with administering the state's charter program were most supportive and very excited about seeing the possibility of collaboration between the traditional public school sector and the charter school movement. We knew if we were successful with our vote at the public school, the Forsyth County delegation was willing to sponsor what is known as a local bill (a change in the law that only applies to one particular situation in a single community) in the state house to allow our partnership with WSFCS to move forward until such time as we could garner enough legislative support to change the state charter law applicable to all charter schools.

"Unfortunately we were viewed as outsiders trying to 'take away a community asset' rather than benefactors trying to bring a unique and positive program to the community school."

On the local scene, we held many meetings at the school to try to win the hearts of the local community. Unfortunately, we were viewed as outsiders trying to "take away a community asset" rather than benefactors trying to bring a unique and positive program to the community school. Our campaign to win the hearts of the community included door-to-door canvassing, meeting with local leaders from the housing project neighborhood, and open meetings at the school. This entire process became a local media story with much unflattering coverage. When the voting was done, the staff of the public school voted in favor of the conversion, but we lost the school-family vote by the slimmest of margins; the vote was almost evenly split. It was now late spring of 2002.

IT'S ALWAYS DARKEST BEFORE THE DAWN

During the time our board spent trying to make the district-run charter work, I formed a cooperative working relationship with Dr. Don Martin, WSFCS superintendent. Don not only cares about the children and the quality of education but is willing to try new things to advance the education options in the county. He deserves a full measure of credit for the ultimate survival of our program, because without his far-reaching support and that of his staff, we would have been defeated at this point.

Excited about the ABES program, Don continued to meet with Jim, Peter, and me to look for a solution that would allow us to implement our program. After much exploration, Don offered to lease us six classrooms in an underutilized public school. Additionally, he offered to provide the administrative support of his organization to allow us to focus on picking up the pieces of our badly battered organization and try to recruit enough students, buy furniture, etc., to salvage our next school year that was to begin in a few short months. Our board decided to take this opportunity to bring our program to life.

"Without [the superintendent's] far-reaching support and that of his staff, we would have been defeated at this point."

Our board went to Atkins Middle School, where we would be leasing the six classrooms. These rooms represented an entire hallway on the ground floor of the three-story middle school. At a meeting held with the facility and administrative staff of the school, many questions were asked about our school and our intentions. There was much concern about what our program might mean for them in the long term. The administration at the school was not sure what to make of this arrangement, which they viewed as "the heavy hand of the central office" imposing its will on their school.

As was our modus operandi by now, we set out to develop a good working relationship with our new hosts. We invited a person of their choosing to join our board of directors. They nominated the assistant principal to our board. This connection turned out to be a valuable resource for us, as she counseled us on many issues related to the school we were in, education law, and the internal workings of our new partner, the WSFCS system, as we set about the job of trying to get our school open. I worked to build a personal relationship with the principal of the school in order to try to create an avenue to promote positive cross pollination and effective conflict resolution, since both would likely be needed during the year.

We obtained donated furniture from many businesses around town and purchased surplus furniture from the WSFCS system. We had to use one classroom for office space, so we decided to open with five classes: one kindergarten, two first grade, one second grade, and one third grade. With our curriculum design providing a target of 15 and a maximum of 18 children per class, we knew the year would be difficult financially, as it would be hard to pay for our administrative staff and other overhead costs with a target enrollment of 75. We opened the school with 68 children, about half of whom were from the original group of parents that had wanted to join our school from the beginning. Jim Sanders served as a part-time principal while continuing to serve as the executive director of the Sawtooth Center. We hired our teaching staff, one full-time administrator, and an administrative assistant. Our total staff consisted of seven full-time employees and Jim as our part-time principal.

"The bathrooms were located on a different hall in a section of the school used by middle school students. We programmed 'bathroom breaks' into our daily routine, lining up the children and trying to make a fun adventure out of our hike down the hall."

Our first year was marked by the normal bumps you would expect with any new business. Through it all, the board and staff focused on creating a successful year for the students. Funding worries plagued our school in the early part of the year; we did not want to spend money we did not have, and thus our program was lean through the first half of the year. The board worked diligently on fund raising, but it was difficult; the community did not yet see our program as stable enough to be worthy of financial support. But the board was committed to making the program a success and worked tirelessly and resourcefully to overcome the challenges and make sure the classroom experience for the children was first rate.

Our "school within a school" at Atkins created additional challenges and opportunities for us during the year. The wing of the school where our classrooms were located was a significant distance from the nearest bathrooms. The bathrooms were located on a different hall in a section of the school used by middle school students. We programmed "bathroom breaks" into our daily routine, lining up the children and trying to make a fun adventure out of our hike down the hall. This procedure had to be coordinated so it would not take place while the middle school students were making a classroom change.

The building had many wonderful attributes that a program like ours could never have afforded. Sterling Garris, the principal of our host school, let us make use of their piano lab, gave us almost exclusive rights to a second gymnasium in the building, and allowed us to put on productions in the school's beautifully renovated auditorium. The staff of the school was very accommodating and gracious, going above and beyond the call of duty to help us.

In making the space available for us, the principal of the school had to relocate all his sixth-grade teachers. In an attempt to let them know we understood and appreciated the sacrifice they made for us, at Thanksgiving we made a gift of a turkey to each sixth-grade teacher and each administrator in the school. This gesture of appreciation and recognition was very warmly received.

THINGS BEGIN TO TURN, BUT CHALLENGES CONTINUE

In early winter 2002, the Office of Charter Schools informed us that we were eligible for a portion of a federal start-up grant that they had applied for and received. We completed an application to the state charter office and were awarded $177,000 in additional funds. It was a major lift to our program. We immediately hired assistants for the classrooms and a curriculum coordinator (Robin Hollis, who would eventually be named full-time principal) to work with our dedicated but nearly burned out crew of teachers. Without constant money worries, things definitely took a turn for the better, and our program began to get legs. Through the remainder of the year, we received four other grants.

"The building owners began to get excited about our school. . . . [They] became our greatest financial benefactors. We worked out a lease arrangement that was very favorable to our school."

During the year, we recruited another facilities expert to our board, Mary Benton, an executive with Novant Health, a large hospital corporation headquartered in our community. It turned out that one of the most promising buildings we had reviewed during our facilities search, the sewing building, was owned by two gentlemen with whom Mary had done a lot of work. Mary opened negotiations with the building owners about moving the school to their building.

The building owners began to get excited about our school, but it was difficult to get them excited about our financial position. We had a very strong board with many community leaders, but a shaky history. The relocation of the school from our five-classroom "school within a school" to their building would be but one more change dynamic in the life of our fledgling organization. Based on the strength of our board, Mary's relationship with the owners, and their excitement for our program, they decided to support our cause and became our greatest financial benefactors. We worked out a lease arrangement that was very favorable to our school, based on a per enrolled student cost (with a minimum lease cost based on 150 children), and a generous upfit allowance.

"The grant was significant not only for its financial support but as a signal that the community now saw our organization as having proved itself worthy of support."

In February 2003, we had a media event to announce our new location and began to recruit our expanded student body for the 2003–04

school year. We decided not to build out the entire space the first year
to help limit our (and the building owners') financial exposure. We decided to expand to 10 classrooms, with a maximum enrollment of 180
students. By mid-June 2003, we had reached 180 enrolled students and
had a waiting list for every class.

Toward the end of the school year, ABES was notified that we had
been granted funds from the Hanes Foundation. The grant was significant not only for its financial support but as a signal that the community
now saw our organization as having proved itself worthy of support.

OTHER FIRST-YEAR PROBLEMS AND BLESSINGS

In the last quarter of the school year, our enrollment fell to 62 students.
Under the state's charter legislation, a school must maintain 65 or more
children or be put on probation. Well, you guessed it; we received a letter from the Office of Charter Schools informing us we were out of compliance.

This followed a string of personnel-related issues that we had to deal
with in our first year. We had to deal with a staff member who left because she was not a good fit for our school. She filed a complaint with
the state, saying that we did not provide services called for by her
child's individualized education plan (IEP) in a timely fashion. We successfully navigated these problems but learned much about the myriad
of education laws and regulations during the year. We also learned what
we wanted the staff and leadership of our school to resemble the following year.

We were blessed to find an exceptional principal that first year. Robin
Hollis, our curriculum coordinator, was named principal in early spring
of 2003. She had fallen in love with our school and was a perfect person
for the job. Through her work with the school during the second half of
our inaugural year, she prepared us well for our second (upcoming) year.
She is largely responsible for the expansion of our student body; she inspired confidence in prospective parents as they toured our school during the student recruitment process for our second year. We also learned
our teacher selection process in the first year was not optimal. We created an abstract from the examples of our most successful classroom

teachers and used that to create a teacher profile as we hired our staff for year two.

Our building continued to be a challenge as we progressed through the upfit. Our plans fell under the newly enacted International Building Code. Code requirements imposed on the renovation by the new international code and our city building department caused the project to run over budget by $75,000. We also ran into problems with the adjacent land owner. The building we were renovating was an all-brick shell. We planned on adding windows as part of the renovation. Because the building sits on the property line, our workers needed to set up their scaffold on the adjacent property to add windows on one side of the building. Despite a campaign of neighborly courtesies by ABES, the neighboring land owner refused the contractor access to his property. Thus, it seems nothing comes easy.

LESSONS LEARNED

Our first year of operations was full of lessons, both positive and negative. As a board and an organization, we have learned the power of persistence and the value of the collective strength that comes from a board composed of dedicated and competent people from a multitude of disciplines. We have learned that parents have innumerable talents and are eager to support their kids' school. We also learned that a process often builds upon its history and that you have to make good decisions that are consistent with your mission from the beginning.

As we talked with our parents at the end of our first year, it became evident that the strength of our curriculum design was sound. Moreover, parents told us that the challenges the school and the board faced were not felt by our children. All of our children passed the required end-of-grade tests (EOGs) mandated by the state.

Making the best use of money is a real challenge for charter schools. Because the charter laws do not provide funds for capital items, obtaining that financing is one of the most critical things a new school must do to help ensure success. Imagine being given a budget for operating your home but no funds to buy, furnish, or remodel it. Regardless, the challenge is worth meeting; there is nothing more rewarding than to see a program work, and to see children who may not have done well in a traditional public school blossom.

We learned that building relationships, large and small, can pay big dividends. Most of our successes came from the fruit that was born by a bridge built along the way. After the first year had ended and we had moved out of Atkins, I went to visit Sterling Garris, the principal. He was very complimentary about the shared experience and what having us there brought to his school, and he indicated he and his staff would miss our group. I invited Sterling to come see our new school and mentioned to him that completing our building would likely take us right down to the first day of school. He replied, "Hey, if you need to open here while you finish your building, just call." Two grown men hugged and parted with a high regard for one another. I can truly say the seven years I have spent involved with this project provided some of the most rewarding experiences of my life and brought me in touch with the most unselfish, caring, and dedicated people I have ever met.

"We learned that building relationships, large and small, can pay big dividends."

I will close with a testimonial from a parent who is now a board member. Gayle Anderson is the president of the Greater Winston-Salem Chamber of Commerce. She came to our board during some of our most challenging days and was a valuable asset in helping get the school started. Gayle has been working with a local immigrant family from Mexico for several years, assisting the children as they began their educational experience in the United States. She saw firsthand the challenges these children were having in a traditional public school and became interested in our program. Here is Gayle's story:

ABES has changed the future for the children I volunteer with. Their experience at a traditional public school was difficult. The teachers did not seem to know them as individuals and were not helpful in allowing me to assist them with their homework. My children are ESL, and they needed more assistance and encouragement from a caring staff. Karla and Rigo both entered third grade at ABES at least one grade behind where they should have been. In addition, Rigo has an audio-processing disability which requires teachers to interact with him in very specific ways, creating opportunities for him to learn kinesthetically. Through the unique method of teaching through the arts, Karla completely caught up with the rest of the third-grade class and passed both the language and math EOGs (end of grade tests). Rigo passed the math EOG, something he never could have dreamed of passing a year ago. His disability makes his language performance more difficult, but he has improved dramatically in language arts his first year (because of his language audio-processing disability, Rigo was not required to take the language EOG). He went from hating school and hating math to loving ABES and truly believing he is the "King of Math."

Carlos entered kindergarten at ABES speaking almost no English. At the end of his first year, he is as fluent in English as his non-Spanish-speaking classmates, and he can read. His teacher says he is completely ready for first grade.

"When I get up to sharpen my pencil, no one yells at me."

All three children love going to school, and they are upset when ABES is on a holiday. But perhaps their experience is best summed up in a conversation I had with Rigo after he'd been at ABES for about a month. I asked him what he liked best about his new school. His answer was, "When I get up to sharpen my pencil, no one yells at me." To me, that says it all. A child cannot learn in an environment where he is afraid, and Rigo has thrived in the ABES environment. This is what this project is truly about; changing the future of these and our other children is an investment that cannot be measured, as the rewards can be infinite!

III

A FUTURE VIEW

16

A CALL FOR LEADERS
OF NEW JOBS

As charter schools confront the inevitable challenges facing any new organization, founders need to look backward and sideways as well as forward. New realities have raised the stakes of schooling for everyone, fostering new approaches to schooling (Chapter 1), and reaffirming enduring issues of leadership (Chapter 2). Too often, new initiatives are launched without mining history for lessons to heed and pitfalls to avoid. As a result, we keep making the same mistakes again and again. Forewarned is very often pre-armed.

Another common error of organizational pioneers is to rivet their attention on parochial issues. This myopia isolates leaders from the experience of others reaching for similar goals. It is all too easy to conclude that "my situation is a unique disaster" when other pioneers are wrestling with similar thorny torments. In this concluding chapter, we first highlight the central and unique issues of our featured schools. We then tease out the cross-cutting themes they share. Even with very different missions, locales, students, sponsors, partners, and other factors, charter schools face many similar trials and tribulations. A sideward look often enlightens what is directly in front of us.

Finally we use our crystal ball to forecast what lies ahead. Will charter schools flourish and change American education? Or will the movement sputter and join the ranks of other noble educational experiments that have fallen flat? Which scenario prevails will ride on the shoulders of leaders and their actions. A look at what has come before and what is going on now should help assure a robust future for some promising new educational initiatives. Each story has unique features: different issues, tactics, and players in differing combinations. No one technical recipe prevails. Pragmatism presumes alternative possible paths to desired ends.

ODYSSEY CHARTER SCHOOL

Odyssey's early years closely parallel those of alternative schools launched in the 1970s. The school was born of passion and dedicated to becoming a student-centered place with a mission of developing soft skills and a commitment to lifelong learning. Like its predecessors, the school quickly ran afoul of latent expectations for what schools should be doing, as well as how they are supposed to look.

Parents, especially, are behind change in schools, as long as their kids are not doing things too differently. Odyssey's power struggle between a group of parents and the school's leadership centered on expectations for what the school was supposed to accomplish. This is a conflict all educational administrators face. Schools are handed a diverse set of goals. Some of these are manifest, such as learning and character development. Others are latent: custody control, sorting, and maintaining tradition. Odyssey's noble mission ran afoul of an iceberg of hidden expectations. Fortunately, the school stood its ground and marshaled political support for the original vision. Most charter schools will face similar challenges. They will be held accountable for outcomes they never intended to pursue. The task is to build a culture that promotes universal belief and faith in the school's unique mission.

The Odyssey case also presents other leadership challenges. Organizational beginnings are never easy. They are rife with ambiguity, chaos, and conflict. A school that weathers these expected rough waters will flourish; those that do not will flounder or fail.

A second leadership quandary is knowing when to let go. In Odyssey's first years, O'Sullivan was working nearly 24 hours a day, seven days a week. Such a demanding schedule can quickly lead to fatigue and burnout. In her case, an accident forced her to turn things over to others. She soon learned that others in the school had leadership talent.

A third leadership challenge centers on the importance of structure. In Odyssey's first year, the school's governance structure consisted of a governing board and a 15-person advisory board, mostly parents. This left confusion about who was really in charge. Confusion, as is typical, led to power struggles. In the second year, this arrangement was streamlined to an eight-person governing body, representing all constituencies. Finding a workable social architecture is something all charter schools must reckon with.

CAMINO NUEVO

Charter schools are founded by a delightful mélange of people, many from outside the field of education. Camino Nuevo was launched by an Episcopal priest/entrepreneur who previously started a janitorial service in Los Angeles. Like other charters, the school had a clear mission or cause that went beyond student learning to empowering a larger neighborhood. Rev. Phillip Lance's credentials for starting a new school were enhanced by his earlier experiences as a community organizer. He was very adept at surveying the political terrain and building coalitions around an agenda. He was smart enough to enlist the assistance of Paul Cummins, an educator with previous private school experience. The name of the new school was a combination of Lance's and Cummins's earlier initiatives, New Roads and Pueblo Nuevo. Political experience and a compelling cause helped secure funding for the new school. Symbolic awareness resulted in a school building that won architectural awards. Structural savvy prompted Lance to turn over the day-to-day operations to the school's principal. Lance now serves as the chair of the school's nonprofit board.

VAUGHN NEXT-CENTURY LEARNING CENTER

Some charter schools begin from scratch; others are existing schools in search of a new identity. Vaughn is one of the latter. Joining the ranks of almost all charter schools, Vaughn is a passionate place dedicated to an ennobling calling. Its commitment to student learning is exemplified in the stories of two brothers. One attended the school prior to its transformation; the other, after. The first brother struggled and ended up dead at the age of 17; the other became a member of the student council and headed for college.

Getting support for the new Vaughn was a highly political undertaking. Yvonne Chan created coalitions wherever she could: at the district, local community, state, and national levels. She and the school staff had a shared agenda and garnered support in any quarter to make it happen. But the real secret to Vaughn's success once the school was launched is its clear, comprehensive, goal-focused structure. This is obvious at all levels. The school is governed by three committees: curriculum and instruction, business and operations, and partnerships. Each committee has a workable membership of 20, half staff and half parents.

The school goes beyond mandated testing to assess how well its multiple goals are being met. Teachers are evaluated regularly, and their pay is tied to how well they meet specific standards. Parents sign a compact specifying their obligations and responsibilities. Decisions are made on the basis of hard data. Fiscal accountability is monitored, with students receiving the highest priority to allocate funds. Teamwork among teachers is one of the school's hallmarks. A close relationship with the community is cemented through a series of specific programs.

Like many other charters, Vaughn has a strained relationship with its sponsoring agency, the Los Angeles City School District, and it operates with unusually intense scrutiny to see how well it measures up.

RYDER CHARTER

Charter schools spring from a variety of sources, pursuing many different agendas. The Ryder initiative is an outlier in this array. The school was established by a corporation with a clear mission of recruiting and retaining employees. It was a natural extension of the company's preschool day-care center. The proposed school also offered the local community some relief from overcrowded facilities. Unlike most charter start-ups, the Ryder project focused on constructing a building before building a program. This quickly enmeshed the project in a political struggle with developers, local agencies, and the local school district.

The educational aspects of the new school were farmed out to a group with a track record in launching new charter initiatives. Over the next months, meetings convened the diverse groups involved in the new school's development. This helped each group know what everyone else was doing. It also solidified a base of political support for the project. These political alliances proved invaluable in working through the multiple political hurdles to get the project approved.

The governing body for the new school was a nonprofit board made up of people with the different expertise needed to get the school up and running. A crisis developed when the new charter had to get support from the local school district. Part of the problem stemmed from structural confusion about who would be running the school, Ryder or the company retained to oversee the actual operations. Another issue was whom the school would serve, children of company employees or others in the local community. Through negotiations, both issues were resolved. A third speed bump materialized over the final charter contract but was resolved through negotiation. The secret of success for the Ryder school was the ability to deal with issues structurally and politically.

FENTON AVENUE

Charter schools have more wiggle room than others in responding to pressing issues. Once described as a "hell hole," the Fenton Avenue school is now recognized as one of California's best. The path from worst to one of the state's first reaffirms that change has a promising chance when an organization is either new or in crisis. Fenton fits both conditions. It was in bad shape and used the charter legislation to start afresh. One of the interesting features of the school's journey is where the new beginning began. Most reform efforts begin with an abstract vision of where we need to go. Fenton Avenue started with the basics: security, equity, and an opportunity to exit. Once these basic needs were addressed, the school moved toward a more noble vision, "Joe Lucente's Dream School." Moving ahead was a blend of structural and political tactics. The school was conceptualized as a business, with appropriate attention to costs and logistics. Structurally, formal leadership was bifurcated: the principal handles fiscal matters; the director of instruction focuses on what happens in the classroom. But it was attention to politics that launched the school on a promising path. Externally, school leaders maneuvered successfully with the sponsoring school district. Internally, everyone was given a voice; 95% of the school's teachers ratified the move to charter status. All constituencies currently have access to important decisions.

SISULU CHILDREN'S ACADEMY

One of the enduring principles of the United States is the separation of church and state. Sisulu Academy, closely aligned with the Canaan Baptist Church of Harlem, was able to walk a middle path based on another American value: pragmatism. The church, among other things, had space the school needed. The founders were astute in welding together the needed political support for launching the school. They were also smart enough to retain outside expertise to deal with educational and operational issues.

Too often, schools center all leadership and management functions in one individual. Sisulu's administrative arrangement was a troika, one person dealing with external relationship, another focusing on the educational program, the third handling operational details. But even this division of responsibilities did not prevent the administrative overload of starting a new enterprise. So often, charter school leaders burn out from the overwhelming number of tasks routine in other public schools. Bureaucracy has its well-known vices, but it also has virtues that become obvious when you are starting a new organization.

One of the interesting features of the Harlem charter was the attention given to the naming of the school for a living international hero, Walter Sisulu. Symbolically, heroes are living logos and their words, deeds, and lore communicate the intangible values that glue a culture together—in the case of Sisulu, liberation and justice. Alongside an obvious commitment of the founders to students and learning, the school has a head start in shaping a focused and meaningful culture.

FEASTER-EDISON SCHOOL

Charter schools sprout from an amazing variety of root stock. Feaster-Edison is part of the Chula Vista school district. It is also part of the Edison Schools. Many charter schools are new initiatives; Feaster is an example of an existing school injected with new blood from outside. The school's performance has benefited from the transformation, but not without a struggle. Trying to coordinate a school, a district, and a for-profit company is not easy. Feaster managed by developing from the get-go a clear operational structure laying out the responsibilities of each participating party. A shared goal of student learning was also part of the pact. In addition, opposition from the teachers' union was formidable. The union did everything possible to block the new arrangement. Their efforts were thwarted by astute political action and coalition-building on the part of supporters. Once again, attention to structure and politics ensured a more positive environment for student achievement.

In addition to creating a more positive learning situation for local students, Feaster has provided a model for other district schools.

WATTS LEARNING CENTER

As noted, heroes and heroines are crucial icons in any successful enterprise. Alive, they provide day-to-day guidance. Dead, their spirit casts a welcome cloak on the enduring purpose or vision. The spirit of Nina Harden Long lives on in the Watts Learning Center. Too often, we put leadership on a temporal plane without realizing that some of the most important influences, in education or elsewhere, flow from history. This is a lesson that has been heeded by Jim Blew, who is smart enough to embrace, rather than fight, a ghost. The Watts Center has a compelling vision, reinforced from the top of the formal hierarchy to the bottom. Teachers are not just invited to participate in making decisions; they are given some real clout. The center's purpose recognizes the centrality of children and believes that those closest to the true clients know best about what is right. Their philosophy is to give people some latitude in making decisions. Teachers are not just empowered to have a say in the status quo; they are also empowered to leave and find employment elsewhere. Even beyond this, the center reinforces teaching as a sacred calling. They struggle with the tension between talent and formal training. In many schools, credentials, not competence, are the basis for determining who is qualified to lead a class.

Most businesses these days realize that the quality of their product rests largely in the hands of suppliers who provide the raw materials. As a renowned French winemaker observes, "good wine begins in the vineyard." Watts Center parents sign a contract that outlines their active role in the educational process.

Like any other charter school, Watts struggles with the relationship with its sponsoring district. It also learned that contracting with an outside agency to manage things all too often leads to conflicts as to who is really in control. While an external management agency can provide needed resources, it can never substitute for local leadership.

ROCKY MOUNT SCHOOL

Rocky Mount is another example of a charter school founded by business people. The group believed that freeing schools from bureaucratic constraints would produce a better learning opportunity for students. The founding group also knew their limitations and hired an outside firm to oversee the educational program. While this arrangement met with initial success, it soon became apparent that the outside firm's approach was out of sync with North Carolina's state standards and testing program. Ultimately, the school and outside firm parted ways.

Similarities between this initiative and other charters are obvious: difficulties in finding space, problems for school leadership in balancing business and educational demands, struggles to find the best teachers (not necessarily those with formal credentials), dealing with rumors about student selection criteria, wrestling with the local school district, trying to maintain student discipline, and getting parents involved. One of the unique challenges the school faced was the destruction of the building by Hurricane Floyd shortly after the school year began. But the disaster brought the entire school community together. Currently the school's curriculum focuses on caring and character development as well as basic academics.

EAST BAY CONSERVATION CORPS SCHOOL

As highlighted again and again, charter schools are launched by a mixed bag of sponsors. The effort of the East Bay Conservation Corps expands the envelope even more. Since 1983, the group has created opportunities to involve inner-city youth in learning by serving. The new charter school was a logical extension of the group's earlier initiatives. The new school's primary mission is to prepare students for a meaningful role in society. Spiritual development and creative expression set the tone for a unique culture that prizes values and ritual. But the school has also successfully balanced culture and caring with rules and responsibilities. Successful organizations know that standards and spirit dance in harmony, not feud in opposition. Creative tension between rationality and spirituality seem to work in this East Bay charter.

As in other charter initiatives, there is a danger that staff commitment and passion can result in fatigue and burnout over the long haul. Another lesson that seems to emerge is the need to bifurcate leadership, splitting operational and educational functions. In most public schools, both are given to the principal, with the result that the enterprise is either overmanaged and underled, or well led and poorly managed. Parceling out these essential functions to different people can strike a workable balance between running a tight ship and creating a beloved institution.

Running across all of our cases is the issue of involving parents. Parents played a heavy role in getting the school building in shape and continue to serve the school in a variety of ways. Parents of diverse backgrounds are encouraged to find common ground around shared values and develop a deep commitment to making the school a cohesive community.

NEW COUNTRY SCHOOL

Charter schools spring up in a variety of locations. New Country School is situated in a rural community of Minnesota. Its evolution follows the scenario of other charter initiatives: conflict with local district, political action in building support, opposition from local teachers, finding a location, and struggling to dovetail innovative practices with state mandated standards. New Country was blessed by having a group of savvy, politically astute founders with experience in educational reform.

The New Country charter is unique in departing significantly from conventional notions of governance and instruction. The vision was to create something special that would spread to other schools. After the school was launched, planners left day-to-day decisions in the hands of teachers, providing oversight, suggestions, and support. To illustrate how far the school departed from the norm, the teaching staff received a lump sum of money and then decided how it would be allocated—including setting their own salaries. The school is still in operation, although the original founders have moved on to other pursuits.

TOMORROWS BUILDERS YOUTHBUILD SCHOOL

Tomorrows Builders YouthBuild School serves troubled youth in East St. Louis. Obtaining support for the new venture provides a classic study in political sensitivity and persistence. In the face of intense opposition, the founders learned how to bypass the local authorities and get what they wanted. Political action was the name of the game. Even students joined in to rally support for the school. Building coalitions and mastering the art of negotiation and compromise, the founders finally claimed success. The school is passionately dedicated to helping students from poor families realize their dreams and become self-sufficient. It provides a rich mixture of skills and hope for students who otherwise would be left behind.

ARTS-BASED ELEMENTARY SCHOOL

The Arts-Based Elementary School took root at the Sawtooth Center, which trained artists. The center's leadership linked up with state charter legislation. Like many other charter schools, ABES found that locating suitable space for a school was a vexing task. Building codes stymied ABES's early efforts. Finally they found space, retained an architect, and were about to start renovation when the building owners reneged. The 120 sets of parents signed up for the inaugural year had to be told the fall's start was no-go. The school's leadership persisted and worked out a joint arrangement with a district middle school. But resistance from the local community quashed that effort. The local school superintendent then found space in another school and ABES began operation. Throughout a frustrating beginning, the founders never lost heart, and their persistence paid off. The founders credit their success to three main things: an early effort to articulate the school's philosophy, their constant attention to relationships, and the consolidation of a broad, diverse political base in the beginning.

COMMON THEMES ACROSS UNIQUE CIRCUMSTANCES

The stories of individual charter school leaders challenge us to reconsider leadership, in particular how much it varies with organizational context. Each story has unique features; at the same time, all represent creative, entrepreneurial acts of major consequence. Given the proliferation of fundamentally different school governance contexts (e.g., charter, voucher, EMO-managed, state take-over, for-profit, traditional public and private, virtual, and networked), the ongoing academic debate over the essence of leadership takes on added importance. Does starting a charter school from scratch require *fundamentally* different leadership skills than taking a position in an existing suburban public school? If so, how do those leadership requirements vary? If not, what are the generic characteristics of school leadership relevant across the full range of situations? The self-reported stories of charter school leaders provide us some clues. If they are in any way representative of others who have elected to create and run charter schools, their experiences suggest some common themes and tendencies. Five themes, in particular, stand out.

Charter Schools Offer Allure, Attraction, and a Chance to "Play"

Despite widely differing backgrounds, leaders are attracted to the unusual challenge of charter schools, accepting a formidable combination of "more to do," but also "more freedom to do it." They embrace the reality that success or failure rests more on their abilities than their circumstances. Those that gravitated to charter schools from traditional school leadership positions saw a chance to create better schools with a lot more work. Others with nonschooling backgrounds who "stumbled onto" charter schools saw an ideal vehicle for carrying out a broader human development mission with K–12 schooling as an integral medium.

Charter schools appear to provide a qualitatively different opportunity for some educational administrators and are attracting more committed, passionate risk takers to the profession. Although their "business" is still schooling, their aptitudes and capabilities are more akin to entrepreneurs and leaders of small businesses than those of traditional educational administrators. Charter schools may be attracting people who would not otherwise have considered K–12 schooling or might have left the profession prematurely.

Enthusiasm, Beliefs, and Experience
Trump Professional Preparation

The leaders in our stories embrace charter schools as a rare, highly valued opportunity to put into practice cherished, firmly held personal beliefs. Their beliefs in the efficacy of what they are about borders at times on an all-encompassing compulsion or fixation. They see themselves as responding to a calling more than filling a job. This passion significantly shapes the character of the schools they lead. Their driving beliefs are often broad and abstract, such as correcting enduring educational inequities and inefficiencies or addressing the depressing plight of the poor. Alternatively, their beliefs may center on the inherent value of a particular curriculum or instructional approach. To charter leaders, values and beliefs take center stage, and their onstage behavior dramatizes daily what the school prizes and holds most dear. Charter school leaders draw heavily on prior experience rather than management fads of the moment. Their formal education and experience are varied, but almost without exception they have been in the "people business." They are educated at the graduate level, though few are products of formal educational administration programs. Charter leaders have a bias toward action and concrete tasks and goals, and they eschew managerial or leadership "techniques" like TQM or visioning.

The issue of what constitutes appropriate professional preparation for school leadership has often been framed in terms of appropriate skills, attitudes, and techniques that can be taught and learned in educational administration programs. The individuals in the preceding stories favor learning by doing and rely heavily on their hearts as well as their heads.

School Leadership Is a Contact Sport

Charter school leaders engender animate and inanimate "enemies": duplicitous school boards, bureaucratic ineptitude and passive aggressiveness of central office officials, conspiring oppositional parents, and recalcitrant unions. As in athletic events, the opponents are real, but their opposition should not be taken personally. Charter leaders need to learn the fine art of tai chi in dealing with contentious individuals or groups: backpedaling under pressure, pushing forward when running room opens up. Although consensus is usually preferable, most important issues have winners and losers. Successful charter school leaders have to "engage in the contest," wrestling, negotiating, winning, and occasionally losing. Temporary failures, setbacks, reverses, and blockages are both inevitable and part of the game.

Engaging many supportive and unfriendly "constituents" is central to leadership in any organization. Successful charter school leaders have learned how to build supportive coalitions, neutralize opponents, and turn conflict into a productive negotiation where bargaining and compromise prevail. You build teams *and* tussle with enemies.

Relentless Optimism Comes with the Territory

The leaders in our stories don't get discouraged easily. They are like pit bulls holding onto cherished values and beliefs. Major and repeated setbacks and disasters don't seem to faze them. Their relentless optimism reflects a bedrock of sound belief in the worthiness of and in the ultimate success of the endeavor. Although objectivity and realism are often desired management traits, charter school leaders often appear to have a nonrational optimistic bias about the likelihood of success.

Unbending Ideologies, Pragmatic Approaches, and Pride Are at a Premium

While charter school beliefs are typically etched in stone, to work they must get off the pad. This is a pragmatic task. Whether it's bringing healthcare to campus, instituting a new compensation system, securing a building, or getting charter approval, leaders end up "making it happen." An unwavering commitment to a small number of immutable ideals potentially opens up a range of ways to move and alternative options to consider. Leaders dream and labor to make dreams come true. They are absorbed in the detailed and successful unfolding story of *one* school. The pride they accrue is from their contribution to the "happy ending" of the story.

IS LEADERSHIP DIFFERENT IN A "TYPICAL" CHARTER SCHOOL?

Reviewing the stories of 13 charter schools and their leaders, we sense that the role of charter school leaders is discernibly different from that of an administrator of a traditional U.S. public K–12 school. The opportunity to *create or shape* something based on one's personal ideas and beliefs is enormously heady and compelling. It is like the rush that drives an entrepreneur who believes she or he has a novel idea for the marketplace. Add to this "sanctioned opportunity" the relative autonomy unavailable to many school leaders to carry it out "my way."

It is the social, cultural, and educational potential of charter schools that attract entrepreneurial leaders. Yet there is a broader array of managerial detail work associated with success: raising money, securing a building, developing effective and efficient personnel and HR systems, assembling a coherent program. All educational administrators have to deal with details. But it is different when a school reflects *your* best efforts, *your* most dearly held beliefs, and the wisdom of *your* experience. It is not surprising that charter leaders radiate relentless optimism, explicit pride, long-run perseverance, and total engagement in the daily contact sport of running a school. All of the narratives (and the storytellers) featured herein are, in a sense, "success stories" if only by virtue of the fact that their schools continue to exist and the leaders have, at least so far, "lived to tell about it."

In what ways would the stories of 13 *traditional* public schools and their leaders differ from our charter school stories? Managing an existing school involves supervising and tweaking things already in place: personnel, facilities, relationships, customs and traditions, and routine. Most of these cannot be changed, even if the principal is fully behind the effort. Launching a charter school, on the other hand, means starting from scratch. There is very little to manage and so much to invent. Traditional school administrators can often squeak by on their management abilities; charter schools require a healthy dose of leadership.

But differences are greater than those between "starting" and "operating" two otherwise identical schools. They involve the range of decisions that *all* organizations end up having to make and remake: (1) the business to be in; (2) how to organize and operate service delivery (or production processes); (3) the kinds of labor to employ and their compensation; (4) customers or clients to be served; and (5) categories of revenues to pursue in what proportions. These decisions are made for both charter and traditional schools, but they are largely made *by the charter school leaders* on the one hand and *are a product of a diffuse system of rules* on the other.[1]

As many traditional school principals point out, the playing field of charters and traditional schools is not level. Constraints emanating from state education codes, school district policy manuals, and union contracts accumulate quickly and leave little room for inspired leadership. This limits both what *has to* be decided and what *can* be decided by school staff and parents. In one urban school district, rules mandate a certain type of vending machine in teachers' lounges, how many damaged floor tiles can be replaced per month (up to 75 in small schools, 200 in larger ones), that custodians can only paint a wall up to 10 feet high (going higher requires the services of the painters' union), that teachers cannot be assigned to patrol hallways, cafeterias, or school yards. Other rules remove hiring decision rights at the school level and ban merit and market pay for teachers.[2]

The undertakings of charter school leaders in these stories are remarkable because the range and freedom of decision-making authority is so different from traditional schools, and serves to attract people with entrepreneurial aptitudes. This contrast is evident in at least five broad categories of decisions:

1. Decisions about the business to be in. This starts with determining the basic mission of the school: who sets the overall mission; who can change it; who can decide to terminate the business; who assumes the risk of failure and captures the benefits of success? Within the broad parameters of K–12 schooling, charter school leaders in these stories created and shaped the nature of their enterprise to a far greater extent than is typical of a traditional public school principal. Basic decisions of mission and direction are made *and owned* locally, creating a school to serve kids having trouble in traditional schools (Odyssey), permitting kids to be with their parents more during the day (Ryder), or providing students an opportunity to learn a trade as well as the 3Rs (YouthBuild).

2. Decisions about how to organize and operate service delivery. This is the embodiment of the mission in real life. Who determines how the organization will function, including who will decide which parts will work together in what ways? Who determines whether these separate parts fit well or need to be changed? Unlike what would be expected of typical principals, these leaders created school programs which run in tandem with skilled trades apprenticeships (YouthBuild), built a school program around performing arts (ABES), grafted conservation and service learning onto a school curriculum (East Bay), and created a complex multi-service education and youth development enterprise (Sisulu).

3. Decisions about the kinds of people to employ and their compensation. While many personnel decisions in public schools are made by district personnel departments, charter leaders are largely on their own in selecting criteria to hire individuals. The range of personnel decisions is great, including determining relevant employee qualifications, eligibility for a position, and actual candidates to be hired, not to mention terminating employees and on what grounds. Decisions must also be made around salaries and benefits: who determines compensation levels; who determines the changes in levels (merit raises); who establishes benefit packages; who decides bonuses in good times and cuts in pay when revenue expectations fall flat? Charter school leaders designed and installed performance-based pay systems (Vaughn), made both teacher development and teacher accountability a high fiscal priority (Watts Learning Center), and even created employee ownership opportunities (New Country).

4. Decisions about customers or clients to be served. Like entrepreneurs in other businesses, charter school leaders make decisions not only about what types of "clients" but also the share of markets served, including quantities, ages, characteristics. They align special program services to their clientele (all charters in the study). Most fundamentally, they actively market their schools and encourage families to enroll their children. Charter school leaders also make myriad student-related decisions: numbers, grade configurations, allocation of services, family relations, and the like. Traditional school principals, on the other hand, don't decide who should attend their school: they deal with those who show up, who also have no choice.

5. Decisions about how to allocate operating revenues. It is a rare charter school that is launched and survives without significant financial support above and beyond per-pupil operating state aid. Charter leaders have to cultivate multiple financial (and other material) resources in order to exist. They have the freedom to pursue additional revenues, and the freedom to fail if they don't. They have to be much more adept on both sides of the ledger—clever in both spending and in revenue generation. There is no "downtown" to hand down an annual budget. When major financial crises hit (Rocky Mount), or major financially related opportunities arose (Fenton, Sisulu, Camino Nuevo), charter leaders swung into action.

In sum, leading a start-up charter is very different from managing a traditional public school. The people attracted to these roles survive despite a barrage of highly ambiguous situations and decisions. Charter school leaders have much greater autonomy, including freedom to fail. Ours were experiences of those who chose the roles and "lived to tell about it"—not the stories of those who tried and failed, nor of those that did not try. But the difference between those who create charter schools and those who assume school leadership positions in traditional public schools is really two contradictions wrapped into one: dissimilarities in jobs combined with deviations in who is attracted to those jobs.

These differences in jobs are often very large—analogous to the difference between starting a business from scratch and assuming a position as department head in a public agency. Different jobs attract different kinds of people: jobs and the people are self-selecting. The "skill sets" required to start and successfully operate a charter school are at a minimum *different from*, possibly *much greater than*, and certainly more entrepreneurial than those required of a principal in a typical public school. Entrepreneurial and managerial talents have little in common.

If so much concern centers on the dearth of well-prepared, skilled school leaders in traditionally governed public schools,[3] is the pool of potential leaders for (more demanding) charter school start-ups even more restricted? It would be, except for one thing: charter schools can draw not only on the talent pool of traditional K–12 educators (like Joe Lucente, Libby Gil, Yvonne Chan, and Doug Thomas), but also on a much larger pool of outsiders without prior educational experience (like Philip Lance, Jim Blew, Judith Price, Joanna Lennon, Michael Lynott, Kathleen O'Sullivan, John Von Rohr, Vickie Forby, and Hal Johnson). This expands the pool of needed leader candidates. Rather than the loss of public school talent to charter schools, the size of the talent pie has expanded. Charter school legislation has created opportunities for entrepreneurial "non-educators"—individuals who have significant professional preparation and experience but who are not a product of formalized credentialing and placement systems.

A LOOMING FORK IN THE ROAD AHEAD?

The essence of public schools has remained remarkably stable over the decades, despite a barrage of extensive and expensive reforms. There are a number of reasons why: (1) the notion of a common school, providing glue to hold a new and diverse country together, was framed by the founders of our country; (2) conventional, romantic images of what a "good" school is are ingrained in the minds of educators, parents, and the public, and deviations are mostly unwelcome; (3) most parents are satisfied with the status quo, and changes are mostly initiated by policymakers and educational reformers. Put all these together and one scenario for charter schools seems evident—a bird that sees clear skies ahead and then hits a glass window. If history is a predictor, that possibility looms large—an initial flurry and an ignominious flop. Opposition to charter schools is already forming and becoming public—both in dramatic prohibitions and by many small cuts. If that pops the balloons of faith, belief, and hope that currently buoy the movement, trouble lies ahead.

There is another reason for a pessimistic prognosis. Pioneers who envision and launch new charter schools are entrepreneurs to their core. But what it takes to sustain a bold new venture is different. The business world is awash in stories of creative geniuses who start with a flourish and then have little interest or talent in instituting routines, rules, and realism that ensure continued success. Our stories are chock full of brilliant leaders who propel things off the pad. But will they stay the course in the out years when details guarantee destiny? If they leave to pursue another dream, who will keep the original flame alive? Once again, history does not paint a promising picture.

The second fork ahead—and the one we lean toward—is much more optimistic. In many ways charter schools are modern, expanded versions of the old one-room schoolhouse where dedicated teachers pursued their calling with parental backing and helped students learn and grow. The secrets of what makes a good school tick, including that one size does not fit all, are well established in the research literature. In a widely circulated study of 1980s school reform efforts, for example, Chubb and Moe identified three factors that accelerated student learning in high schools: (1) the involvement of parents, (2) autonomy for the local site to respond to its clientele without bureaucratic interference from above, and (3) a sense of cohesion and shared focus among administrators, teachers, and staff.[4] Laying these findings against the experiences of our 13 schools, we see an almost perfect fit. This pattern, if duplicated in other charter schools, augurs well for a promising future.

Another take on the future of charters comes from the work of Bolman and Deal, who point to four characteristics of effective organizations across the board. Successful organizations: (1) create a caring climate that allows all constituencies to satisfy basic human needs; (2) design a clear and outcome-oriented structure that lets everyone know what the goals are, their role in making things happen, and how their efforts relate to others; (3) accept power and conflict as natural by-products of cooperative activity and encourage coalitions and active bargaining; and (4) shape a culture that gives work meaning and bonds people together in a shared noble quest. A look at many of today's public schools highlights a shortfall in most of these areas. Our collection of charter schools demonstrates mastery in all four. If this continues to hold true for present and future efforts, we may see a welcome and uplifting development in the ability of our nation's schools to serve the best interests of students and parents.

The deciding factor in how the charter movement fares will depend on exemplary leadership from common people who are able to do uncommon and noble things while learning as they go along. Enabling (permissive) charter school legislation (despite some handicapping conditions in some states) is creating leadership opportunities for people who want the greater freedom, risk, responsibility, and pride of ownership that comes from creating and managing charter schools. Many of these individuals were never attracted to the highly restricted role of public school principal, and they have different tastes and aptitudes from traditional administrative roles. They see a very different job and a different role for themselves. Far from being more demanding and less attractive, charter schools are attracting people to school leadership who seem to thrive on "daunting opportunities." Our goal is to extend an invitation to entrepreneurs with a passion for fulfilling the most sacred calling of all—to create places where every child can learn and grow. The pathway will never be clear, and the going is always tough. But human history has always shown that a few bold pioneers will give a worthy task their best effort. They are the ones who really make a difference. Nowhere is such courage and dedication needed more than in education.

NOTES

1. See Davies, B., and Hentschke, G. (1994) for one taxonomy on decision making.

2. "Witness Protection for Teachers" (2003).

3. See the National Association of Elementary School Principals Fact Sheet at http://www.naesp.org/ContentLoad.do?contentId=1097.

4. Chubb, J. E., and Moe, T. M. (1990).

REFERENCES

Abelmann, C., Elmore, R., Even, J., Kenyon, S., & Marshall, J. (1999). When accountability knocks, will anyone answer? Report for the Consortium for Policy Research in Education (Report Number RR-42). Philadelphia, PA: University of Pennsylvania Graduate School of Education.

Advantage Schools. (2001, March). Annual report on school performance: 1999–2000 school year. Boston, MA.

Arsen, D., Plank, D., & Sykes, G. (1999). School choice policies in Michigan: The rules matter. East Lansing, MI: Center on School Choice and Educational Change, Michigan State University.

Ascher, C., et al. (2001). Going charter: New models of support. New York: Charter School Research Project, New York University.

Ascher, C., Jacobowitz, R., McBride, Y., & Wamba, N. (2000, December). Reflections from New York City's charter schools and charter authorizers. Report for the Institute for Education and Social Policy, School of Education, New York University.

Baldridge, J. V., & Deal, T. E. (Eds.). (1975). *Managing change in higher education.* Berkeley, CA: McCutchan.

Barton, P. (2003). Parsing the achievement gap: Baselines for tracking progress. Princeton, NJ: Educational Testing Service. Available from http://www.ets.org/research/pic

Betts, J. R., Kim, R. S., & Danenberg, A. (2000). Equal resources, equal outcomes? The distribution of school resources and student achievement in California. San Francisco: Public Policy Institute of California.

Bierlein, L. (1997). The charter school movement. In Ravitch, D., & Viteritti, J. (Eds), New schools for a new century (pp. 37–60). New Haven, CT: Yale University Press.

Billingsley, L., & Riley, P. (1999). Two steps forward, one step back: The battle for California's charter schools. San Francisco: Pacific Research Institute for Public Policy.

Bolman, L., & Deal, T. (2003). Reframing organizations. San Francisco: Jossey-Bass.

Bulkley, K. (2001, October). Educational performance and charter school authorizers: The accountability bind. Education Policy Analysis Archives, 9(37).

Bulkley, K., & Fisler, J. (2002). A decade of charter schools: From theory to practice. Available at http://www.cpre.org/Research/Research_Project_B-2.htm

Bulkley, K. E., & Wohlstetter, P. (2003). Taking account of charter schools: What's happened and what's next? New York: Teachers College Press.

California Department of Education. (1999). Types of alternative classroom instruction in California charter schools. Available at http://www.cde.ca.gov/charter/

Center for Applied Research and Educational Improvement. (1998). Minnesota charter schools evaluation. Minneapolis: College of Education and Human Development, University of Minnesota.

Center for Education Reform. (1999). Making school work better for all children. Available at http://www.edreform.com/charter_schools/

Center for Education Reform. (2001). Survey of charter schools. Washington, DC: Author. Available at http://www.edreform.com

Center for Education Reform. (2003). What the research reveals about charter schools: Summary and analysis of the studies. Washington, DC: Author. Available at www.edreform.com/_upload/research.pdf

Chaddock, G. (1999, February 22). Hands-on politicians are up to their elbows in education. Christian Science Monitor. Available at http://search.csmonitor.com/durable/1999/02/02/p20s1.htm

Charter Friends National Network. (2001a). Charter schools and the education of children with disabilities. Available at http://www.charterfriends.org

Charter Friends National Network. (2001b). Charting a clear course: A resource guide for building successful partnerships between charter schools and school management organizations. Available at http://www.charterfriends.org

Charter Schools Development Center. (1998). Beyond the rhetoric of charter school reform: A study of ten California school districts. UCLA Charter Study. Sacramento: California State University Institute for Educational Reform. Available at www.cacharterschools.org

Charter Schools Institute. (2002). Charter schools in New York: A new choice in public education. New York: State University of New York.

Chavez, S., & Morain, D. (1993, November 3). In wake of defeat, voucher backers vow a stiffer fight. *Los Angeles Times*.

Chubb, J. E., & Moe, T. M. (1990). *Poliltics, markets, and America's schools*. Washington, DC: Brookings Institution.

Christenson, C. (1997). *Innovator's dilemma: When new technologies cause great firms to fail*. Boston, MA: Harvard Business School Press.

Clark, B. (1975). The organizational saga in higher education. In Baldridge, J. V., & Deal, T. E. (Eds.), *Managing change in higher education* (pp. 75–97). Berkeley: McCutchan.

Davies, B., & Hentschke, G. (1994). School autonomy: Myth or reality—Developing an analytical taxonomy. *Educational Management and Administration, 22*, 96–103.

Deal, T. E. (1975). Alternative schools: An alternative postmortem. In Baldridge, J. V., & Deal, T. E. (Eds.), *Managing change in higher education* (pp. 467–481). Berkeley: McCutchan.

Deal, T. E., & Jenkins, W. A. (1994). *Managing the hidden organization*. New York: Warner Books.

Deal, T. E., & Nolan, R. R. (Eds.). (1978). *Alternative schools: Ideologies, realities, guidelines*. Chicago: Nelson Hall.

DelVecchio, R. (1999, May 22). Jerry Brown blasts teacher unionization bill; charter schools' self-determination at stake, he says. *San Francisco Chronicle*, A17.

Dianda, M., & Corwin, R. (1993, April). An early look at charter schools in California. Report prepared for the Southwest Regional Laboratory. San Franciso: WestEd.

Education Commission of the States. (2001). Charter schools ECS state notes: Charter school teachers. Retrieved July 12, 2002, from http://www.ecs.org

Finn, C. E., Manno, B. V., Bierlein, L. A., & Vanourek, G. (1997). *Charter schools as seen by those who know them best: Students, teachers, and parents*. Charter Schools in Action Project, Part 1. Washington, DC: Hudson Institute.

Finn, C. E., Manno, B. V., & Vanourek, G. (2001). *Charter schools in action: Renewing public education*. Princeton, NJ: Princeton University Press.

Fitzgerald, J. (2000). 1998–99 Colorado charter schools evaluation study: The characteristics, status and performance record of Colorado charter schools. Report for the Colorado Department of Education. Available at http://www.cde.state.co.us

Fuller, B. (2001). *Inside charter schools: The paradox of radical decentralization*. Cambridge, MA: Harvard University Press.

Gabel, M., & Bruner, H. (2002). *Global, Inc.: An atlas of global corporations.* New York: New Press.

George Washington University. (2001). Growing pains: An evaluation of charter schools in the District of Columbia, 1999–2000.

Gill, B. P., Timpane, M., Ross, K., & Brewer, D. J. (2001). Rhetoric versus reality: What we know and what we need to know about vouchers and charter schools. Available at: http://www.rand.org/publications

Good, T., & Braden, J. S. (2000). *The great school debate: Choice, vouchers, and charters.* Mahwah, N.J.: Lawrence Erlbaum.

Griffin, N., & Wohlstetter, P. (2001). Building a plane while flying it: Early lessons from charter schools. *Teachers College Record, 103*(2).

Hart, G., & Burr, S. (1996). The story of California's charter school legislation. *Phi Delta Kappan, 78*(1), 37–40.

Hassel, B. (1999). *The charter school challenge: Avoiding the pitfalls, fulfilling the promise.* Washington, DC: Brookings Institution.

Hendrie, C. (2003, December 10). Suit accuses Walton foundation of torpedoing new charter group. *Education Week.* Retrieved March 25, 2004, from http://www.edweek.org/ew/newstory.cfm?slug=15Charter.h23

Henig, J. R., Moser, M., Holyoke, T. T., & Lacireno-Paquet, N. (1999). *Making a choice, making a difference? An evaluation of charter schools in the District of Columbia.* Washington, DC: George Washington University, Center for Washington Area Studies.

Hentschke, G. (1997). Beyond competing reforms: A redefinition of public in public schooling. *Education and Urban Society, 29*(4), 474–489.

Hentschke, G., Oschman, S., & Snell, L. (2003). Trends and best practices for education management organizations. *Policy Perspectives.* San Francisco: WestEd. 16pp.

Hill, P. T., & Lake, R. (2002). *Charter schools and accountability in public education.* Washington, DC: Brookings Institution.

Horn, J., & Miron, G. (2000). An evaluation of the Michigan charter school initiative: Performance, accountability, and impact. Kalamazoo, MI: Evaluation Center at Western Michigan University. Retrieved March 18, 2003, from http://www.wmich.edu/evalctr

Izu, J., Carlos, L., Yamashiro, K., Picus, L., Tushnet, N., & Wohlstetter, P. (1998, June 30). The findings and implications of increased flexibility and accountability: An evaluation of charter schools in Los Angeles Unified School District. Report for LAUSD.

Khouri, N., Kleine, R., White, R., & Cummings, L. (1999). Michigan's charter school initiative: From theory to practice. Report for the Michigan Department of Education. Lansing, MI: Public Sector Consultants and MAXIMUS.

Knowledge Universe. (2004). Human capital. Retrieved March 24, 2004, from http://www.knowledgeu.com/human_capital.html

Kolderie, T. (1990). Beyond choice to new public schools: Withdrawing the exclusive franchise in public education. Washington, DC: Progressive Policy Institute.

Koppich, J., Holmes, P., & Plecki, M. L. (1998). *New roles, new rules? The professional work lives of charter school teachers.* Washington, DC: Center for the Advancement of Public Education, National Education Association.

Legislative Analyst's Office. (1993). Proposition 174: Analysis by the legislative analyst. Sacramento, CA: State of California.

Loveless, T. (2002). The 2002 Brown Center report on American education: How well are American students learning? With sections on arithmetic, high school culture, and charter schools. Retrieved February 20, 2003, from http://www.brookings.edu

Martinelli, F. (2001). How community-based organizations can start charter schools. Charter Friends National Network. Available at http://www.charterfriends.org/cfi-financing-oct01.html

McCluskey, N. (2002). Beyond brick and mortar: Cyber charters revolutionizing education. Washington, DC:Center for Education Reform. Available at http://www.edreform.com

McQueen, A. (2000, February 11). Charter schools movement growing. Associated Press.

Mergers: Let's talk turkeys. (2000, December 11). *BusinessWeek.* Available at http://www.businessweek.com/@@@893W4cQl@cUDQgA/archives/2000/b3711142.arc.htm

Metcalf, K. K., Theobald, N. D., & Gonzalez, G. (2003, March). State university roles in the charter school movment. *Phi Delta Kappan,* 543.

Meyer, J., & Rowan, B. (1983). The structure of educational organizations. In Meyer, J. W., & Scott, W. R. (Eds.), *Organizational environments.* Beverly Hills: Sage.

Milken Institute. (2002, April 22–24). 2002 global conference briefing book. See http://www.milkeninstitute.org and www.knowledgeu.com/human_capital.html

Mintrom, M. (2000). Leveraging local innovation: The case of Michigan's charter schools. East Lansing: Michigan State University.

Miron, G. (2000). The initial study of Pennsylvania charter schools. Report for the Evaluation Center at Western Michigan University, Kalamazoo.

Miron, G., & Nelson, C. (2001). Student academic achievement in charter schools: What we know and why we know so little. New York: National Center for the Study of Privatization in Education. Retrieved April 5, 2003, from http://www.wmich.edu/evalctr/

Miron, G., & Nelson, C. (2002). What's public about charter schools? Lessons learned about choice and accountability. New York: National Center for the Study of Privatization in Education.

Moeller, J. (1968). Bureaucracy and teachers' sense of power. In Bell, N. R., & Stub, H. R. (Eds.), *Sociology of education*. Florence, KY: Dorsey Press.

Nathan, J. (1996). *Charter schools: Creating hope and opportunity for American education*. San Francisco: Jossey-Bass.

Nathan, J. (1996). Possibilities, problems, and progress: Early lessons from the charter movement. *Phi Delta Kappan, 78*(1): 18–23.

National Conference of State Legislatures. (1998). The charter school roadmap. Available at http://www.ed.gov/pubs/Roadmap/title.html

Nelson, B., Berman, P., Ericson, J., Kamprath, N., Perry, R., Silverman, D., & Solomon, D. (2000). The state of charter schools, fourth year report. RPP International. Retrieved April 5, 2003, from http://www.ed.gov/pubs/charter4thyear/

Nelson, H., Muir, E., & Drown, R. (2000). Venturesome capital: State charter school finance systems. Washington, DC: National Charter School Finance Study. Office of Educational Research and Improvement, U.S. Department of Education.

New Jersey Department of Education. (2001). Evaluation of New Jersey charter schools. Available at http://www.nj.gov/njded/chartsch/evaluation/

Nordquist, J. (2000). *The privatization of public education: Charter schools and vouchers: A bibliography*. Santa Cruz, CA: Reference and Research Services.

Office of Educational Research and Improvement. (2000, January). The state of charter schools 2000. Report for the U.S. Department of Education.

Office of the Press Secretary, The White House. (2000, February 11). White House releases study showing boom in charter schools and announces $30 million increase in charter school funding. Washington, DC: Author.

Pacific Research Institute. (2001). The fight to save the Edison charter in San Francisco. See http://www.pacificresearch.org/

Patterson, D. (2000). California Network of Educational Charters (CANEC). Available at http://www.canec.org

Powell, J., Blackorby, J., Marsh, J., Finnegan, K., & Anderson, L. (1997, December 11). Evaluation of charter school effectiveness. Report for SRI International, Menlo Park, CA.

Premack, E. (1996, September). Charter schools: California's education reform "power tool." *Phi Delta Kappan,* 60–64.

Premack, E. (1999). Charter Schools Development Center (CSDC). Available at http://www.csus.edu/ier/charter/charter.html

Premack, E. (2000, February 16). Personal communication.

Riley, P. (2000). A charter school survey: Parents, teachers, and principals speak out. Pacific Research Institute. Retrieved from http://www.pacificinstitute.org

RPP International. (1999). The state of charter schools. Washington, DC: Office of Educational Research and Improvement, U.S. Department of Education. Available at http://www.ed.gov/pubs/charter3rdyear/

RPP International. (2000). The state of charter schools: 2000. Washington, DC: Office of Educational Research and Improvement, U.S. Department of Education.

Scheffel, D. (2002). Special education services in Colorado charter schools. Denver: Colorado Department of Education.

Shore, R. (1997). New professional opportunities for teachers in the California charter schools. *International Journal of Educational Reform, 6*(2), 128–138.

Slovacek, S., Kunnan, A., & Kim, H. (2002). California charter schools serving low-SES students: An analysis of the Academic Performance Index. Program Evaluation and Research Collaborative, Charter College of Education, California State University at Los Angeles.

SRI International. (1997, December 11). Evaluation of charter school effectiveness. Sacramento, CA: Office of the Legislative Analyst.

SRI International. (2002, November). A decade of public charter schools. Washington, DC: Author.

Texas Public Policy Forum. (2001). Navigating newly chartered waters: An analysis of Texas charter school performance.

Tirozzi, G., & Uro, G. (1997). Education reform in the United States: National policy in support of local efforts for school improvement. *American Psychologist, 52*(3), 241–249.

U.S. Department of Education. (2000). Evaluation of the public charter schools program: Year one evaluation report. Washington, DC: U.S. Department of Education.

U.S. Department of Education. (2004). Stronger accountability. Retrieved March 26, 2004, from http://www.ed.gov/nclb/accountability/schools/edpicks.jhtml?src=ln

U.S. General Accounting Office. (2000). Charter schools: Limited access to facility financing. Washington, DC: Author.

Vanourek, G., Manno, B., & Finn, C. (1997, April 30). The false friends of charter schools. *Education Week, 60,* 64. Available at http://www.edweek.org/ew/1997/31vanour.h16

Wells, A. S. (1998, December). Charter school reform in California: Does it meet expectations? *Phi Delta Kappan,* 305–312.

Wells, A. S., Artiles, L., Carnochan, S., Wilson Cooper, C., Grutzik, C., Jellison Holme, J., Lopez, A., Scott, J., Slayton, J., & Vasudeva, A. (1999). Beyond the rhetoric of charter school reform: A study of ten California school districts. UCLA Charter School Study.

Witness protection for teachers. (2003, November 24). *Wall Street Journal*, A-14.

Wohlstetter, P., & Anderson, L. (1994). What can U.S. charter schools learn from England's grant-maintained schools? *Phi Delta Kappan*, 75: 486–491.

Wohlstetter, P., & Griffin, N. (1998). Creating and sustaining learning communities: Early lessons from charter schools. CPRE Occasional Paper Series. Philadelphia: University of Pennsylvania, Consortium for Policy Research in Education. Available at http://www.cpre.org/index_js.htm

Wohlstetter, P., Malloy, C. L., Hentschke, G., & Smith, J. (in press). Improving service delivery in education through collaboration: The role of cross-sectoral alliances in the development and support of charter schools. *Social Science Quarterly*.

Wohlstetter, P., Malloy, C. L., Smith, J., & Hentschke, G. (in press). Incentives for charter schools: Building school capacity through cross-sectoral alliances. *Educational Administration Quarterly*.

Wohlstetter, P., Wenning, R., & Briggs, K. L. (1995). Charter schools in the United States: The question of autonomy. *Educational Policy*, 9(4), 331–358.

Zimmer, R., Buddin, R., Chau, D., Daley, D., Gill, B., Guarino, C., Hamilton, L., Krop, C., McCaffrey, D., Sandler, M., & Brewer, D. (2003). *Charter school operations and performance: Evidence from California*. RAND Education. Retrieved July 8, 2003, from http://www.rand.org

INDEX

ABOUT THE AUTHORS AND CONTRIBUTORS

AUTHORS

Terrence E. Deal is currently a free agent—writing, speaking, and making wine. He has served on the faculties of Stanford, Harvard, and Vanderbilt Universities and was most recently Irving R. Melbo Scholar at USC's Rossier School of Education. Prior to his academic career, he taught high school in Pomona and was a teacher and school principal in Pacific Grove, California. In addition to his public school experience, he was the director of the Athenian School Urban Center in San Francisco. He is author of many books and articles on educational leadership.

Guilbert C. Hentschke is the Richard T. and Mary Catherine Cooper Chair in Public School Administration and former dean at the University of Southern California's Rossier School of Education. In addition to teaching and writing, he serves on the boards of several U.S. K–12 education organizations. He served as faculty member and education dean at the University of Rochester, and prior to that was on the faculty at Columbia University Teachers College. He taught high school in San Jose, California, and was a school administrator in the Chicago public schools.

Kendra Kecker is currently a principal at Camino Nuevo Charter Academy in Los Angeles. She is originally from Minnesota and received her undergraduate degree in elementary education from the University of Wisconsin–Madison. She taught grades 2–5 and has been involved in various curriculum development projects, including designing a program in environmental education. She has a master's degree in educational policy and administration from the University of Southern California.

Christopher Lund is the principal at Robert F. Kennedy Elementary School in the Los Angeles Unified School District and also teaches in the educational leadership program at Pepperdine University. He received his doctorate from the University of Southern California, his MS from Pepperdine, and his BA from Northwestern University. Dr. Lund is author of *A Longitudinal Comparative Study of the Effects of Charter Schools on Minority and Low-SES Students in California*.

Scot Oschman is a PhD candidate at USC's Rossier School of Education. He has taught in the public school system for seven years and has managed international distance learning, online education programs, and course management software implementation for USC's Marshall School of Business, where he holds an MBA. He contributed to a paper on educational management organizations, as well as a paper on the relationship between school facilities and student performance.

Rebecca Shore is the former principal of Los Alamitos High School, a three-time national blue-ribbon school. She is author of *Baby Teacher: Nurturing Neural Networks from Birth to Age Five* (Scarecrow Education, 2002) and producer of the *Bach & Baby* and *Bach & Kids* CD series. She currently teaches educational leadership at Wake Forest University and the University of North Carolina at Greensboro.

CONTRIBUTORS

Lowell Billings has spent 26 years in public education as a K–6 teacher, was principal of West View School, and director of research and technology in the South Bay Union School District. In 1991, he was appointed assistant superintendent for instructional services, was subsequently appointed assistant superintendent for business services, and is now superintendent for the Chula Vista Elementary School District.

Jim Blew helped found the Watts Learning Center charter elementary school in 1997 and continues to serve on the school's board. He has worked since 2000 with the American Education Reform Council and its companion advocacy organization, the American Education Reform Foundation. He attended LAUSD public schools, received his BA from Occidental College, and earned an MBA from Yale University.

Yvonne Chan immigrated alone to the United States from Hong Kong at the age of 17, and since 1968 has worked as a teacher and administrator in the Los Angeles Unified School District, earning her master's and doctorate degrees along the way. Under her leadership, Vaughn Street Elementary School became Vaughn Next Century Learning Center, a California distinguished school and National blue-ribbon school, which has been recognized and visited by dignitaries from around the globe.

Dennis M. Doyle has served as an assistant superintendent in the Chula Vista Elementary School District, the largest K–6 district in California. Prior to this, he was director of educational partnerships for Lightspan, Inc., a multimedia educational technology company, and served as an administrator in the San Diego Unified School District for eight years.

Vickie Kimmel Forby received her master's degree in architecture from the University of Illinois at Urbana–Champaign while participating in the East St. Louis Action Research Project from 1990 to 1994. She has been the executive director of the Emerson Park Development Corporation since 1996 and has a proven commitment to the revitalization of the East St. Louis region and support of its residents.

Libia S. Gil began her teaching career in the Los Angeles Unified School District and is the former superintendent of the Chula Vista

Elementary School District. Under Dr. Gil's leadership, the district was recognized for continuous student achievement gains through multiple school and systemwide change efforts, including charter schools. More recently she has taken on leadership responsibilities with the New American Schools Development Corporation.

Hal Johnson has been an executive vice president for BB&T since 2001, being a part of over 100 acquisitions and the company's growth in asset size from $20 billion to over $90 billion. In 1994, he became involved with the Sawtooth Center for Visual Art in Winston Salem, North Carolina, which originated the concept of an Arts-Based Elementary School (ABES). He presently serves as treasurer on the ABES board.

Philip Lance is a nationally recognized leader in the field of community development and the founder and executive director of Pueblo Nuevo Development, a nonprofit community development corporation focused on the MacArthur Park neighborhood near downtown Los Angeles. He began his career as a minister in the Episcopal church and now works full-time developing community-based organizations, including charter schools.

Joanna Lennon is the founder and CEO of the East Bay Conservation Corps (EBCC) in Oakland, California, and has worked for over 25 years in education, environmental stewardship, and youth development. Ms. Lennon was the founding board president for the National Association of Service and Conservation Corps in Washington, D.C., and in 2001 received the Peter E. Haas Public Service Award from the University of California, Berkeley, where she had earned a master's of science degree and secondary teaching credential. She has taught at the middle, high school, and university levels.

Richard Lodish is the associate head at Sidwell Friends Lower School and has been the lower school principal for over 25 years, having previously taught in the Cleveland public school system. He holds a doctorate from the Harvard Graduate School of Education, has published widely on educational matters, is the recipient of a National Distinguished Principal Award from the U.S. Department of Education, and helped to establish a bilingual, intercultural school in Beijing, China. From 2001 to 2002, he spent a sabbatical year serving as the founding head of school for the elementary level of the EBCC charter school.

Joe Lucente is a national leader in the charter school movement. In addition to running one of the largest and most successful elementary charter schools in the nation, he has also been president of California's Charter School Association. Mr. Lucente has been recognized for his positive contributions to the charter school movement by the white house, the California state legislature, the California state superintendent of public instruction, and the mayor of Los Angeles.

Michael Lynott is a former partner in the law firm of Mershon, Sawyer, Johnston, Dunwody & Cole. He was serving as assistant general counsel for Miami-based Ryder System, Inc., an international, $5 billion, integrated logistics and transportation services company, when he became involved in opening Florida's first workplace charter school, the Ryder Elementary Charter School.

Cathleen Micheaels is a currently consultant with the East Bay Conservation Corps and the EBCC's Institute for Citizenship Education and Teacher Preparation. She served as director from 2001–2003 and supported the opening and ongoing implementation of the elementary level of the EBCC Charter School. From 1991 to 2001, Ms. Micheaels facilitated the planning for the school and managed EBCC's school-based service-learning program, Project YES (Youth Engaged in Service).

Kathleen O'Sullivan has brought 25 years experience in corporate, nonprofit, and public-sector administration, sales and marketing, fund development, human resources, and workforce preparation to her work with charter schools over the past six years and now with her consulting practice Think-Up! Inc. She is a Eureka communities fellow, a graduate of Leadership Pasadena, and currently serves on the boards of Leadership Pasadena, Odyssey Charter School, and CharterVoice. Her professional affiliations include the Rotary Club of Pasadena, the Pasadena Chamber of Commerce, and Women of Pasadena.

Judith Price is a native New Yorker and was educated at the Richman Country School and City College of New York's School of Business Administration. She has spent more than 35 years in senior management positions working for major corporations and nonprofit organizations and continues to be an active business developer with civic and community interests, including the Urban League Black Executive Exchange Program, Louise Wise Services, Big Brothers, New York YWCA, ICBO, and OIC. She received a three-year gubernatorial appointment to the New York State Economic Development Board and Project Greenhope Services for Women.

Paul H. Seibert is a nationally recognized figure in education reform. As the director of Charter Consultants, he works with individuals and groups, including parents, teachers, for-profit and nonprofit corporations, public and private schools, and state universities in their quest to improve education. He supported the passage of Illinois' charter public school law and later assisted in the development of Missouri's charter school legislation.

Doug Thomas is director of the Gates–EdVisions Project and president of EdVisions, Inc., a nonprofit corporation hosting the effort funded by the Bill and Melinda Gates Foundation to replicate the learning model of the New Country School and the teacher-owner model of EdVisions Cooperative. Thomas was the University of Minnesota's Center for School Change outreach coordinator for southern Minnesota for ten years and served four terms on the LeSueur–Henderson Board of Education.

Ana Tilton is a senior vice president of the School Division for Edison Schools Inc., the largest educational management company in the United States. She oversees all school operations for the western division of the company. Prior to working for Edison, Dr. Tilton had a long career as a California public school administrator.

John von Rohr is superintendent of North Carolina's largest charter school. Test scores have continually gone up during his five-year tenure, and his school is recognized as the "flagship charter school" for the state of North Carolina. Dr. von Rohr returned to education after a twenty-one year career in the U.S. military.

Rick Werlin received his bachelor's degree in elementary education from the State University of New York and a master's in educational administration from Texas Southern University in Houston. He has worked in human resources in three major districts in Texas and has served as the assistant superintendent for human resources services for Chula Vista in California.